Essential SCO® System Administration

Keith Vann

Prentice Hall P T R
Englewood Cliffs, New Jersey 07632

Library of Congress Cataloguing-in-Publication Data

Editorial/production supervision: *Mary P. Rottino*
Cover design: *Karen Marsilio*
Cover photographs: *Westlight Computer Graphics Collection*
Manufacturing manager: *Alexis Heydt*
Acquisitions editor: *Mark L. Taub*

© 1995 Prentice Hall P T R
Prentice-Hall, Inc.
A Simon & Schuster Company
Englewood Cliffs, New Jersey 07632

Text printed on recycled paper

Open Desktop, the Open Desktop logo, SCO, the SCO logo, the The Santa Cruz Operation are registered trademarks of The Santa Cruz Operation, Inc. in the USA and other countries. Open Server and MPX are trademarks of The Santa Cruz Operations, Inc. MPX was jointly developed by SCO and Corollary, Inc. Corollary is a trademark of Corollary, Inc. SCO TCP/IP was developed by Lachman Technology, Inc. SCO TCP/IP is derived from LACHMAN SYSTEM V STREAMS TCP, a joint development of Lachman Technology, Inc. and Convergent Technologies. LACHMAN is a trademark of Lachman Technology, Inc. SCO NFS was developed by Lachman Technology, Inc. based on LACHMAN SYSTEM V NFS. LACHMAN is a trademark of Lachman Technology, Inc. Sun, Sun Microsystems, and NFS® are trademarks or registered trademarks of Sun Microsystems, Inc. UNIX is a registered trademark of Unix System Laboratories (a wholly owned subsidiary of Novell, Inc.) in the United States and other countries.

The publisher offers discounts on this book when ordered in bulk quantities.
For more information contact: Corporate Sales Department, Prentice Hall P T R,
113 Sylvan Ave., Englewood Cliffs, NJ 07632.
Phone (800) 382-3419   Fax (201) 592-2249   email: dan_rush@prenhall.com

The author and the publisher make no warranty of any kind, expressed or implied, with regard to these programs or the documentation contained in this book. The author and publisher shall not be liable in any event for incidental or consequential damages in connection with, or arising out of, the furnishing, performance, or use of these programs.

All rights reserved. No part of this book may be reproduced, in any form or by any means, without permission in writing from the publisher.
Printed in the United States of America

10 9 8 7 6 5 4 3 2

ISBN 0-13-290859-X

Prentice-Hall International (UK) Limited, *London*
Prentice-Hall of Australia Pty. Limited, *Sydney*
Prentice-Hall Canada Inc., *Toronto*
Prentice-Hall Hispanoamericana, S.A., *Mexico*
Prentice-Hall of India Private Limited, *New Delhi*
Prentice-Hall of Japan, Inc., *Tokyo*
Simon & Schuster Asia Pte. Ltd., *Singapore*
Editora Prentice-Hall do Brasil, Ltda., *Rio de Janeiro*

Contents

Essential SCO System Administration

Preface	v
Acknowledgements	vii
About This Book	ix
Road Map	x
Conventions	xi
Chapter 1: Orientation to SCO UNIX	1-1
Chapter 2: A First Install	2-1
Chapter 3: Overview of System Administration	3-1
Chapter 4: Looking Under the Hood	4-1
Chapter 5: Configuring Your System	5-1
Chapter 6: The Art of System Administration	6-1
Appendix A: List of Supplemental Resources for SCO Systems	A-1
Appendix B: SCO Online Support BBS Access	B-1
Appendix C: Relevant SCO Software Supplements	C-1
Index	Index-1

Preface

This book, *Essential SCO System Administration*, is an annotated guidebook to the essential features of a powerful applications platform named SCO UNIX. SCO UNIX (hereafter simply referred to as SCO) underlies all of SCO's system products, including Open Server and Open Desktop. It is, by turns, an experienced guide, a pocket companion, and a compendium of useful tables and diagrams. I have designed it to, hopefully, meet the needs of a broad range of SCO system administrators.

Within a relatively few pages are distilled the key administrative secrets of a very complex operating system. It is a book filled with tips, strategies, suggestions, and workarounds. There is something for everyone, no matter what your experience.

Highlights include:

- an overview of the key tasks and goals of SCO system administration
- road maps in each chapter, directing you to key topics and tables
- friendly and concise vocabularies free of technical jargon
- abundant hands-on exercises that you can perform as you read
- scores of short and sweet how-to-do-it tips and reminders
- easy-to-read checklists to help you successfully complete key operations
- tips to prepare you for a successful product installation
- copious cross-references to related topics in the SCO online documentation

Some of the interesting topics you'll find include:

> How an Operating System Works for You
> How to Assess the State of Your System
> How To Configure High-speed Modems
> Easy Filesystem Configuration
> Data Access Optimization
> How and When to Back Up Your Data
> Painless SCO UNIX Security
> Keeping Users Happy
> Planning for Future Growth

The introductory sections should comfort those new to the system, while the key configuration sections will inform even experts.

Essential SCO System Administration

This small book cannot and will not replace the SCO product documentation. It was not designed to do so. It is humbly offered as a valuable supplement. Of course, humility only going so far, I would hope that this book alone will help most of you to resolve your most common system problems.

The text itself is simple and direct. Clearly marked digressions, providing greater detail are peppered copiously throughout the manuscript. Chapter road maps steer you precisely to areas of personal interest. In short, if this book looks like it might be for you, skim further. You may be pleasantly surprised.

Version Information

This book describes the features (and eccentricities) of SCO UNIX Release V/386 version 4.2. This is the exact same operating system that underlies Open Desktop 3.0 and Open Server 3.0 (both use the same OS code tree). This version of SCO UNIX incorporates features of BSD UNIX, and USL UNIX Release 3.2, and SCO XENIX. In many cases, I have described extra functionality provided by the various software supplements available from SCO for this version of the product.

Open Desktop and Open Server Users!!

This book addresses the configuration of the SCO UNIX base system underlying your product. Look for the follow-on book to present administration strategies for the graphical, networking, and MS-DOS components of the Open Desktop and Open Server products.

Acknowledgements

I am greatly indebted to a host of people who have assisted me in the completion of this book. But, first and foremost, I must express my profound gratitude to a company - The Santa Cruz Operation, Ltd. SCO most graciously offered me both desk space and system access so that I could complete this manuscript while away from home in Europe. In tribute to SCO, I sincerely hope that this manuscript does justice to their deservedly successful products.

My tireless technical reviewers included Alec Parker, Don Draper, and Steve Pate of SCO. I also owe a world of thanks to Paul Hurford of SCO Technical Support, whose informed comments helped me to restructure the book after I submitted the initial prototype for his review.

I have nothing but praise for my copy editor, Mary Lou Nohr, who provided wonderfully witty comments and reams of typographical corrections. Please, do not hold her responsible for any typos or problems that might remain, since the onus was on me (with my primitive tools) to generate camera-ready copy.

Certainly, I cannot forget to mention my Engineering Services stablemates at SCO London. These included Paul Culley, Nick White, Jill Pryse-Davies (whose photos of her radiant sons shall be forever fixed in my memory), Stefan Polzer, and Sandra Holder (equestrienne extraordinaire). They have all bravely tolerated many long weeks of my bulky presence toiling in their midst. Of course, the person most responsible for my encroachment into his corporate domain is their capable manager, Iain Gray. He has been more than understanding.

I also offer a warm thank you to the wonderful folks at Corporate Services, especially Lynn Snoxall and Nina Howells. They offered me much needed hospitality and accommodation upon my arrival at SCO London.

It is with great delight that I express my sincerest acknowledgment for the invitation extended by David Taylor (Director of Services, SCO) and conveyed by Diana Foster (SCO Corporate), both who so warmly welcomed me back to SCO London.

There are not words enough to thank Lesley MacDonald (SCO Marketing Communications) for the many years of friendship and professional guidance. Lesley was instrumental in making my stay at SCO London possible.

Essential SCO System Administration

I could not fail to mention the competent and courteous women at SCO reception, Julia Smith and Michele Temple. They treated me like family (no, just the good bits) during my entire stay. I must also express my thanks to the two gentlemen taking turns managing the night security desk, Alan Lyon and Ernie Element. They were always happy to open the doors for me, even on those wet and stormy British summer nights.

Another of my sustaining contacts at SCO London was Maria Blasi, who refreshes the company house. Her wonderful humor and vibrant energy boosted me many a dreary morning before making my way to my desk.

Additionally, I'd like to offer thanks to Alex Tuninga and his brother, who both helped me to blow off needed steam (at the pub and at the house) during the early stressful weeks. Thank you as well to Hugh Dickens of SCO Engineering who kept me company during some very long nights at the keyboard.

My debt shall probably never be repaid to my long-term friend, Henry Goldstein, senior member of SCO Legal Services, who was my primary interface to the company during my weeks of preliminary roaming in Europe. He and his gifted wife, the poet Joyce Goldstein, graciously adopted me into their family and their home for the bulk of my stay in London.

Back in Tucson, Arizona, where this project took early form, I offer warm and heartfelt recognition for the support offered by my friends Roberta Bush, Judy Miller, Arlene Sigel, William Meyer, and Laureen Lee. They all provided precious spiritual and moral sustenance during the long hot desert months.

With great love, I offer a joyous paean to my mom, Norma Sharp, without whom none of this would be possible.

And finally, my deepest thanks go out to Mark Taub, UNIX technical editor at PTR Prentice Hall, who pushed and prodded me to finally complete a project that I would have been hard-pressed to finish on my own. We've finally done it! Yes!!

About This Book

This book is both an introduction to and condensed reference of operating system administration on SCO systems. It is not, however, an introduction to generic UNIX end-user concepts (e.g. command line creation, file editing, or directory upkeep). Users in need of such instruction should consult the *User's Guide* that is packaged with the SCO product. There are many fine commercial books, as well, that describe the basic use of UNIX.

The book consists of the following chapters.

- Chapter 1: Orientation to SCO UNIX

    Answers the question - what is an operating system? Provides an overview of product features and capabilities. Includes a detailed orientation to SCO UNIX for administrators coming from MS-DOS systems.

- Chapter 2: A First Install

    Presents ways to effectively prepare for a trouble-free system configuration (and installation). Introduces the system administration shell. Investigates basic system startup and structure.

- Chapter 3: Overview of System Administration

    Lays the foundation for the key administration tasks and skills. Guides you through an initial system configuration. Provides an overview of other tasks that should be undertaken.

- Chapter 4: Looking Under the Hood

    Summarizes the skills and commands that enable you to comprehensively assess the state of the operating system and your system hardware.

- Chapter 5: Configuring Your System

    Provides the fundamental skills and concepts to effectively configure your system. All aspects from hardware to system security and user accounts are addressed. Unlike generic UNIX books, careful attention is focused on the mechanics of properly preparing hardware for use in an SCO system. Numerous preventative configuration tips are included.

Essential SCO System Administration

- Chapter 6: The Art of System Administration
    Introduces the art of maintaining, analyzing, and troubleshooting your SCO system. Emergency recovery and access skills are included. The chapter concludes with an introduction to the art of performance tuning.

Users desiring in-depth mastery of performance tuning skills on SCO systems are advised to consult the PTR Prentice Hall book, *SCO Performance Tuning Handbook*, by Gina Miscovich and David Simons.

Road Map

Novice system administrators should start with Chapter 1, proceeding on to Chapter 2. Many foundation concepts and skills are presented within the context of preparing for product installation. Next, novice administrators should proceed to Chapter 3. This chapter guides you through the craft of SCO system administration. Finally the novice should select topics of interest in Chapters 5 and 6. Essential topics are indicated in the road maps of those chapters. Chapter 4 functions primarily as a condensed reference of system monitoring commands and procedures.

Experienced system administrators may want to proceed directly to Chapter 5. There are many aspects of system configuration addressed in greater depth. Chapter 4, as mentioned above, can serve as a handy reference for assaying the state of your system. Chapter 6 presents the key skills and an overriding philosophy to keep your system healthy. Essential emergency recovery information is intrinsic to this chapter. The information presented is useful to both new and experienced system administrators.

Conventions

The conventions used in this book are as follows.

- file names, command names, and the names of SCO utilities are in bold
- command lines are in bold, except for user-supplied objects in italic
- words of emphasis or warning and new technical terms are in bold italic
- technical terms mentioned for the first time, but not defined, are in italics
- comments, book references, and section or table references are in italics (except within an italicized comment, book references are normal text)
- shell programming code tends to be in bold, but may vary by context
- fictional prose and dialogues are in 11 point Palatino italic font
- within exercises and tables, underlined words indicate user actions

Special notations include:

- **command**(SECTION)   reference to the SCO online **man** pages
- System ⇨ Software ⇨ Remove   system administration shell menu path
- **command** (⇨ 2)   selection to be made from a menu presented by command

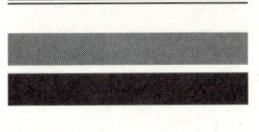

used to bracket technical strategies
used to bracket hands-on exercises
used to bracket technical demonstration and technical background text
used to bracket (some) shell script examples

Notations indicating digressions from the text include:

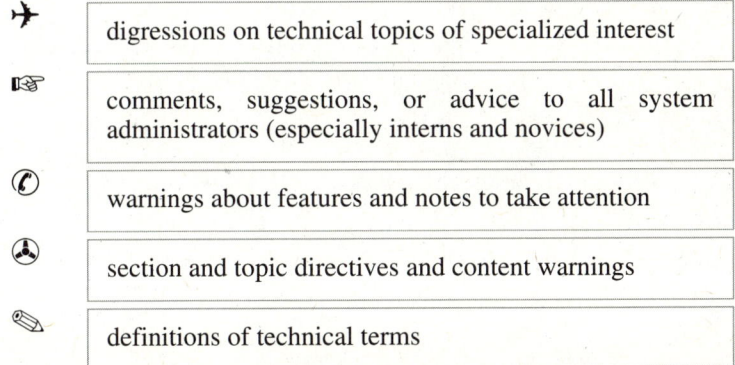

✈ digressions on technical topics of specialized interest

☞ comments, suggestions, or advice to all system administrators (especially interns and novices)

🄒 warnings about features and notes to take attention

⚙ section and topic directives and content warnings

✎ definitions of technical terms

Chapter 1

Orientation to SCO UNIX

	Page
Introduction	1-3
Road Map	1-4
What is SCO UNIX?	1-5
A Home Video Analogy	1-5
Installed System Intelligence	1-6
SCO UNIX is an Operating System	1-7
Application Services	1-7
Basic Terminology and Concepts	1-8
Files	1-8
Directories	1-9
Processes	1-10
Accounts	1-11
The Shell and the Kernel	1-12
Commands	1-12
Basic Product Information	1-13
Support for Industry-standard PCs	1-13
Hardware Support and Integrated Device Drivers	1-14
Application Support and Value-Added Utilities	1-14
Layered Product Support	1-17

Essential SCO System Administration

	Page
Orientation for MS-DOS Users	1-20
Major Differences Between MS-DOS and SCO UNIX	1-20
Power-up, Power-down, and Reset	1-20
System Configuration and Start-up	1-21
Access to Disks	1-21
The Command Line	1-21
Files and Directories	1-22
Command Execution	1-23
File Management	1-23
Printing	1-24
Port Access	1-24
Memory Allocation	1-25
Graphics	1-26

Tables

1-1:	SCO Value-added Utilities	1-15
1-2:	Standard Included UNIX Utilities	1-16
1-3:	Summary of Other Features in SCO UNIX	1-18
1-4:	Key Operative Differences from Other UNIX Systems	1-18
1-5:	End User Features of SCO UNIX	1-19
1-6:	Differences between MS-DOS and SCO UNIX File Names	1-22
1-7:	MS-DOS to SCO UNIX Port Mappings	1-25
1-8:	MS-DOS -> SCO UNIX Command Map	1-26

Diagrams

1-1:	Directory Tree Structure	1-10

Chapter 1   Orientation to SCO UNIX

Introduction

> *"What happened?", Paul wondered aloud. Before stepping away from his desk, a nice, friendly screen with graphics, windows, and color had lit up his monitor. His second week at the office, Paul was really enjoying this new system. "UNIX" they called it. Yeah, this UNIX system was really nice. Now, all that was left was a dismal, dun-colored display with a single symbol "#" in the upper left corner. And his mouse had stopped working. It must have been Justine, his supervisor. Paul had felt that she and he were just beginning to understand each other; and now this. "Why?"*
>
> *Just then he noticed a thin cream-colored manual on his desk. It was titled "SCO UNIX Tutorial". Beside it was an enrollment notification. Paul was to report to an accelerated UNIX class the next morning. At the bottom was a handwritten note. It read "I hope you're going to enjoy being our new SCO UNIX system administrator." It was signed "Justine."*

Welcome to the administrative face of SCO UNIX and SCO Open Desktop, its graphical persona. Like Paul, you are about to discover the hidden face of this powerful multiuser application environment. It is a face that your end-users will never see (on a properly configured system). It is one that you will come to know and, hopefully, love as you master the art of maintaining, administering, and tuning your busy SCO systems. It is the powerful world accessible from the SCO UNIX administrative (**root** superuser) command line – the "#" prompt.

It is on the command line that UNIX system administrators like you, no matter how fancy the system, still perform their day-to-day work. Although many UNIX tools and utilities now run in friendly, mouse-driven graphical environments, there is still much administrative and diagnostic power available only from the command line.

This chapter presents the basic principles and concepts underlying the SCO UNIX system. Wherever possible, analogies will be made to MS-DOS as well as to other UNIX systems.

Essential SCO System Administration

Road Map

 Those already familiar with the basics of SCO UNIX may skip this chapter.

Notes to New Administrators and Recent Transfers

The prospect of administering an SCO UNIX system may be daunting at first, but, take heart. You may find that you already understand the fundamentals of this powerful software system. If so, it is simply a matter of time before you become fluent in the basic vocabulary of SCO UNIX.

Essential Sections for All New Administrators

    What is SCO UNIX
    Basic Terminology and Concepts

Supplemental Section for MS-DOS Users: Orientation for MS-DOS Users

Strongly Recommended: Basic Product Information

 Users with experience on other UNIX systems may benefit from the section "Basic Product Information."

Chapter 1   Orientation to SCO UNIX

What is SCO UNIX?

You might already know SCO UNIX as a multitasking operating environment for open-systems multiuser applications and services. But if you understandably find yourself reeling from that dizzying stream of jargon, this section is for you.

A Home Video System Analogy

To best describe SCO UNIX, consider your home video system. For most of you this includes some video *hardware*:

- a television
- a video cassette recorder (VCR)
- a cable converter box with connected cable
- one or more remote controls

Your video *software* may include:

- a cable feed
- video cassettes
- local television broadcast signals

Assuming that you connect everything properly, the built-in intelligence of that system lets even the youngest child effortlessly enjoy a vast array of video software. You simply press the right buttons on the remote, and things work.

Now consider your current computer system (or the one you'd like to have). It may include the following system hardware components:

- a computer case enclosing:
    - one or more floppy disk drives
    - at least one hard disk drive
    - other mysterious pieces (e.g. CPU, RAM)
- a keyboard
- a video monitor
- a printer

If you were lucky, you bought your system already assembled. In that case it should, theoretically, be ready to use and operate as simply and as friendly as your VCR. Unfortunately, that is a rare exception. Once you get it home and turn it on, you find yourself phoning in a frenzy for help, subjecting yourself to needless abuse (trying to decipher the vendor's manuals), or pacing desperately in frustration.

But let's assume, for simplicity, that the system was set up properly, and initially works when you turn it on. The keyboard seems to respond properly. The computer may have initialized the printer. The screen on the monitor appears legible. But this is nothing like your VCR. Where is the "PLAY" button? Which button prints? Is it tuned to the right computer "channel"?

In desperation you type something at the keyboard and press the ENTER key ...

```
HELP ME
```

and, lo and behold, the system responds ...

```
HELP: not found
```

But what type of help is that? Where is the "intelligence" in this system?

Installed System Intelligence

The questionable "intelligence" of your computer system is a form of software. This software was designed to logically respond to specific processing requests, but apparently its logic seems to escape us humans.

Computer components are intrinsically dumb. The "intelligence" has to be added (or installed). The fortunate ones among you had it installed by someone else (e.g. the dealer you bought your system from). SCO UNIX is one type of "installed intelligence" for computer systems.

While your video equipment works well as a system, computer components are not generally designed for intelligent interconnection. That's where SCO UNIX comes in. It orchestrates the various computer components into a functional system. You install SCO UNIX to let you to "play" your software on the system.

> Computer software is typically marketed in packages called *applications*. It is these software applications (e.g. spreadsheets, databases, word processors) that enable you to perform useful work on your computer system.

Chapter 1   Orientation to SCO UNIX

SCO UNIX Is an Operating System

As you may be aware, SCO UNIX is one of many varieties of installed system intelligence. MS-DOS and OS/2 are other examples. There are competing varieties of UNIX as well. The technical term that applies to all of these examples of "installed system intelligence" is *operating system* (or OS).

Each operating system is unique, with key differences from the others. Yet, one overall purpose is common to all – to make it easy for software applications to talk to the attached computer system components.

For example, SCO UNIX takes care of the details of talking to the printer when an application wants to print. It ensures that the video monitor accurately displays the messages and graphics that an application generates. SCO UNIX manages the complex tasks of writing to and reading from the disk whenever an application needs to save or retrieve data. All of these functions require substantial system intelligence. This is the power of an operating system.

Application Services

Applications talk to the operating system. Specifically they ask the operating system to perform various services for them (e.g. printing). Conversations typically might go something like this:

    App: *Honored OS, please print this stuff.*
    OS: *Okay, I'll get the printer ready; and I'll tell you when I'm done.*

(The OS engages the printer in productive interaction.)

    OS: *Hey application! It's done.*

(The application now happily proceeds on its way, while the ever busy
    OS responds to other requests.)

Applications tend to have common system needs; so the various operating systems offer similar basic application services. Such services include:

- displaying text and graphics
- preparing and queuing data for the printer
- translating keystrokes into usable text or signals
- managing data transfers to and from the disk(s)
- allocating memory (RAM) for application use

Essential SCO System Administration

These basic services keep the majority of software applications fairly happy.

One service that SCO UNIX offers that many operating systems (e.g. MS-DOS) do not, is the ability to share the CPU among multiple competing applications. This is called *multitasking*. When implemented properly, as with SCO UNIX, multitasking gives the impression of multiple applications all running feverishly at once.

Yet, what about applications that need to work closely together, for example, electronic mail and network file transfer? What about huge, complex applications, like airline reservations systems? No problem. SCO UNIX, an advanced operating system, was designed to meet the needs of those applications as well.

Some of the advanced services of SCO UNIX are listed in the box below.

Some Advanced SCO UNIX Application Services

- sharing computer memory among multiple applications
- conveying data and signals between applications
- scheduling application access to one or more central processing units (CPUs)
- supporting virtual memory (for large applications)

Basic Terminology and Concepts

The key concepts underlying SCO UNIX (and UNIX in general) are:

files	directories	processes	accounts
shell	kernel	commands	

Files

The *file* is one of the two fundamental abstractions (a fancy word for concepts) underlying UNIX. The other is the *process*.

Chapter 1   Orientation to SCO UNIX

UNIX files are extremely flexible objects. A *file* is anything that can receive or originate data. Using this definition, printers are files. A VGA screen is a file. The hard disk is a file. Subdivisions of the hard disk are files. Collections of data on floppy or hard disks are files. What other OSs (such as MS-DOS) refer to as "files" (collections of data) are merely a single type of file under SCO UNIX.

A file under SCO UNIX has several key components:

- a name   (some files have several names)
- attributes   (e.g. who owns it, who can access it, its type)
- data   (optional for some files)

Like manila office files, UNIX files can be opened for reading, writing (adding data), or both. Unauthorized users can be kept out by the access restrictions.

Applications store their data as files. For example, individual WordPerfect documents are saved as files. John's document will be a separate file from Susan's document.

Even applications themselves are treated as files. This turns out to be very useful. For instance, the SCO UNIX utility, **divvy***(ADM)*, which reformats the UNIX portion of the hard disk, must only be used by the system administrator. No one else must use it. The file abstraction makes it easy to enforce this.

There is much more to learn about files than can be covered here. You will come to understand the true power of this concept as your mastery of SCO UNIX grows in the chapters that follow. *[Files are discussed in greater detail in Chapter 5.]*

Directories

A *directory* is a file used to look up other files. It's like a phone directory for files.

A UNIX directory is a lookup table. It is a table of file names and where to find them. Directories are very useful for grouping files under a common name – that of the directory. Technically, UNIX directories do not contain any files, but for most of us, it is useful to pretend that they do.

By design, a UNIX directory may reference other directories. These are called *subdirectories*. Subdirectories make it possible to build a hierarchy of

Essential SCO System Administration

directories, also known as a *directory tree*. Incidentally, a directory tree is a great structure for organizing, accessing, and naming files.

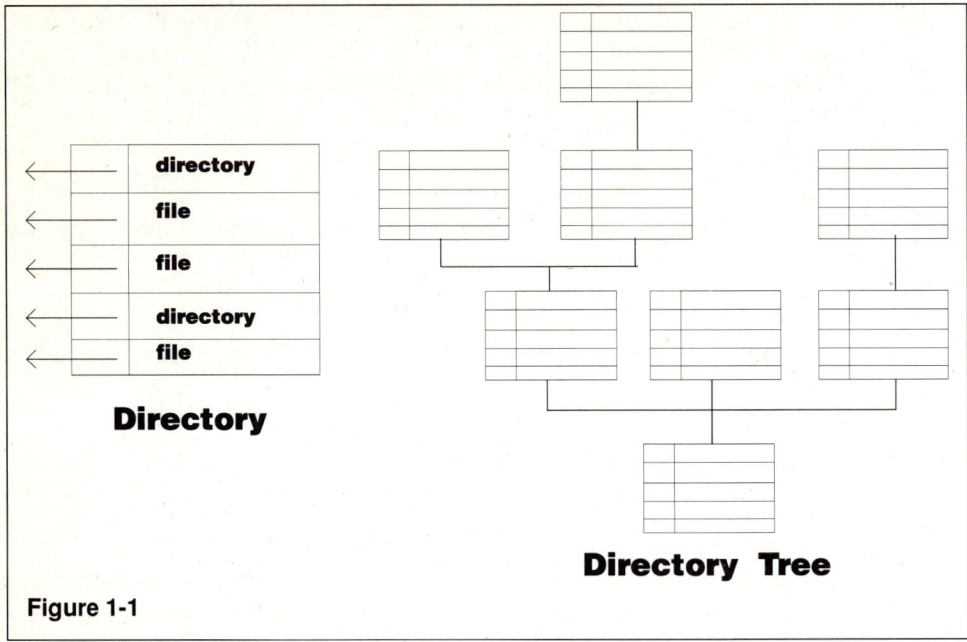

Figure 1-1

Built into the SCO UNIX product is a particular directory tree – the *root filesystem*. The shape of this tree and the names of its directories are well known to SCO UNIX utilities and applications. It makes it extremely easy for software to find specific files. How? Well, SCO UNIX files are uniquely named by the path of the directories used to reach them.

Processes

All activity on an SCO UNIX system is grouped into objects called *processes*. A *process* is stream (sequence) of operations generated by running an application.

 Technically, each application binary file generates a process. Many applications generate several processes in the course of completion.

For example, a user named Martin runs Microsoft Word. This may, in fact launch a series of processes, but one, in particular, controls the main tasks that

Chapter 1   Orientation to SCO UNIX

Word performs for Martin. These tasks belong to the process. This includes the tasks that access files, those that interpret Martin's keystrokes, as well as those that format Martin's work.

As with files, the process concept is extremely powerful. When multiple users run the same application, each user is associated with a unique process. To suspend or terminate an instance of the application run by a particular user, the system administrator merely needs to signal that user's process. Even user login sessions (started when a user requests access to an SCO system) are processes.

Accounts

A special feature of SCO UNIX is that it supports multiple users. In other words, SCO UNIX is a *multi-user operating system*. To run applications, a user must have an account on the system. The *account* is a record in a special database, the *password database*, that authorizes the user to access the system.

SCO UNIX keeps track of users through their accounts. Each account is numbered, and assigned a password. Passwords help to prevent system access by unauthorized users. The authorized user of the account is the *account owner*.

The system administrator assigns a private work area to each account. The work area is simply a specific directory in the UNIX directory tree. Most of the user's work on the system will be stored in this private directory (the user's *home directory*) or any subdirectories the user chooses to create.

A user's request to access the system is called *logging in*. Once the user supplies a valid account name and its password, he or she is granted system access. Immediately, the system places the user in the user's home directory. Typically, the user remains there until he or she decides to *log out* (exit the system).

One account on the system has special privileges. It is the **root** account. The root account is where the system administrator logs in. It even has a special home directory, *I*, which is the base (or *root*) of the *root filesystem*. The **root** user has unlimited access to any file, directory, or other system resource.

The Shell and the Kernel

Once a user logs in, a process is started for that user. This process is the user's *shell*. The shell translates user requests (e.g. running an application, deleting a file) into system calls to the *kernel* – the processing heart of the SCO UNIX operating system. The shell also conveys responses from the kernel to the user.

The UNIX kernel coordinates the activities of the operating system. It stays extremely busy managing users, and, generally, trying to do everything at once.

Several types of shells are integrated into the SCO UNIX product. You, as system administrator, assign a specific shell when setting up a user's account.

Commands

The most common SCO UNIX shells are the *command-line shells*. Command-line shells respond to special instructions called *commands*. A command is a sequence of words entered into the system. It is a request to perform a system operation, such as renaming a file.

> Some SCO UNIX shells can respond to mouse operations or keystroke selections from special screens (e.g. SCO Shell).

Some simple examples of SCO UNIX commands follow:

date	Instructs the shell to create a process to run the **date** program. The **date** program displays the time and date. The process terminates when **date** completes.
lp report	Creates a process to run the **lp** program, which spools files for printing. **report** is the name of a file that has been submitted for printing.
kill 2865	Tells the shell to *kill* (terminate) process # 2865.
echo "HELLO"	Transmits the message "HELLO" to the display.
exit	Tells the shell to terminate. If the shell was started when the user logged in, this ends the login session.
sleep 60	Tells the shell to *sleep* (suspend operation) for 60 seconds.

Chapter 1   Orientation to SCO UNIX

Commands may be issued by users or read from files called *shell scripts*. A shell script is a previously prepared file containing a structured list of commands. Some may know them better as *batch files*.

Below is an example of a simple shell script:

>   echo "Please wait for your document to print."
>   lp document
>   sleep 10
>   echo "Please pick-up your document now."

Basic Product Information

The SCO UNIX operating system is a powerful multitasking, multiuser application environment, whose features include:

- support of industry-standard PCs using Intel processors
- extensive hardware support enabled by integrated device drivers and a boot-time loadable driver facility
- wide application support (including support for MS-DOS and Windows applications)
- numerous SCO value-added utilities
- layered product support for advanced applications
- conforms to industry-approved open systems standards

Support for Industry-standard PCs

SCO UNIX runs on industry-standard computers using Intel 80386, 80486, and Pentium processors. This includes not only ISA (industry-standard architecture), EISA (extended ISA), VESA (Video Electronics Standards Association), and MCA (Micro Channel architecture) machines, but multiprocessor and server-class systems, as well. SCO's continuing system support will include newer technology platforms such as Intel's PCI (peripheral component interconnect) and Intel's proposed Plug-and-Play architecture.

Essential SCO System Administration

Hardware Support and Integrated Device Drivers

SCO UNIX supports a broad range of the most popular hardware devices and peripherals for Intel-based systems. To a large part, SCO's integrated device drivers make this possible.

Essentially, a *device driver* is a special software module that manages the communications between the operating system and a specific type of peripheral (e.g. a tape drive).

> Unlike MS-DOS, SCO integrates a wide range of device drivers into the distributed product. Furthermore, many SCO drivers are specially designed to support a wide spectrum of hardware makes and models. This greatly facilitates installing existing hardware onto SCO systems. Contrast this with MS-DOS device drivers, which must be acquired separately, and which typically support only a single model of a given peripheral (e.g. graphics card, tape drive). To support existing hardware on MS-DOS systems requires tracking down the requisite drivers from the hardware vendors.

For example, the SCO UNIX SCSI$_1$ tape driver, **Stp**, understands a wide range of QIC (quarter-inch cartridge), 8mm (video), and DAT (digital audio) tape drives. To use a specific make or type of SCSI tape drive, you simply identify it to the system. The device driver automatically translates generic control commands (i.e. rewind, erase, read) into the instructions expected by the specific device.

> The success of the **Stp** driver relies upon the existence a driver for the SCSI host adapter supporting the tape device. Fortunately, these also are integrated into the SCO product.

Application Support and Value-Added Utilities

Thousands of commercial applications have been created for SCO UNIX. Through COFF$_2$ binary support and IBCS-2 conformance, many applications designed for other UNIX versions (e.g. BSD, IBM, AT&T, Interactive) run under SCO UNIX. And with SCO Merge installed, thousands of MS-DOS and Windows applications run under SCO UNIX, as well.

---

1   a popular high-speed peripheral interface (pronounced "scuzzy")
2   the AT&T UNIX Release 3 binary application format

Chapter 1 Orientation to SCO UNIX

Integrated into the SCO UNIX product are scores of "value-added" utilities, many exclusive to SCO. These SCO "value-added" utilities include:

Table 1-1:   **SCO Value-added Utilities**

- a window/menu-based system administration shell (**sysadmsh**(ADM))
- a heuristic kernel-tuning interface (**tunesh**(ADM)) [Open Desktop only]
- SCO Shell, a configurable window/menu-based end-user shell (**scosh**(C))
- intelligent, menu-based software installation utility (**custom**(ADM), **fixperm**(ADM))
- a tool to migrate standard UNIX accounts to SCO (**addxusers**(ADM))
- a tool to easily migrate SCO accounts between systems (**ap**(ADM))
- a powerful, multiprotocol, mail delivery system (**mmdf**(ADM))
- extensive local language support, including message files (**locale**(M))
- extensive kernel and device driver configuration tools (**idbuild**(ADM))
- extensive hardware and resource installation tools (**mkdev**(ADM))
- disk partition and virtual disk management (**fdisk**(ADM), **divvy**(ADM))
- extensive MS-DOS disk, file, & file conversion tools (**doscmd**(C))
- full C2-level security maintenance system w/ system audit facility (**tcbck**(ADM), **authck**(ADM), **subsystem**(M))
- controlled setuid shell script execution capability (**asroot**(ADM))
- semi-automated periodic filesystem backup (**fsave**(ADM), **fsphoto**(ADM))
- unattended backup facility (**cbackup**(ADM))
- console and serial terminal multiscreens (**multiscreen**(M), **mscreen**(M))
- floppy disk recognition and management (**dtype**(C), **diskcp**(C), **format**(C))
- magnetic tape management (**tape**(C), **mcart**(C), **tapecntl**(C), **tapedump**(C))
- high-speed modem dialer support [see the SCO UNIX v4.2 release notes]
- system activity reporting (**uptime**(C), **mpstat**(ADM), **vmstat**(ADM), **w**(C))
- configuration reporting (**hwconfig**(C), **swconfig**(C), **netconfig**(ADM))
- boot-time loadable driver support (**boot**(HW), **btld**(F))

Other SCO value-added utilities include:

lock(C), **lprint**(C), **goodpw**(ADM), **mapchan**(M), **mapkey**(M), **setkey**(C), **sg**(C), **crypt**(C)$_1$, **purge**(C), **translate**(C), **rmb**(M), **idleout**(ADM), **getserno**(C), **kbmode**(ADM), **setcolor**(C), **vidi**(C), **usemouse**(C), **sfmt**(ADM), **eisa**(ADM), **scanon**(M), **scanoff**(M), **badtrk**(ADM), **dparam**(ADM), **haltsys**(ADM), **setclock**(ADM), **scsibadblk**(ADM).

---

1   crypt is available upon request from SCO Support

Essential SCO System Administration

Standard UNIX utilities supplied with SCO UNIX include:

Table 1-2:	Standard Included UNIX Utilities
• the base UNIX utilities	[not listed here]
• on-line manual pages	(**man***(C)*)
• file/directory management	(**mkdir***(C)*, **rmdir***(C)*, **mvdir***(ADM)*, **copy***(C)*, **settime***(C)*, **touch***(C)*, **chmod***(C)*)
• shells	(**sh***(C)*, **csh***(C)*, **ksh***(C)*, **rsh***(C)*, **rksh***(C)*)
• shell tools	(**getopts***(C)*, **line***(C)*, **test***(C)*, **env***(C)*, **wait***(C)*, **xargs***(C)*)
• text editing	(**ed***(C)*, **ex***(C)*, **vi***(C)*, **sed***(C)*, **bfs***(C)*, **csplit***(C)*, **split***(C)*, **exrecover***(C)*)
• calculation	(**bc***(C)*, **dc***(C)*, **expr***(C)*, **random***(C)*, **factor***(C)*, **units***(C)*)
• output filters	(**tee***(C)*, **cut***(C)*, **paste***(C)*, **join***(C)*, **col***(C)*, **pr***(C)*, **nl***(C)*, **tr***(C)*)
• file display	(**pg***(C)*, **dd***(C)*, **od***(C)*, **hd***(C)*, **newform***(C)*, **strings***(C)*)
• archival	(**tar***(C)*, **cpio***(C)*, **dd***(C)*, **ptar***(C)*, **pcpio***(C)*, **pax***(C)*, **sum***(C)*, **xtract***(C)*, **labelit***(C)*, **volcopy***(C)*)
• compression	(**compress***(C)*, **uncompress***(C)*, **zcat***(C)*, **pack***(C)*, **unpack***(C)*, **pcat***(C)*)
• filesystem	(**mkfs***(ADM)*, **fsck***(ADM)*, **fsdb***(ADM)*, **fstyp***(ADM)*, **fsstat***(ADM)*, **ncheck***(ADM)*, **fuser***(ADM)*, **ff***(ADM)*, **df***(C)*, **dcopy***(ADM)*, **clri***(ADM)*, **link***(ADM)*, **unlink***(ADM)*, **pipe***(ADM)*, **swap***(ADM)*, **sync***(ADM)*, **fsba***(ADM)*, **backup***(ADM)*, **restore***(ADM)*)
• mounting	(**mount***(ADM)*, **umount***(ADM)*, **mountall***(ADM)*, **umountall***(ADM)*, **setmnt***(ADM)*, **devnm***(C)*, **chroot***(ADM)*)
• login-related	(**getty***(M)*, **login***(M)*, **uugetty***(M)*)
• users & accounts	(**who***(C)*, **whodo***(C)*, **finger***(C)*, **ps***(C)*, **passwd***(C)*, **id***(C)*, **newgrp***(C)*, **su***(C)*)
• user communication	(**write***(C)*, **mesg***(C)*, **wall***(ADM)*)
• electronic mail	(**mail***(C)*, **mailx***(C)*, **rmail***(ADM)*, **execmail**
• system monitoring	(**crash***(ADM)*, **sar***(ADM)*, **sag***(ADM)*, **sadc***(ADM)*, **pstat***(C)*, **dmesg***(ADM)*, **prof**$_{iler}$*(ADM)*, **strace***(ADM)*, **timex***(ADM)*)
• print spooler	(**lp***(C)*, **lpadmin***(ADM)*, **lpsched***(ADM)*, **lpshut***(ADM)*, **lpfilter***(ADM)*, **lpstat***(C)*, **lpforms***(ADM)*, **lpmove***(ADM)*, **accept***(ADM)*, **reject**(ADM), **enable***(ADM)*, **disable***(ADM)*, **lpusers***(ADM)*)
• startup/shutdown	(**init***(M)*, **telinit***(M)*, **reboot***(ADM)*, **rc0***(ADM)*, **rc2***(ADM)*, **shutdown***(ADM)*)
• process & disk use accounting	(**quot***(C)*, **acct**$_{(ADM)}$, **acctcom***(ADM)*, **acctcon***(ADM)*, **acctprc***(ADM)*, **acctsh***(ADM)*
• task scheduling	(**cron***(C)*, **crontab***(C)*, **at***(C)*, **batch***(C)*)
• uucp	(**cu***(C)*, **ct***(C)*, **uucp***(C)*, **uuname***(C)*, **uuencode***(C)*, **uudecode***(C)*, **uustat***(C)*, **uuinstall***(ADM)*, **uucico***(ADM)*,

1-16

Chapter 1   Orientation to SCO UNIX

•	terminal-related	**uuto**(C), **uupick**(C), **uux**(C), **uuxqt**(ADM), **uusched**(ADM), **uudemon**(ADM), **uulog**(C), **uucheck**(ADM), **uutry**(ADM)) (**stty**(C), **tty**(C), **tabs**(C), **tput**(C), **tset**(C), **enable**(ADM), **disable**(ADM), **tic**(C), **infocmp**(ADM))
•	installation	(**displaypkg**(ADM), **installpkg**(ADM), **removepkg**(ADM), **installf**(ADM), **pkg***(ADM), **removef**(ADM))
•	shell layers	(**shl**(C), **layers**(C), **jterm**(C), **jwin**(C), **ismpx**(C), **relogin**(ADM))
•	graphing	(**spline**(C), **tplot**(C), **graph**(C))
•	programming support	(*processor-type booleans*, **ctags**(C), **ld**, **adb**$_2$)
•	miscellaneous	(**awk**(C), **news**(C), **calendar**(C), **uname**(C), **nlsadmin**(ADM), *games*)

The text formatting tools (**nroff**, **troff**, etc.) are not available from SCO.

Layered Product Support

More than just another pretty OS, SCO UNIX is a powerful platform for advanced system and network services. Layered system products can be installed onto SCO UNIX to greatly enhance its capabilities.

Advanced system products such as SCO Open Desktop and SCO Open Server have selected product layers already integrated.

Some of the key layered products available from SCO are listed below:

AHS	supplementary hardware drivers and configuration support
MPX	symmetric multiprocessing support
Merge	MS-DOS 5.0 and Windows 3.1 application support
LLI	network (link level) interface card support
TCP/IP	network applications support
NFS	network filesystem support
IPX/SPX	Novell network client support
LAN Manager	networked MS-DOS and OS/2 workstation support
Xsight	X11-based Motif GUI (graphical user interface) support

---

2   **adb** is supplied (but not supported) in the base SCO UNIX OS as **/etc/_fst**

Essential SCO System Administration

Scores of layered products are also available from third-party vendors, providing services ranging from transaction processing to network management.

Table 1-3:   Summary of Other Operating System Features in SCO UNIX

- hard disk OS coexistence (MS-DOS, OS/2)
- keyboard scan-code support (including keyboard remapping)
- demand paging and virtual memory
- ACER fast filesystem
- long file names (256 character)
- symbolic links
- uucp protocol support (g/e/f/x/t)
- asynchronous raw disk I/O
- scatter/gather disk I/O
- I/O character mapping support [see **mapchan**(M)]
- network transport interfaces (TLI, BSD sockets, XTI)
- process signalling and job control
- interprocess communication
- standards conformance (POSIX 1003.1, XPG3, IBCS-2)

Table 1-4: Key Operative Differences from Other UNIX Systems

- system installation
- system boot
- SCSI device autosensing
- multi-user initialization
- kernel configuration and linking
- built-in hardware support
- hardware and device driver configuration
- hardware device names
- filesystem support
- DOS partition and floppy support
- filesystem backup
- print spooling and administration
- security and auditing
- local language support
- command defaults directory

Chapter 1 Orientation to SCO UNIX

> The box below lists user-oriented features of SCO UNIX. It is included mainly for comparison with operating systems such as MS-DOS and OS/2.

Table 1-5:   End User Features of SCO UNIX

- command-line editing (BACKSPACE, CTRL-U)
- command-line prompt customization
- input command-line history (**csh** and **ksh** only)
- configurable command search path
- configurable directory search path
- exportable shell environment variables
- selectable execution shell (**#!**) *[known as **hashpling**]*
- output redirection and command line pipes
- signal keys to terminate input or processes (DEL, CTRL-D)
- wildcard searching on file names (*****, **?**, [ ])
- access permissions on files (read, write, execute)
- multiple access permission levels (owner, group, others)
- screen scrolling control (CTRL-S, CTRL-Q)
- console screen dump
- selectable screen color
- true ANSI support on console
- keyboard and output character mapping
- background and batch processing
- configurable user login start-up scripts

Essential SCO System Administration

Orientation for MS-DOS Users

The intent of this section is to provide you with essential comparative information to ease your transition from MS-DOS to UNIX.

Major Differences between MS-DOS and SCO UNIX

Differences are addressed in the following areas:

- power-up, power-down, and reset
- system configuration and start-up
- access to disks
- the command line
- files and directories
- command execution
- file management
- printing
- port access
- memory allocation
- graphics

Power-up, Power-down, and Reset

When a DOS system is powered up, the DOS kernel and a few device drivers are loaded. Overall, the power-up stage is short and sweet.

Power-up of a UNIX system involves a lot more. A much larger kernel must be loaded. Much of its size is due to the pre-configured device drivers integrated into the kernel binary. Additional time is spent verifying the integrity of the logical UNIX disks. Not to be overlooked are various processes that must be initialized for use by multiple users. This especially applies to printing and networking. Finally, after all this, the user sees a login prompt. You determine if the wait is worth it.

DOS systems can be powered down at the DOS prompt. UNIX systems, on the other hand, have quite a bit to clean up. Under UNIX, the safe way to power down is with the **shutdown**(ADM) command. That ensures that the proper clean-up will be performed.

Chapter 1   Orientation to SCO UNIX

> Much of the SCO UNIX clean-up requires that data cached (kept) in memory gets written to the hard disk. Caching disk data in memory is a common technique for expediting access to disk data.

DOS systems can be easily reset with CTRL-ALT-DEL. Fortunately, this does not work with UNIX systems. The same reasons apply.

System Configuration and Start-Up

DOS systems read **CONFIG.SYS** to determine where to load the DOS kernel and which device drivers to load. Further initialization is performed by **AUTOEXEC.BAT**.

With SCO UNIX, the kernel configuration and driver selection is a more complex procedure involving several system utilities, culminating in the creation of a new kernel. That kernel reflects the desired configuration changes.

The SCO UNIX system initialization files are clustered into special directories accessed before user logins are enabled. Start-up shell scripts can be specified for individual users. These are consulted at login time.

Access to Disks

DOS users become quite comfortable memorizing drive letters to access floppy disks and logical hard disks. As long as you keep the letters straight, files can be copied easily from one device to another.

As a rule, there are no drive letters in SCO UNIX. Yes, there are logical hard disks, but they must undergo a procedure called *mounting* before they can be accessed. Floppies are another story entirely. You can look forward to learning new techniques to store and access files on floppies under UNIX.

The Command Line

The command line in SCO UNIX basically operates similar to that in MS-DOS. There are some differences, though. These include the special keyboard keys.

Essential SCO System Administration

> Do not use arrow keys on a UNIX command line! They confuse the shell.

Special keys (i.e. arrow keys, function keys, insert/delete, hot-keys) are not recognized by the command line shells. Hot-keys are supported, but only in special shells such as SCO Shell or the system administration shell.

> Another difference is the choice of command-line shells available in SCO UNIX. These range from **sh***(C)* (Bourne shell) to the fuller-featured **ksh***(C)* (Korn shell). The wonderful functionality of the **DOSKEY** program is provided, to a large extent, by the Korn shell.

The flexibility of the DOS prompt to display the current device and directory is echoed in the Korn shell and the C-shell, **csh***(C)*, but not in the default Bourne shell.

Files and Directories

How different can files and directories be between DOS and UNIX? A file is a file, right? Yes, and no. As you may have gleaned from the basic terminology, files in UNIX are special. Fortunately, most UNIX files are just ordinary files.

Directories are similar, but different in the respect that UNIX directories don't actually contain any files. UNIX directories are more like tables of contents.

Other differences are listed in the table below:

Table 1-6: Some Differences Between MS-DOS and SCO UNIX Filenames

	MS-DOS	SCO UNIX
max file name length	8	255
file name extension?	yes	none
path name separator	"\"	"/"
name case-sensitive?	no	yes
file name wildcards	* ?	* ? [ ]

Chapter 1   Orientation to SCO UNIX

Filename Notes
- Be aware that SCO UNIX, like most versions of UNIX, is case-sensitive! With few exceptions, UNIX file and command names are all lowercase.
- Be extremely careful to use "/" in SCO UNIX filenames! When UNIX shells see "\", they treat the character that follows as special. The results will certainly not be what you expected.
- Since filename extensions are not special in SCO UNIX, "." is treated as just another character. This makes "*.*" virtually useless. Instead, use "*" to refer to all files in a UNIX directory.

Command Execution

Here again DOS and UNIX are basically similar. UNIX commands support options, as well as redirection and pipes. Even the simplicity of **DOSSHELL** is echoed in the SCO Shell, **scosh***(C)*.

A key difference is that UNIX is multitasking. A user can run multiple UNIX processes. One will run in the foreground, the others in the background. In UNIX you can't hot-key to a TSR, but job control (supported by the Korn shell) does allow processes to be shifted between background and foreground.

Canceling a command is different, as well. Foreground commands are easy enough to stop, but a special utility, **kill**, must be used to cancel aberrant background commands.

   The SCO UNIX cancel key is DEL, not CTRL-C.

SCO UNIX batch files, aka *shell scripts*, are much more powerful than those under DOS. A major part of administering a UNIX system is either changing or creating shell scripts.

File Management

Besides different command names, there are few differences in the way that files are copied, renamed, moved, or deleted. A key exception is that SCO UNIX files cannot be undeleted.

Essential SCO System Administration

> Some vendors (e.g. Norton) offer UNIX products that support undeletion. These programs work, but use special tricks that don't actually delete the files in the first place.

SCO UNIX has a totally different concept of file attributes. UNIX files have twelve attribute bits which can be set independently. Access to UNIX files can be restricted to a specific user or a group of users. Three types of access can be granted (read, write, execute). UNIX directories have the same number of attribute bits.

DOS File Attribute	SCO UNIX Equivalent
hidden	deny read access on directory
readonly	deny write access on file
archive	*[not applicable]*
system	restrict file access to system user

> UNIX has the concept of a special system user, called the ***superuser*** or ***root*** user. The superuser has unrestricted access to all files and directories on the system.

Printing

Nearly all printing in UNIX is managed by a master print spooler. UNIX uses the **lp***(C)* command for print spooling. Output can also be piped to **lp**. There is practically no limit to the number of printers that can be configured.

Although you can copy files to the printer in DOS, this is not done in UNIX. There is no SCO UNIX equivalent to PRN. SCO UNIX printers are referred to by name, instead of by port or destination.

The concept of mapping the default printer to another port does not exist in UNIX. Use the UNIX print configuration utility to specify the port of the default printer. To use a printer other than the default, simply specify the name as an option to **lp**.

Chapter 1   Orientation to SCO UNIX

Port Access

As a rule, users seldom access ports directly in UNIX. The convention is to access ports through a controlling application, such as the print spooler (**lp**) or the communications manager (**uucp**).

SCO UNIX port names differ from their MS-DOS counterparts. The parallel and serial ports are special files, *device files*, that reside in the UNIX **/dev** directory.

The table below maps DOS ports to their default SCO UNIX device files.

Table 1-7:	MS-DOS to SCO UNIX Port Mappings	
DOS Port	**SCO Device**	**Function**
LPT1	**/dev/lp0**	first parallel port
LPT2	**/dev/lp2**	second parallel port
LPT3	**/dev/lp1**	parallel port on mono card
COM1	**/dev/tty1a**	first serial port
	/dev/tty1A	modem interface to first serial port
COM2	**/dev/tty2a**	second serial port
	/dev/tty2A	modem interface to second serial port
CON	**/dev/tty**	current terminal or console port
PRN	*no equivalent*	

> On an SCO UNIX system, there can be multiple serial device interfaces configured as COM1 or COM2. This is possible, because SCO UNIX supports multiport adapters.
>
> Since COM3 and COM4 conflict with COM1 and COM2, they are not supported. To use them requires special configuration.
>
> The SCO UNIX parallel devices, **/dev/lp0** (LPT1) and **/dev/lp1** (LPT3) conflict as well. Only one or the other may be used at any time.

Although most ports in SCO UNIX are configured automatically, all can be explicitly configured using special utilities.

Memory Allocation

Relax. There is no 640K barrier in UNIX. Installed RAM is treated as one giant stretch of memory. This is also known as a *flat memory space*. Even better, SCO UNIX supports a concept called *virtual memory*. Virtual memory combines

Essential SCO System Administration

installed RAM and dedicated disk space to create more usable memory. The net result is that lots of programs can run comfortably together.

Graphics

Unlike DOS, SCO UNIX programs not are free to take control of the graphics adapter. If you require graphics, you'll need to purchase an advanced systems product like SCO Open Desktop or install a layered product like SCO XSight that supports graphical applications.

Table 1-8:   MS-DOS -> SCO UNIX Command Map

Command Description	MS-DOS	SCO	Notes
change directories	cd	cd	
display current directory	cd	pwd	
copy a file	copy	cp	
delete a file	del	rm	
rename a file	ren	mv	
move a file	move	mv	copy + del (in MS-DOS 5.x)
print a file	print	lp	
list files	dir	ls -l	
display a file	type	cat	
display a file page-by-page	more	more	
edit a file	edit	vi	SCO shell has a friendly editor
searching for text	find	grep	
create a directory	md	mkdir	
remove a directory	rmdir	rmdir	
copy a directory	xcopy	copy	
checking a logical drive	chkdsk	fsck	
clear the screen	cls	clear	
display current date	date	date	
change current date	date	asktime	
set command search path	path	PATH=	SCO UNIX shell variable
set command line prompt	prompt	PS1=	SCO UNIX shell variable
display the environment	set	env	

1-26

Chapter 2

A First Install

	Page
Introduction	2-4
Road Map	2-5
Basic Terminology and Concepts	2-6
Disk Partitions	2-7
Partition Size, Tracks, and Cylinders	2-7
Divisions and Filesystems	2-8
Booting	2-9
Hardware Configuration	2-9
SCSI	2-10
Preparing to Install	2-11
Verifying Hardware Support	2-11
Verifying Required System Resources	2-12
Recording the Existing System State	2-13
General Hardware Preparation and Preconfiguration	2-14
Creating an Initial MS-DOS Partition	2-17
Installation Overview	2-18
The Boot and Media Installation Floppies	2-18
Installation Options	2-18
Fresh Installation	2-19
Update Installation	2-19
Initializing the Hard Disk	2-20
Automatic Disk Installation	2-21
Fully Configurable Disk Installation	2-21
Installing the SCO Product	2-22
Considerations for a Fresh Installation	2-24
Considerations for an Update Installation	2-25
Installation Follow-up	2-25
Preventative Installation Planning	2-27

Essential SCO System Administration

Survival Recipes and Tutorials   **Page** 2-28

Survival Recipes

SR2.1:	Creating an Initial MS-DOS Partition	2-17
SR2.2:	Booting the System	2-28
SR2.3:	Booting to Single-user Mode	2-29
SR2.4:	Booting to Multiuser Mode	2-30
SR2.5:	Shutting Down the System	2-32
SR2.6:	Shutting Down to Single-user Mode	2-33
SR2.7:	Introduction to the System Administration Shell	2-34
SR2.8:	Configuring the Default Backup Device	2-37
SR2.9:	Creating a Root/Boot Floppy Set	2-39

Procedures and Suggestions

Recording an Existing System Configuration	2-13
System Hardware Preconfiguration	2-14
Fresh Installation Options	2-24
Update Installation Options	2-25
Installation Follow-up	2-26
Preventative Installation Tips	2-27

Titled Digressions

✆	Supported or Not Supported?	2-11
✈	Disk Allocation Guidelines	2-12
✈	Overriding Default Configuration Values Using Boot Strings	2-15
✈	Boot-time Loadable Drivers	2-16
☞	Allocating Swap Space	2-21
☞	Trusted Security Levels	2-23
☞	Aborting the Fresh Installation	2-24
☞	Restarting the Fresh Installation	2-24
☞	Aborting the Update Installation	2-25
☞	The Initial System Backup	2-26
☞	Emergency Root/Boot Floppies	2-26
✈	Avoiding System Time Loss	2-31
✈	Names of Tape Devices on the Updated Root/Boot Floppy Set	2-38

Chapter 2   A First Install

Page

Tables

2-1:	Required Resources for Installation	2-12
2-2:	Recommended Configuration of Supported SCSI Adapters	2-15
2-3:	Hard Disk Initialization Steps	2-20
2-4:	Highlights of the SCO Installation	2-22
2-5:	Final Installation Checklist	2-23

Diagrams

2-1:	Hard Disk Partitions	2-6
2-2:	Disk Tracks and Cylinders	2-7
2-3:	Disk Divisions (Virtual Disks)	2-8

Essential SCO System Administration

Introduction

It was half-time on Sunday, an off day. Incredibly, the lowly Sharks were leading their hockey opponents, albeit only by a goal. Sierra and her sister, Shasta, rushed to raid the office icebox before undertaking their task.

The two had a small, but growing, organic produce business. They were adding new employees and had decided to upgrade their DOS machine to UNIX. Since they were supposed to be here working, Sierra reluctantly started to install the new UNIX, which had arrived the day before.

"Great gherkin!" she groaned as she opened the product box. "What is all this stuff!?" Sierra started to panic, then remembered how much junk had accompanied the database software for her DOS system. Most of it she hadn't even used. She had survived that; she would survive this.

Fortunately, the first thing out of the box was an installation roadmap. It illustrated very clearly the order of installation and what would happen at each step. Sierra was able to get started before the second half commenced.

During each subsequent time-out, Shasta and Sierra took turns inserting the next installation disks. It just wouldn't be fair for either to miss those crazy beer commercials. As it turned out, the entire process was quite easy. They finished the installation with minutes to spare, only to see their ungrateful Sharks give up the winning, and final, goal.

This chapter presents the skills and knowledge to enable you to successfully complete a basic SCO UNIX installation. This initial configuration will enable you to receive hands-on experience learning to administer this powerful operating system.

Chapter 2   A First Install

Road Map

This chapter targets users who have minimal experience with installing an SCO system product. This includes the following categories of users:
- users who are new to SCO (perhaps from MS-DOS)
- users with primarily runtime SCO experience
- experienced administrators with minimal SCO exposure
- administrators of older SCO systems (e.g. XENIX)

[Important Caveat]

This chapter provides effective planning and implementation strategies for a successful SCO installation. It supplements the *Installation Guide* that comes with your SCO product. For precise guidance and detailed installation troubleshooting, you may need to consult that guide directly. Simply consider this chapter as a friendly and intelligent guide to the installation.

Essential Sections for All New Administrators

Preparing to Install
Installation Overview
Performing the Installation

Strongly Recommended: Basic Terminology and Concepts
SR2.7: Introduction to the System
Administration Shell

Suggested Topics for Experienced Administrators

General Hardware Preparation and Preconfiguration
SR2.1: Creating an Initial MS-DOS Partition
SR2.8: Configuring the Default Backup Device
SR2.9: Creating a Root/Boot Floppy Set
ℂ   Supported or Not Supported?
☞   Allocating Swap Space
✈   Avoiding System Time Loss

2-5

Basic Terminology and Concepts

Before letting you loose to install the SCO product, a few basic system concepts may be in order.

partition	track	division	filesystem
booting	hardware configuration		SCSI

Disk Partitions

Let's start with the obvious – where you install SCO UNIX. You install it onto the hard disk, right? Well, partially yes. On Intel-based systems you actually install the operating system onto a disk *partition*.

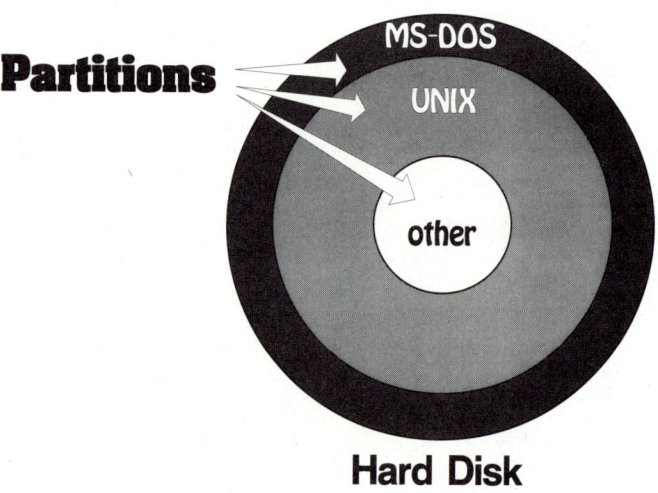

"Huh!?", you say, "What's a partition?" Well, here are some examples on your right. This disk is divided into three of them. One is for MS-DOS, another for SCO UNIX, and the third is still to be determined.

Hard disks are often divided into one or more partitions. Each OS resides on its own partition.

 On DOS systems, there may be a primary DOS partition, plus a separate extended DOS partition. In contrast, there is typically a single UNIX partition on SCO systems. A maximum of four partitions can be defined per hard disk.

Okay, good, but why do this? One reason is to have a choice of computing environments on the same system. For instance, I often work in MS-DOS for fast graphics response. Yet, I still prefer SCO UNIX to create my manuscripts.

Chapter 2   A First Install

> Only one partition may be *active* at any time. The *active partition* determines which operating system will be in force. While an SCO partition is active, DOS partitions may still be accessed. With SCO Merge installed, you can even execute files on a DOS partition while the SCO partition is active.

Partition Size, Tracks, and Cylinders

Partition size is commonly measured in megabytes (MB). One MB can hold just over one million bytes or characters (roughly 436 typewritten pages). In SCO UNIX, partitions are measured in disk units called *tracks*.

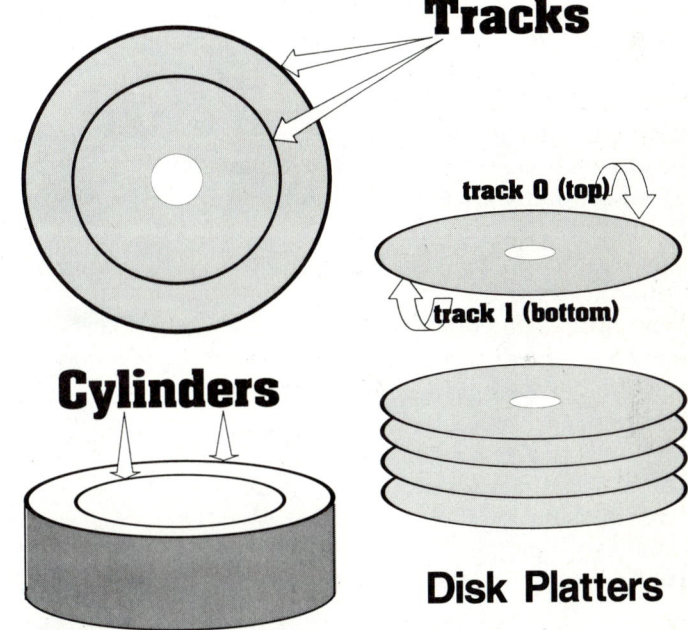

Tracks, as you can see from the diagram, are like the grooves on a vinyl record. Each track is circular. Tracks are extremely narrow, just wide enough for a single bit (eight bits forming one byte). Yet, tracks may be thousands of bits long.

A single disk can hold thousands of tracks, each with the same number of data bits. The actual size varies by hard disk. Fortunately, this is not critical for the initial installation.

Other units encountered when discussing disk partitions are *cylinders*. As the diagram indicates, hard disks are actually stacks of disk platters. Both the top and bottom surface of each platter can store data.[1] A *cylinder* is, effectively, a vertical stack of tracks, one from each platter surface.

---

1 Inside the hard disk assembly are read/write heads, one per platter surface.

2-7

Essential SCO System Administration

> Three of the specifications shipped with every hard disk are the numbers of cylinders, heads, and sectors per track. Multiply cylinders times heads to yield the total number of tracks. Each sector contains 512 bytes.
>
> Beware that many disks controllers, especially ESDI and the newer IDE, remap the number of physical cylinders and heads to logical values allowed by the PC BIOS firmware. Since SCO UNIX accesses the disk through the controller, it is only interested in the logical specifications.

Divisions and Filesystems

Disk partitions may themselves have their own subdivisions. MS-DOS users call them *logical drives*. On SCO UNIX systems, logical drives are known as *divisions*. Divisions that contain files and directories are called *filesystems*.

At several points in the UNIX installation procedure you may be asked about divisions (or filesystems). As the diagram to the right illustrates, they are simply distinct sections of the disk belonging to a single partition.

Virtual Disks (on a partition)

Hard Disk

The diagram identifies three divisions on the UNIX partition.
Two, **root** and **u**, are SCO UNIX filesystems. The third, **swap**, is special.

> SCO UNIX uses **swap** to supplement the installed random access memory (RAM). The combination of **swap** and RAM is called *virtual memory*.

In many respects the OS treats each division as a separate hard drive. Each division can have its own format. Disk data errors can be confined to a single division. Divisions can be taken off-line or put back on-line. And, like real disks, multiple divisions can be used concurrently.

Booting

When you turn on the machine, the operating system gets initialized to enable users to start computing. This process is known as *booting*.

The machine seems to know exactly how to start up the operating system. Even more interesting is when multiple partitions are defined, the machine knows the correct operating system to boot.

This wizardry is performed by the ROM-BIOS, a special read-only memory (ROM) chip in the computer. The ROM-BIOS uses special information on the first track of the hard disk to locate and run the right operating system.

> The first track (track 0) is where the table of partitions is located. It is also where the **masterboot** program lives. **masterboot**'s job is to find the active partition, then run the special boot program at the start of that partition. It is the boot program's job to load and run the operating system.

During the installation process, the system may *boot* more than once. This is necessary, because after each installed modification to the operating system, the computer must be *rebooted* to take advantage of those changes.

Hardware Configuration

A good operating system must be able to locate the installed hardware. Devices that the ROM-BIOS knows about (e.g. disk drives, video monitors, RAM) are relatively easy to sense. Others (e.g. serial adapters, tape drives, CD-ROM drives) are more reliably found using information provided by the system administrator – you.

You will need to determine the current *device configuration parameters* for each hardware device, then communicate this to the OS. The process is called *hardware configuration*. As you might expect, this is the most critical part of the SCO UNIX installation procedure.

Essential SCO System Administration

SCSI

SCSI – an unpronounceable acronym striking terror in the minds of anyone within hearing distance! Actually, not quite. It's pronounced "scuzzy".

SCSI is short for *small computer systems interface*. SCSI is a fast data pathway connecting certain hardware devices with the computer. It is a popular way to add peripherals to Intel-based systems.

As the primary installation authority on your SCO system, you will need to know whether a SCSI interface is installed and how it is configured. This is especially important when you have tape drives, CD-ROM drives, or hard disks connected to the SCSI adapter.

Chapter 2   A First Install

Preparing to Install

Essential preparation for a trouble-free installation includes the following:

- verifying hardware support
- verifying required system resources
- recording the existing system state
- preconfiguring hardware for the actual installation

Verifying Hardware Support

The most thorough preparation can't help you if the hardware you plan to use is not supported (or supportable) under SCO. For installation, in particular, you'll need to verify support for the following devices:

- computer system   *[note the motherboard version and system bus]*
- hard disk controller   *[note the controller type (e.g. IDE, SCSI, ESDI)]*
- SCSI host adapter   *[note the base chip set]*
- video adapter   *[note the underlying chip set]*
- QIC tape controller

Supported or Not Supported?

SCO publishes a list of hardware that it has tested in the *SCO Hardware Compatibility Handbook*. This handbook also contains hardware that has been reported by the vendor to work with SCO. Such hardware may listed as supported by the vendor. Yet, hardware tested by SCO will, with few exceptions, be supported by SCO. Support for a specific system or device implies that SCO takes responsibility to help you resolve system-related problems involving that hardware. This responsibility usually extends through the warranty period, even longer if you purchase extended support.

Although many devices not specifically listed in the *SCO Hardware Compatibility Handbook* may actually work with SCO systems, you are generally on your own when problems develop from the use of these devices. Support is more an insurance policy than anything else. If you even slightly value the data on your system, supportability is insurance well worth having.

<u>If in doubt about the supportability of any hardware you might consider using with a SCO system, you can always contact SCO directly at the following numbers:</u>

               (North America)   800-726-8649
               (Europe/Asia)   +44 923 816344

Verifying Required System Resources

There is little point installing the operating system if you haven't allocated sufficient resources for successful operation. Consult table 2-1 below to determine the system resources required for your installation.

Table 2-1:	Required System Resources for Installation			
		Minimum Required	Recommended Resources SCO	Author
Free disk space	(SCO UNIX)	40MB *	80MB *	120MB *
	(Open Desktop)	108MB *	200MB *	300MB *
Total system RAM	(SCO UNIX)	2MB	4MB	8MB
	(Open Desktop)	8MB	16MB	24MB
Processor power		386SX/16	-------	486DX/25
			* - add 60MB for the Development System	

A floating point unit is required to run SCO Open Desktop. This is standard with the Intel "DX" and Pentium Processors.

Disk Space Allocation Guidelines

Beyond the minimum required disk space you should allocate:

- 10-20 MB file storage space per system user
- 10-12 MB swap space per Open Desktop user
- 10-15% of the root filesystem size for temporary files

Recording the Existing System State

This section especially applies to those who have an existing operating system installed on their machines.

As most auto mechanics quickly learn, one takes special care to record the configuration and interconnection of the engine components <u>before</u> making any major adjustments. This applies no less to computer systems.

If you have an existing operating system configured, you'll want to record the states of both your software and hardware. The hardware information will greatly facilitate proper configuration of the new (or revised) operating system.

Chapter 2 A First Install

At best, the software information will help you to properly initialize and allocate resources on the new system. At worst, you can use the software information to restore the system to a known state for troubleshooting purposes.

Recording an Existing System Configuration

1) Back up all system and application software currently installed on your system. Yet, do not remove any software at this time.

    If no native backup utility is available, simply copy the installed files to floppies or tape (if configured).

2) Print out the contents of relevant operating system configuration files

MS-DOS	**SCO UNIX**
CONFIG.SYS	/etc/default/boot
AUTOEXEC.BAT	/etc/inittab
	/etc/conf/cf.d/stune
	/etc/conf/cf.d/mscsi

3) Record the current hardware configuration parameters for your system and its installed peripherals. These include:
    - hardware IRQ values (interrupt vectors)
    - base hardware addresses (I/O base addresses)
    - DMA channels
    - controller RAM addresses (memory-mapped I/O addresses)
    - port names for attached printers, mice, and modems
    - makes and models of attached or installed hardware

    ☞ It is not important to understand the various configuration terms (i.e. IRQ, base address, DMA, controller RAM) now. They are explained in detail in chapter 5. For now, you simply need to record any values reported by your system for these terms. This information will be invaluable when reconfiguring your hardware for use with SCO.

    ☞ Although you can determine the relevant settings for many hardware devices from DIP switches, it may be easier to run the hardware-specific setup and configuration programs to display these values for you.

4) Label all attached and internal cables, clearly indicating the device or port to which each cable end is connected.

Essential SCO System Administration

General Hardware Preparation and Preconfiguration

> Although this section targets those who have no operating system installed on their machines, many of the recommendations apply universally.

Although PC hardware configurations vary widely, a few general preparatory recommendations (courtesy of SCO Technical Support) may greatly minimize technical problems during your SCO product installation.

System Hardware Pre-Configuration

1) Verify that the floppy disk is correctly configured.

   Use the CMOS setup program (available when the system first powers up) or, on EISA systems, the EISA configuration disk.

2) Through the CMOS setup program, disable the system's shadow RAM, shadow BIOS, and high-speed cache.

3) If booting from a SCSI disk, adjust the CMOS settings so that no disks are configured. This allows the SCSI BIOS to find and boot the SCSI disk.

   > ☞ If installing multiple SCSI host adapters, make sure that the adapter hosting the boot hard disk has its BIOS enabled. Disable the BIOS on all other adapters.

4) For the duration of the installation, slow the machine's processing speed to 33MHz.

   > ☞ A slower speed is recommended to allow the operating system to correctly locate and identify system hardware. The speed can be restored once installation is complete.

5) Disable any caching on your disk controllers and SCSI adapters.

6) Put your SCSI adapter in standard mode (32-bit modes may cause problems).

7) Verify that your installation hardware devices are set up properly.

SCSI adapters	[consult table 2-2]
SCSI CD-ROM	confirm target ID = 5, LUN (logical unit number) = 0
SCSI tape	confirm target ID = 2, LUN = 0
QIC-02 tape	[note the configured IRQ, base address, and DMA]

Chapter 2   A First Install

Table 2-2: Recommended Configuration of Supported SCSI Host Adapters

Supported SCSI Adapter	Code	IRQ	Base Addr	DMA	ID
Western Digital WD7000-FASST2	wdha	12	0x350	6	7
Western Digital WD7000EX	wdex	15	a/c	a/c	7
DPT 2011	dpt	14	0x1F0	5	7
DPT 2012	dpt	14	a/c	a/c	7
Adaptec AHA-152x	spad	11	0x340	0	7
Adaptec AHA-154x/164x	ad	11	0x330	5	7
Adaptec AHA-174x	eiad	11	a/c	a/c	7
Future Domain TMC-845/850/860/885	tmcha	5	a/c	a/c	6
Future Domain TMC-1660/1680,MCS-700	fdha	14	0x140	a/c	6
Storage Plus SUMO	sumo	14	0x310	a/c	7
386/486 CBUS SCSI	ciha	*	*	*	
IBM Hard File	hf	*	*	*	
Olivetti ESC-1	esc	*	*	*	
Compaq SCSI		5	0x130	7	7

a/c = autoconfigured (either on-board or by software)
* - consult vendor's documentation

Overriding Default Configuration Values Using Boot Strings

Boot strings can be used to override the configured defaults for hardware adapters and SCSI devices. This includes SCSI host adapters. For example, to override the defaults for the WD7000 host adapter, you could enter the following at the boot prompt *[see SR2.2 for an example of the boot prompt]*:

defbootstr adapter=wdha(0x350,14,6)

This example accepts the default boot parameters, but indicates base address 0x350, IRQ14, and DMA channel 6 for the WD7000 host adapter.

For another example, to override the defaults for the installation CD-ROM drive, you could enter the following boot string:

defbootstr Srom=spad(0,6,0)

This example also uses the default boot parameters, but indicates that the default CD-ROM drive is connected to the first (#0) Adaptec 152x host adapter, and is configured at target ID 6, LUN 0. *[See boot(HW) for details]*.

Essential SCO System Administration

> **Boot-time Loadable Drivers**
>
> Some hardware vendors supply special drivers to support their hardware under SCO. For the most part, these are boot-time loadable drivers (BTLDs). These are drivers that can be specified and loaded during the boot phase of the operating system installation. *[Consult the vendor's documentation for detailed instructions on loading BTLDs].*

8. Remove extraneous cards not required for installation.

9. Ensure that your video adapter is supported.

    Consult the *SCO Hardware Compatibility Handbook* for specific makes and models. If unsupported, set adapter for standard VGA mode. Disable EGA autoswitching.

10. For the duration of the installation, install the video adapter into an 8-bit slot to avoid DMA conflicts. This applies to ISA (standard architecture) systems only.

11. When using SCSI host adapters:
    a) Ensure that the terminating resistors are correctly seated and placed. Only the adapter and the last attached device are terminated.
    b) Ensure that the target ID of the SCSI hard disk is jumpered correctly.

> For most SCSI adapters, the target ID of the primary disk should be 0. Consult your SCSI adapter hardware manual for specific details.

12. Verify that the add-on memory chips or modules have the same speed and size.

13. For the duration of the installation, put 2.88MB floppy drives into 1.44MB mode.

14. If your hard disk has more than 1024 physical cylinders, make sure that you enable translation mode (to use logical cylinders and sectors/track instead).

> After the installation, you can:
>
> - return your system to full speed
> - re-enable CPU and adapter caching
> - restore your floppy to 2.88MB mode
> - restore the video adapter to a 16-bit (or 32-bit) slot
> - re-install cards for devices not required for the installation

Chapter 2 A First Install

Creating an Initial MS-DOS Partition

> This section is optional, but highly recommended.

An MS-DOS partition is useful for several reasons. Three are listed below:

- You can store MS-DOS, Windows, and SCO-based files on the same disk.
- You have the choice of running MS-DOS, Windows, or SCO-based applications.
- Most diagnostic and configuration software is available only for MS-DOS.

The last point is arguably the most important for your SCO software installation.

> Much of your hardware configuration can be performed under MS-DOS. Once relevant configuration parameters have been set using a DOS configuration program, they will remain set until the system is turned off or reset. This especially applies to hardware that is software-configurable.

The steps to create an initial MS-DOS partition are provided in the recipe below:

Quick Recipe SR2.1   **Creating an Initial MS-DOS Partition**

If desired. an MS-DOS partition must be created before installing the SCO product distribution

1. Boot from an MS-DOS floppy.
   If the installation program starts up, either quit or abort by pressing CTRL-C
2. Run: **fdisk c:**
   This lets you allocate all or part of your disk to MS-DOS.

   > Pay close attention to the units used to allocate the DOS partition. Be sure to allocate at least 2.5MB for the DOS partition. Remember to leave sufficient disk space for the SCO operating system. It is alright to make the DOS partition active.

3. Next, run: **format /s c:**
   This formats the DOS partition allocated in step (2) as bootable.
4. Reboot from the MS-DOS floppy and install MS-DOS onto the hard disk.

Essential SCO System Administration

Installation Overview

A little background beforehand can save you hours of configuration and administration headaches later. Topics to facilitate a happy installation include:

- the boot and master installation floppies
- installation options (update or fresh installation)
- initializing the hard disk (for SCO system files)

The Boot and Media Installation Floppies

Regardless of the actual distribution media (3.5" or 5.25" floppies, DC6xxxx cartridge tape, or CD-ROM), every installation kit contains three special floppies:

N1 - the SCO distribution boot disk
N2 - the SCO distribution boot filesystem disk
M1 - the SCO distribution media installation disk

The two boot floppies (N1 and N2) effectively kickstart the installation. These floppies initially load a small SCO UNIX kernel into RAM. This kernel, in turn, launches a special UNIX program to manage the installation process.

Their job is to prepare the hard disk for the contents of the SCO product distribution. This requires that:

- a suitable portion of the disk be reserved for SCO
- a **root** filesystem exist to hold the installed system files
- a minimum set of files be installed on the hard disk in order for it to boot

Once the hard disk is ready, the media installation floppy (M1) takes control.

Installation Options

For those of you without SCO UNIX or Open Desktop already installed on your system, the choice is very simple: fresh installation.

[SCO First-timers]

Perform the fresh installation. Proceed next to "Initializing the Hard Disk".

Chapter 2   A First Install

Fresh Installation

As you might imagine, the fresh installation loads a pristine SCO system onto your hard disk (or the active partition). It overwrites all existing files. This includes all configuration information. Select fresh installation if you:

- are a new user of SCO
- are updating a version of SCO UNIX prior to Release 3.2 version 2.0
- are updating a version of SCO Open Desktop prior to version 2.0
- suspect that your current SCO system might be corrupt
- are upgrading a relaxed SCO system to a C2 trusted security level

Otherwise, you may find the update installation a preferable option.

Update Installation

The update installation preserves your existing configuration. Features include:

- all user data and directories are retained
- all system data and directories are retained
- all SCO-supported drivers are retained
- system files not modified since the last install are silently replaced

Although intelligent, the update is not 100% seamless. Some files may not be modified. These will include:

- any system files on non-root filesystems

    This especially applies to systems with separate **/usr**, **/usr/spool**, **/usr/lib**, or **/usr/man** filesystems. Only files on the root filesystem are modified.
- most **uucp** files (especially the dialer files: **/usr/lib/uucp/dial***)
- the master shell start files (**/etc/cshrc**, **/etc/profile**)
- the terminal database source files (**/usr/lib/terminfo/terminfo.src**, **/etc/termcap**)

> A complete list of the files left unmodified can be found in your SCO product *Installation Guide*.
>
> Most of the files left unmodified will have update versions bearing ".new" or "_" extensions. The system leaves it to you to insert the changes to unmodified system files from the updated versions.

2-19

Essential SCO System Administration

Initializing the Hard Disk

Before copying any files, the system will attempt to allocate sufficient space for the primary disk divisions – the *root filesystem* and the **swap** space. This process is called *hard disk initialization*. You may well want to have input into this process.

> Hard disk initialization is only performed for fresh installs.

The SCO UNIX installation provides two levels of control over disk initialization: fully configurable and automatic.

> *[SCO First-Timers]*
>
> For fast and easy initialization, select automatic installation. Simply beware that the associated disk scan takes nearly one minute for every 10MB of hard disk partition (except on SCSI disks, which do not require scanning). Proceed to "Highlights of the SCO UNIX Installation".

The hard disk initialization steps are summarized in the box below.

Table 2-3:	Hard Disk Initialization Steps
1. Verify hard disk parameters.	*[not done for SCSI disks]*
2. Determine disk partitioning.	
3. Map bad disk tracks.	*[not done for SCSI disks]*
4. Set the size of the **swap** division.	
5. Size the default filesystems (**root**, **u**)[1].	
6. Adjust size and position of default and new divisions.	
7. Build the defined filesystems.	
8. Mount the hard disk **root** filesystem, and copy the boot software onto it.	

Once disk initialization is complete, the system is ready to install the basic operating system from the distribution disks.

---

[1] A **u** filesystem (virtual disk) is created by default only on partitions of 240MB or larger.

Chapter 2 A First Install

Automatic Disk Initialization

The system uses reasonable defaults to automatically perform the above steps. You simply sit and watch. You might want to brew yourself some tea while the system carefully scans the hard disk for flaws.

Advantages	Disadvantages
Easy	Slow
Relatively goof-proof	No chance to customize
Retains existing filesystems and partitions	Cannot reallocate disk

Fully Configurable Disk Initialization

The fully configurable installation lets you verify or modify the suggested configuration defaults at each stage of the process. This affords you the best opportunity to customize the allocation of the hard disk according to the unique needs of your site.

Advantages	Disadvantages
Fast track scanning possible	Manual intervention required
Can redefine filesystems and partitions	Some risk of overwriting data
Can segregate user data from OS	Must precisely size root filesystem
Configures nonstandard disks	
System performance tunable via swap	Need to know system usage patterns

> **Allocating Swap Space**
>
> The amount of swap space that you allocate can govern the performance of your system. This is especially critical for Open Desktop systems, where each user may be allocated up to 10MB of dedicated virtual memory. As multiple users and processes compete for limited RAM and CPU resources, the kernel is obliged to move the virtual memory of sleeping or inactive processes out to swap. This frees RAM for newly activated dedicated processes.
>
> Minimally, you should allocate as much swap as you have RAM. Optimally, you should allocate 1.5-2.0 times the RAM amount for your swap space.

Essential SCO System Administration

Installing the SCO Product

> Specific installation steps are explicitly detailed in your SCO product's *Installation Guide*. The installation is merely summarized here. The goal of this section is to offer orientation and troubleshooting tips for a successful installation. Open Desktop users should be aware that your installation steps may differ from those described here.

Preparation complete, there are just a few more considerations before you actually begin your installation.

First, you'll need to open the SCO product box and set aside the following items:

- the SCO product's *Installation Guide*
- the SCO product's *Release Notes*
- the *SCO Hardware Compatibility Handbook*
- the *SCO Open Systems Software Hardware Configuration Guide*
- a colored card-stock sheet titled "Activation Key"
- a small box containing boot and master installation floppies (N1,N2,M1)
- your SCO software distribution media (i.e. floppies, tape, CD-ROM) *[consult the* Release Notes *for a specific list of contents]*

Table 2-4:	Highlights of the SCO Installation
A.	You insert the N1 floppy to commence the installation.
B.	The system displays the boot prompt. You can press ENTER or supply an appropriate boot string.
C.	The system loads a kernel specially preconfigured with the device drivers required for installation.
D.	The system initializes the hard disk, then reboots.
E.	You insert the SCO distribution media.
F.	The system extracts the SCO runtime system files.
G.	You supply the product activation key and serial number.
H.	You can elect to install the remainder of the distribution.
I.	You christen your newly installed system with a name.
J.	You select one of four security levels for your system.
K.	You choose a password for the **root** super user.
L.	The machine reboots as a virgin production SCO system.

Chapter 2   A First Install

> **Trusted Security Levels**
>
> During the installation you will be asked to select a trusted security level for your system. The four defined levels are:
>
> **high**   resource restrictions so tight, even grandma wouldn't approve.
> **improved**   a nice starting point, granting reasonable protection
> **traditional** the usual, run-of-the-mill UNIX file and password security
> **low**   imagine South Central LA, with no gun control *[it's your system!]*
>
> The rule of thumb is to start high, then "relax" to lower security levels until you feel comfortable. I prefer to start with **improved**.

Consult the checklist in table 2-5 to determine whether you are sufficiently prepared for a trouble-free installation.

Table 2-5:   **Final Installation Checklist**

- ❒ existing operating system (including user files) is backed up
- ❒ product installation option (fresh or update) selected
- ❒ disk initialization procedure (automatic or fully configurable) determined
- ❒ SCO boot floppies and distribution media within reach
- ❒ SCO serial number and activation key handy
- ❒ previously logged hardware configuration parameters accessible
- ❒ suitable system name (8 character maximum) chosen
- ❒ trusted security level (high, improved, traditional, low) determined
- ❒ non-obvious root password selected
- ❒ accurate time and date ready to be entered
- ❒ correct local timezone known
- ❒ local applicability of daylight saving time determined

- ❒ two new floppies for the root/boot floppy pair put aside
- ❒ a blank tape (or ample floppies) for the initial system backup ready

2-23

Considerations for a Fresh Installation

For a fresh installation I recommend the following options:

Fresh Installation Options

A. Select automatic hard disk initialization.

   This is appropriate for new users, because the system uses intelligent defaults to configure reasonable utility and performance.

B. Directly install the entire set of extended utilities.

   It is faster and simpler to install the entire distribution and later delete what you don't require.

C. Use "improved" as the initial trusted security level.

   If "improved" proves too restrictive, you can safely relax to "traditional".

D. Decline to run the system administration shell when prompted.

   Running the system administration shell when requested is not necessary and may actually complicate subsequent user and application configuration.

Please consult the notes below in case of unanticipated problems.

Aborting the Fresh Installation

If, for any reason, you must prematurely exit the fresh installation, the system lcts you resume from the point of exit. Simply follow the instructions below:

1. Reboot from the N1 floppy.
2. Press ENTER at the "Boot:" prompt.

To exit the installation, select "quit" when next available as a prompt option. Otherwise, abort by pressing the DEL key.

Restarting the Fresh Installation

If at any time you need to restart the installation from the beginning, follow the instructions below:

1. Exit the installation *[as described in the previous box]*.
2. Reboot from the N1 floppy.
3. At the boot prompt, enter: **restart**

Chapter 2 A First Install

Considerations for an Update Installation

There are six main phases in the update installation:
- initial boot phase   (saves current version system files)
- run-time install phase   (extracts new run-time system files)
- activation phase   (activates the new OS)
- extended install phase (extracts extended utilities)
- wrap-up phase   (adjusts packages, sets security level)
- manual update phase   (<u>you</u> update any unmodified system files)

For the update installation, I recommend the following options:

Update Installation Options

A. Update both existing and new packages. (run-time install phase)

    It is easier to install everything now, then delete what you don't need later.

B. Reply "n" when prompted for relaxed security mode. (wrap-up phase)

    Replying "n" sets the security level to "improved". Beware, though, that the resource access permissions of existing users will be unaffected.

> **Aborting the Update Installation**
>
> If, for any reason, you prematurely exit the update installation, your system must be restored to the previous OS version. This will be done automatically anytime before the system begins to extract and install the run-time system. After that point, you'll need to manually restore the previous OS. *[Consult your SCO product* Installation Guide *for specific instructions]*.

Installation Follow-up

> You are strongly advised to consult this section immediately after completing your installation.

2-25

Essential SCO System Administration

Installation Follow-up

1. Reboot the system to single-user mode. *[see SR2.3]*
2. Log all information from the following tables:

    - the disk partition table   (run: **fdisk**)
    - the division table   (run: **divvy**)

3. Configure your default backup device into the kernel. *[see SR2.8]*
4. Create a set of emergency root/boot floppies for your system. *[see SR2.9]*
5. Enter the system administration shell. Perform an unscheduled backup of your root filesystem, **/dev/root**. *[see SR3.11]*
6. Quit the system administration shell and shut down the system. *[see SR2.5]*

> Since you'll use the system administration shell, **sysdamsh**, to perform step 3 (and many other tasks), you may find the hands-on introduction in SR2.7 quite useful.

☞
> **The Initial System Backup**
>
> This initial backup will be a snapshot of your virgin (or newly updated) SCO system. The main purpose of this backup is assurance. It will save you the time and effort of having to reinstall in case file or directory corruption renders your system inaccessible. You can also use this backup to restore the system to a known state in case you have confounded your system with too many incompatible device configurations or modifications.

☞
> **Emergency Root/Boot Floppies**
>
> The emergency root/boot floppies let you access your system in an emergency. For example, if you forget the root password (a real emergency!) you would still be able to access your system. The root/boot floppy set is especially useful for restoring the entire root filesystem from a backup.
>
> The advantage to creating these floppies now is that the kernel is small enough to fit on the boot floppy. As new devices and resources are configured, the kernel will dramatically increase in size.

Chapter 2 A First Install

Preventative Installation Planning

The tips below may help you to avoid some uncommon, but frustrating installation problems.

Preventative Installation Tips

A. Avoid the 1024 cylinder boundary.

This boundary is imposed by the BIOS on Intel-based systems. The BIOS is unable to reference files beyond this limit. Although SCO partitions may extend beyond the 1024 cylinder boundary, the SCO kernel may not. To guarantee that the kernel stays within this limit, make sure that the root filesystem lies inside the 1024 cylinder boundary.

Apply the following formulas to the hard disk parameters (i.e. cylinders, heads, sectors/track) recorded in your system log.

```
tracks         = cylinders * heads
size in bytes  = tracks * (sectors/track) * 512
size in MB     = (size in bytes) / (1024 * 1024)
```

☞ | SCO users can use the command below to report the disk parameters:
fdisk   /dev/rhd00

B. Start the SCO partition on a cylinder boundary.

If you choose to manually initialize the hard disk, make sure to start the SCO partition on a cylinder boundary. This avoids wasting precious disk space. It also prevents potential filesystem corruption when abutting an MS-DOS partition.

C. Before using any non-root filesystems created during the installation, you must explicitly mount them.

If you create other filesystems (for example, to hold user directories), be aware that none of those filesystems will be mounted during the installation process. Only the root filesystem is mounted during installation. To place data on the other filesystems, they must be explicitly mounted. You can use **mount** *(ADM)* or you can run **mkdev fs** [see SR3.2 for instructions].

Essential SCO System Administration

Survival Recipes and Tutorials

The following recipes and tutorials are included in this section:

SR2.2	Booting the System
SR2.3	Booting to Single-user Mode
SR2.4	Booting to Multiuser Mode
SR2.5	Shutting Down the System
SR2.6	Shutting Down to Single-user Mode
SR2.7	Introduction to the System Administration Shell
SR2.8	Configuring the Default Backup Device
SR2.9	Creating A Root/Boot Floppy Set

Quick Recipe SR2.2   **Booting the System**

This exercise demonstrates how to boot SCO UNIX system. It proceeds to the point where you can select either single-user or multiuser mode.

1. Make sure that the system and monitor are turned on and that no floppies are in the floppy drives.

   If the *power off message*, below, is displayed, press the ENTER key.

   ```
   ** Safe to Power Off **
              -or-
   ** Press Any Key to Reboot
   ```

   The system will proceed to display hardware ROM startup messages.

   > ✈ The system also reports the key to press to enter CMOS configuration mode. This key must be pressed fairly quickly before booting starts.

2. At the SCO *boot prompt*, below, press ENTER:

   ```
   SCO UNIX System V/386 on i80486   ①

   Boot
   :
   ```
   ① – the actual string will indicate your processor type

   The system will proceed to display various system messages, including an initial copyright notice, and the OS *version id message* below:

2-28

Chapter 2   A First Install

> **Avoiding System Time Loss**
>
> Many systems experience significant time loss due to this prompt. The longer you wait before pressing ENTER, the more inaccurate the displayed time becomes. A smart strategy is to enter the time one or two minutes ````a
> NTER at the moment your clock (or watch) hits that time. Other administrators prefer to configure their systems to *autoboot*. This effectively displays the time without waiting for a response.

The system next displays:
- a series of copyright messages
- some security status messages
- the message: `The system is coming up. Please wait.`
- filesystem status messages
- initialization status messages from installed software (including **cron**, print services, networking software)

Finally the system displays an initial login message (similar to that below).

```
Welcome to SCO Open Server Multiuser System Release x.y

sirius99!login:
```

> The pre-login lines are the contents of the file **/etc/issue**. The format of the login prompt is specified by the applicable line in **/etc/gettydefs**.

> If your system is Open Desktop, Open Desktop Lite, or Open Server Enterprise, the graphical **scologin**(X) screen is displayed instead.

3. To log in, enter: **root**

   Then enter **root**'s password.
   Once the password has been accepted, the system displays:
   - two login status lines
   - a short version message
   - some required system copyright messages
   - the system name
   - the message of the day
   - the status of your electronic mailbox

> These lines are not printed when **hushlogin** *[see **login**(M)]* is enabled.

> The message of the day is the contents of the file **/etc/motd**.

Finally the system displays the *root shell prompt*.

2-31

Essential SCO System Administration

```
   #
```

4. You may enter any desired commands from this point.
5. To log out, enter: **exit**

Quick Recipe SR2.5   Shutting Down the System

To turn off the system, you must shut it down. You must perform this in a controlled manner to safely recover filesystem data and other allocated system resources.

1. From single-user mode, run: **haltsys**

   The system displays the *power off message*, below:

   ```
   ** Safe to Power Off **
              -or-
   ** Press Any Key to Reboot
   ```

   You may now safely turn the system off or reboot.

2. From multiuser mode, if just root is logged on, run: **init 0**

   Otherwise, for general multiuser shutdown, run: **shutdown**

> The **shutdown**(ADM) command gives users 5 minutes to log out before terminating their processes. Once all users have logged out (or been terminated), the procedure invokes: **init 0**

Shortly, the system displays a new run-level message and some down messages:

```
INIT: New run level: 0
The system is coming down.  Please wait.
System services are now being stopped.
```

This is followed by:

- termination status messages from installed software
- the message: `The system is down`

> Software termination status messages may print for 30 seconds or longer. This especially applies to networking software, which needs to carefully deallocate any "borrowed" system or remote resources.

Finally the power off message is displayed.

You may now safely turn the system off or reboot.

Chapter 2   A First Install

Quick Recipe SR2.6   **Shutting Down to Single-user Mode**

Occasionally you'll need to perform some system software maintenance.   This is best done from the safety of single-user mode.

1. From multiuser mode, if just root is logged on, run: **init 1**
   Otherwise, for general multiuser shutdown, run: **shutdown -i1**

   Shortly, the system displays a new run-level message and some down messages:

   ```
   INIT: New run level: 1
   The system is coming down.  Please wait.
   System services are now being stopped.
   ```

   This is followed by:
   - termination status messages from installed software
   - the message: The system is down

   Subsequently, the system displays:

   ```
   The system is down.

   INIT: New run level: S
   ```

   Finally comes the single-user prompt.

   ```
   INIT: SINGLE-USER MODE

   Type Control-d to continue with normal start-up,
   (or give the root password for system maintenance):
   ```

2. Enter **root**'s password to enter single-user mode.

Essential SCO System Administration

<u>Quick Recipe SR2.7</u>   **Introduction to the System Administration Shell**

Many useful tasks can be performed from the system administration shell. This exercise provides an essential introduction to its structure and use.

1. At the root shell prompt, run: **sysadmsh**

   This initiates the system administration shell and displays the initial menu.

```
                                                                    SysAdmSh
System Backups Accounts Printers Media Jobs Dirs/Files Filesystems Users Quit
Administer and configure system resources and report system status
/                                          Wednesday, January 19, 1994  10:58
```

This is the main screen of **sysadmsh**. It is one of many screens accessible from the system administration shell. **sysadmsh** screens are organized as follows:

```
                                                          Menu/Context Indicator
Menu Line
Description Line
[Current Directory]              Status Line                       [Date/Time]

                          Command/Form Name

                             Display Area

```

Let's interpret the main (or top-level) **sysadmsh** screen:

```
                                                                    SysAdmSh
System Backups Accounts Printers Media Jobs Dirs/Files Filesystems Users Quit
Administer and configure system resources and report system status
/                                          Wednesday, January 19, 1994  10:58
```

The menu (or context) is "SysAdmSh". The highlighted word, "System", is the *current menu option*. The *description line* displays information about the current menu option: "System".

You can highlight any of the 9 other menu options by pressing the SPACE bar. Pressing the left or right arrow keys also works.

2-34

Chapter 2   A First Install

2. Press the SPACE bar to highlight the option "Backups".
   The display should now look like this:

                                                                        SysAdmSh
System **Backups** Accounts Printers Media Jobs Dirs/Files Filesystems Users Quit
Performs backup of files, filesystem, or the entire system
/   Wednesday, January 19, 1994   10:59

Notice how the description line changes with the current menu option.

3. Press ENTER to select the current menu option: "Backups".
   This yields the screen below:

                                                                          Backups
Create Restore Schedule View Integrity
Creates backups
/   Wednesday, January 19, 1994   11:00

Notice what has changed:
- the menu/context is now "Backups"
- the new menu line has a new current option: "Create".
- the description line explains the "Create" menu option.

Apparently, selecting "Backup" has dropped us down a level to another menu.

☞ > The terms "up" and "down" indicate directions of movement in the
    > hierarchy (or tree) of **sysadmsh** menu/context levels.

4. Press the letter "c" (or "C") to select the option "Create".
   A new screen with the menu/context "Create" is displayed.

                                                                          Create
Scheduled Unscheduled
Performs scheduled filesystem backups with fsphoto(ADM)
/   Wednesday, January 19, 1994   11:01

You may have noticed that in **sysadmsh** menu lines, no two options begin with the same letter. Pressing the first letter of an option is a rapid way to select it.

"Create" is the *current context*. The current context is our location in the tree of **sysadmsh** menus. We can represent it with the following notation:

       Backups ⇨ Create

This indicates the order of menu selections, starting at the main menu.

In fact, this notation implies that you must first run **sysadmsh**.

2-35

Essential SCO System Administration

5. Press the right arrow key to highlight "Unscheduled".
   The screen should now look like this:

```
                                                                    Create
Scheduled Unscheduled
Perform unscheduled filesystem backup
/                                       Wednesday, January 19, 1994  11:02
```

We could select "Unscheduled" by pressing ENTER, but we won't. Instead we'll back up to the previous screen.

6. Press the ESC key to back up to the previous screen.

```
                                                                    Backups
Create Restore Schedule View Integrity
Creates backups
/                                       Wednesday, January 19, 1994  11:10
```

Optionally, we could hit ESC again to back up to the main menu, but for demonstration purposes we'll try a different method.

7. Press the F2 function key. The following screen is displayed:

```
                                                                       Quit
Yes No
Leaves the system administration shell
/                                       Wednesday, January 19, 1994  11:13
```

The F2 key is used for quick exits from **sysadmsh**. It works from any screen at any level in the system administration shell.

8. From here, press ENTER to exit **sysadmsh** and return back to the root prompt.

Chapter 2 A First Install

Quick Recipe SR2.8 — Configuring the Default Backup Device

In order to create your root/boot floppy set, you'll need to first configure your default backup device. This exercise configures a default tape backup device, and updates the root/boot floppy set with the configuration.

> The root/boot floppy creation procedure ignores default SCSI and QIC-40/80 (mini) tape configurations. Error-correcting (ECC) QIC-02 devices are ignored, as well. *[Consult chapter 5 for more about tape and ECC].*

There are three primary cases to consider:

> A. You used the tape device to install your SCO product.
> *The tape driver is already configured! Simply update the root/boot floppy set.*
> B. You performed an update installation; the tape was already configured.
> *The tape driver is still configured! Simply update the root/boot floppy set.*
> C. You installed from floppies or CD-ROM.
> *You must configure a tape driver, then update the root/boot floppy set.*

1. Run: **mkdev tape**

   > In **sysadmsh**, go to: *System ⇨ Hardware (⇨ Tape)*

   This verifies an existing tape configuration or configures a new tape device. Make sure to configure the new tape device as the default device. *[Consult "Configuring Tape Devices" in chapter 5 for details of tape configuration].*

   Make sure to relink the kernel and to reboot before creating the root/boot floppies.

2. Create the root/boot floppy set *[see SR2-9].*
3. Modify the root/boot floppy set as follows:
   a) Mount the root floppy: **mount /dev/install /mnt**
   b) Execute the relevant command line:
      - QIC-40/80:   **ls ./dev/[rx]ctmini | cpio -pmu /mnt**
      - SCSI: **ls ./dev/[rx]ct0 | cpio -pmu /mnt**
      - QIC-02:   **ls ./dev/[rx]ct0 | cpio -pmu /mnt**

Essential SCO System Administration

☞ If you want to use an error correction (ECC) tape device as the default, run the relevant commands first:
- QIC-O2: **ln /dev/erct0 /dev/rct0**
- SCSI: *execute the shell script below*
- QIC-40/80: *not necessary; these devices use ECC automatically*

4. Unmount the root floppy: **umount /dev/install**

✈ **Names of Tape Devices on the Updated Root/Boot Floppy Set**

Tape Driver	Data Device	Control Device
SCSI	/dev/rct0	/dev/xct0
	/dev/rStp0	/dev/xStp0
QIC-02/36	/dev/rct0	/dev/xct0
QIC-40/80	/dev/rctmini	/dev/xctmini

```
: Shell script to create a default SCSI ECC device
IFS=,$IFS                        # make shell skip commas as well as spaces
cd /dev                          # change to device directory
set `ls rct0`                    # need device major and minor numbers
newminor=`expr $6 + 32`          # must add 32 to minor number to enable ECC
mknod rctecc c $5 $newminor      # now creating SCSI ECC device node
mv rctecc rct0                   # replacing default device with ECC device
```

☞ Make certain to use reverse quotes `` `` in the above shell script.

2-38

Chapter 2 A First Install

Quick Recipe SR2.9   **Creating a Root/Boot Floppy Set**

It is essential to create a root/boot floppy pair for emergency access to your system. The set is especially useful for restoring an entire root filesystem from a backup. These floppies should be created immediately after your installation, but not until you've configured your tape backup device into the kernel *[see SR2.8]*.

You'll need two blank floppies for this exercise.

1. Run: **mkdev fd**

   ☞ | In **sysadmsh**, go to: *Filesystems* ⇨ *Floppy*

   This displays four choices of floppy format.

2. Select **2** or **4**, as appropriate.

   This displays three options for the floppy filesystem.

3. Select **2** ("Bootable only") to create the boot floppy.

   The system then responds as follows:

a)	prompts you to insert a blank floppy into the drive.
b)	asks if you want to format the floppy first. *Respond "no" if the floppy is already formatted for SCO.*
c)	formats the floppy, as needed.
d)	builds the relevant floppy filesystem (boot or root); copies the relevant files to the floppy.
e)	verifies the consistency of the newly built filesystem
f)	returns you to the menu of three floppy filesystem options

4. Select **3** ("Root filesystem only") to create the root floppy.

   The system responds as in step (3).

5. Enter **q** to quit and return to the root prompt (or **sysadmsh**).

Chapter 3

Overview of System Administration

	Page
Introduction	3-3
Road Map	3-4
A Brief Job Description	3-5
What the Operating System Does	3-6
What To Do After You Install	3-7
Removing Unwanted System Packages	3-7
Configuring the Remaining System Hardware	3-9
Configuring Software and Services	3-10
Initializing Filesystems	3-11
Configuring Basic System Services	3-12
Installing Supplemental Software and Applications	3-14
Configuring Security	3-15
Customizing the Kernel	3-16
Configuring User Accounts	3-17
Determining Groups	3-17
Selecting User Shells	3-18
Determining User Space Requirements	3-20
Specifying User Home Directories	3-20
Creating User Accounts	3-21
Customizing User Accounts	3-23
Backing Up the System	3-24
What To Do Next	3-25

Essential SCO System Administration

Survival Recipes

		Page
SR3.1:	Removing Software Packages	3-7
SR3.2:	Initializing Filesystems	3-11
SR3.3:	Configuring a Default Printer	3-13
SR3.4:	Installing SCO Software	3-14
SR3.5:	Changing Kernel Parameters	3-16
SR3.6:	Relinking the Kernel	3-17
SR3.7:	Adding Groups	3-18
SR3.8:	Customizing the SCO Shell Template	3-19
SR3.9:	Situating User Home Directories	3-20
SR3.10:	Creating User Accounts	3-22
SR3.10b:	Capturing an Encrypted Password	3-23
SR3.11:	Backing Up Your System	3-24

Titled Digressions

☞	User ID Ranges	3-21
✈	About User Mailboxes	3-21

Tables

3-1:	Packages in the Extended Operating System Utilities	3-9
3-2:	Hardware Configuration Summary	3-10
3-3:	Supplemental Software and Applications	3-14
3-4:	SCO Trusted Security Parameters	3-15
3-5:	Key Kernel Parameters for New Installs	3-16
3-6:	SCO System Shells	3-18
3-7:	SCO System Shell Login Templates	3-19
3-8:	User Account Creation Checklist	3-22
3-9:	SCO UNIX Subsystems	3-25
3-10:	Summary of System Administration Tasks	3-26

Chapter 3 Overview of System Administration

Introduction

"Let's see," mused a contented Andrew, "the DAT drives are configured. In fact all the SCSI devices are finally online. The modems are working. The filesystems are healthy. And the mailer is up and running. This must be my lucky day!"

"Even that pesky Brenda was happy. I finally fixed her desktop problems. Renardo was ecstatic that we now have daily backup. The folks in finance were especially relieved to have all their security holes plugged. And that new account manager, Lydia, even complimented me on my attire. Am I a god or what?"

"Earlier a freak storm had flared up; and we lost all power. But right on cue, the UPSs clicked in long enough to get the auxiliary generators revved. The network recovered flawlessly. My manager was impressed, in fact, impressed enough to offer me a 20% raise. I had to pinch myself for reassurance...."

"Hey! Snap to it" grunted Tracy, his boss. "Been here all night again, huh? Well, Andy, you sure do work hard. Just think, some day soon you'll fix all of our problems; and you might even get a chance to take a day off. What do you think about that?" Andrew groggily rubbed his eyes; and muttered weakly "Yeah, great, really great." "Oh yes, when you get a moment in the next ten seconds, I'd appreciate it if you could help me get into my mailbox. I'm locked out again."

"Another miserable day from hell!," sighed Andrew. "I wonder if SCO is as much trouble as this overtaxed NT system."

Although it takes a little effort to administer an SCO system, you may find yourself well off, considering the alternatives. This chapter will give you some idea of what to expect, including a survey of the powerful tools at your disposal.

Anyway, to make a long story short, Andrew finally convinced his company to migrate to an SCO server-based network. And although he's not yet received that raise, at least he has most of his weekends free.

Essential SCO System Administration

Road Map

Experienced administrators need not spend too much time here. Chapter 4 may be a better starting point for you.

This chapter is an informal overview of SCO system administration. Primarily, it addresses the key tasks to perform after you complete the product installation. New and apprentice administrators should find this chapter extremely useful.

Most topics introduced here are covered in greater detail in chapter 5.

Essential Sections for All New Administrators

    A Brief Job Description
    What To Do After You Install
    What To Do Next

Essential Recipe: SR3.11:   Backing Up Your System

Suggested Topics for Experienced Administrators

    Removing Unwanted System Packages
    Configuring Security
    SR3.10:   Creating User Accounts   *[an efficient way]*
       ☞   User ID Ranges

Chapter 3   Overview of System Administration

A Brief Job Description

Be honest. If you saw this ad in your local newspaper, would you be interested?

> *Wanted:*   **Enthusiastic system administrator for a medium-sized server. Responsibilities include:**
>
> - maintaining efficient access to data and applications
> - configuring, monitoring, and tuning system hardware
> - customizing system and application software
> - protecting sensitive information from unauthorized access
> - ensuring a high degree of system availability
> - automating system procedures wherever possible
> - implementing simple, but powerful, end-user environments
> - monitoring and tuning system performance
> - managing local and remote printing
> - regularly upgrading system with latest software versions
> - minimizing data loss through regular backups and other procedures
> - maintaining efficient data communications (especially via modem)
> - configuring and managing electronic mail and network access
> - responding quickly and accurately to user and system problems
> - maintaining a comprehensive log of system configuration and changes

I would be surprised if you weren't. It's a fairly good description of the role you have undertaken as you apply the skills presented in this book.

Granted, you will be busy, but the job isn't all responsibility. There are authority and prestige, as well. Effectively, you rule the roost (or stop the buck). You have the power to grant or deny your users' wishes. All the privileges of almighty *root* are yours. No file or command can resist you. No directory can refuse you. And excepting occasional folly, who would dare to judge you? What a job!

Whether you manage a modest desktop or a serious super-server, your basic goal is the same. You must keep your system up and running, and your users happy.

   Never forget the golden rule of system administration – ***Keep a log!*** Every hardware and software installation, removal, or modification must be noted. No strange event must go unlogged. The log will save your job. Period.

Essential SCO System Administration

What the Operating System Does

> *Warning!!*
>
> *The following section is strictly tongue-in-cheek. Yet, don't be surprised if much of it rings true. The main intent is to give you some idea of the kernel's priorities. You'll most likely want to position yourself to work in concert rather than in conflict with the kernel.*

Sometimes it helps to know that someone is working even harder than yourself. Well here's a resumé from somebody who probably *is* busier - the SCO system kernel.

- continuously rates processes for promotion to the CPU
- ceaselessly evicts lowlife from the CPU
- sends wake-up calls to sleeping processes
- disposes all user hardware requests
- maintains perpetual message babble among processes
- tolerates hardware interrupts and exceptions
- conveys fatal signals to processes
- keeps disks and filesystems extremely busy
- fastidiously allocates virtual memory
- generally refrains from heavy swapping
- zealously enforces resource access restrictions
- repels visitors without valid visas
- won't let cron daemon rest for even a minute
- detects and (usually) resolves resource contention
- generates and generates audit records
- maintains many system logs
- condones child labor
- revives deceased login processes
- maintains constant lookout for network messengers
- chokes when Windows applications run under Merge
- baffles the system administrator
- exercises patience of heavy system users

Makes you feel a whole lot better, doesn't it?

Chapter 3   Overview of System Administration

What To Do After You Install

With the operating system installation complete, the real fun begins - set-up and configuration. You'll need to configure the rest of your system hardware, as well as application software, system services, and users.

Here's a high-level view of the tasks ahead (in the suggested order of attack):

- remove unneeded system packages
- configure remaining hardware
- configure software and services
- configure security
- customize the kernel (to your system needs)
- configure user accounts
- backup the configured and customized system

Removing Unwanted System Packages

 This task can be performed right away.

As recommended, you should have installed the entire SCO extended utilities. Now is your chance to remove the packages you don't intend to use.

A summary of the most likely candidates for removal are listed in this section. Table 3-1 lists all the packages in the SCO base system Extended Utilities.

Here is the general procedure for removing packages.

Quick Recipe SR3.1:   **Removing Software Packages**

1. Run the system administration shell: **sysadmsh**
2. Proceed to the following menu: *System ⇨ Software ⇨ Remove*
3. From the display area, select (in sequence):

   SCO UNIX System V Operating System
   Service Components
   SCO UNIX System V Extended Utilities
   You should now see a list of packages in a scrollable window.

3-7

Essential SCO System Administration

4. As you use the arrow keys to scroll through the list, press SPACE as a toggle to select (or deselect) the packages you wish to remove.
5. Press ENTER to commit your selections.
6. Press F2 to exit the system administration shell.

Little used packages:

LAYERS	System V layers (not much used, predates multiscreens)
TPLOT	raster graphics plotting tools (for special terminals, plotters)

Optional hardware-dependent packages:

DIAL	high speed modem dialers for **uucp** [modems @ 9600+ baud]
MOUSE	mouse and graphic input devices files
UUCP	**uucp** and **cu** communications utilities [modems, network links]

Optional tools/utilities:

CSH	the C-shell (some prefer Korn shell)
OAMPKG	installation tools for generic UNIX SVR3 applications
DOS	MS-DOS utilities for reading and writing DOS disks
SCOSH	the SCO Shell (window/menu-oriented user shell)
KSH	the Korn shell (combines best of Bourne and C-shells)

Optional, but indispensable for savvy administrators:

LINK	System V kernel Link Kit tools and files
LPR	multiple line printer spooler
MAN	operating system manual pages
FILE	supplemental tools such as **strings**, **hd**, **test**, **egrep**
SYSADM	supplemental tools such as **quot**, **finger**, whodo, **ncheck**
VI	the **vi** and **ex** editors

Required for some layered products (e.g. Merge, XSight, TCP/IP) and applications

NETCFG	base network configuration tool, **netconfig**
VIDEO	video graphics configuration
AIO	synchronous raw I/O admin (used by third-party database systems)

Critical package, not to be removed:

MAIL	electronic mail (**mmdf**, **sendmail**); used for system diagnostics

3-8

Chapter 3   Overview of System Administration

Table 3-1: Packages in the Extended Operating System Utilities

Package	Blocks	Function
ALL	33962	entire extended utilities
AIO	48	asynchronous raw I/O administration
BACKUP	272	system backup and recovery tools
BASE	1106	basic extended utility set
CSH	132	the C-shell
DIAL	170	high speed modem dialers for uucp
DOS	384	DOS utilities
FILE	320	file manipulation tools
KSH	254	The Korn shell
LAYERS	128	System V layers
LPR	2370	multiple line printer spooler
MAIL	6990	electronic mail and micnet
MAN	2856	operating system manual pages
MOUSE	172	mouse and graphic input devices files
NETCFG	94	netconfig
OAMPKG	1802	office automation and maintenance package
SCOSH	3416	SCO shell
SYSADM	726	additional system administration tools
TPLOT	134	tplot, graph, and spline
UUCP	2442	uucp and cu communications utilities
VI	426	the vi and ex editors
VIDEO	570	video graphics configuration
LINK	8946	System V Link Kit files

1 block = 512 bytes

Configuring the Remaining System Hardware

The ease of configuring your hardware depends upon the device. Table 3-2 lists the most common system hardware, plus the commands to configure them.

For typical systems, the most critical devices to configure at this point are the parallel and serial ports. These are required for user terminals, printers, serial mice, and modems. Next in importance is your tape backup device.

 As of version 4.0, SCO UNIX no longer preconfigures any parallel ports. Only the standard serial port at COM1 is preconfigured. COM2 is not.

Essential SCO System Administration

☞
> You might appreciate a few hardware fundamentals before trying to configure any
> devices. *[Consult chapter 5 for hardware configuration details].*

Table 3-2:   **Hardware Configuration Summary**

device	command	manual reference
serial ports	mkdev serial	serial*(HW)*
parallel ports	mkdev parallel	**parallel**(HW)
additional SCSI adapters	mkdev .scsi	**scsi**(HW)
noninstallation SCSI devices	mkdev cdrom	**cdrom**(HW)
(e.g. 9-track, DAT, Exabyte, 8mm)	mkdev tape	**tape**(HW)
non-SCSI tape backup devices	mkdev tape	**tape**(HW)
mice	mkdev mouse	**mouse**(HW)
vendor-supported third-party hardware *[see vendor-supplied instructions]*		

☞
> To configure hardware with **sysadmsh**, go to: *System ⇨ Hardware*

> *Attempt to configure your serial and parallel ports now.*
> Consult Chapter 5 if you experience problems. If you have an intelligent serial board, follow the instructions that came with the board.

Configuring Software and Services

The next layer to configure after the hardware is services. The system services provide consistent and efficient means for applications to access both hardware and system resources such as virtual memory and virtual disks.

The outline below summarizes the major software configuration tasks.

- initialize filesystems
- configure basic system services:
    - terminal I/O
    - modem communications
    - print spooling
- install additional software and applications
- customize utilities and applications

Chapter 3   Overview of System Administration

Initializing Filesystems

> *This task can be performed right away.*
> If you are absolutely certain that no other filesystems (besides root) were created, you may skip this section (but it won't hurt to read it anyway).

This sounds complex, but is rather simple. You are going to make any previously created filesystems (from the installation) automatically available. Every time the system starts up, those filesystems will be ready to use. In technical terms, the filesystems will be checked and *mounted*.

Quick Recipe SR3.2   **Initializing Filesystems**

1. Run the following to display the created filesystems: **divvy**

    This produces a display somewhat like the one below. Yours will be different.

```
+---------------+---------------+--------+---+-------------+------------+
| Name          | Type          | New FS | # | First Block | Last Block |
+---------------+---------------+--------+---+-------------+------------+
| root          | EAFS          | no     | 0 |           0 |      93999 |
| swap          | NON FS        | no     | 1 |      198439 |     214438 |
| man           | EAFS          | no     | 2 |       94000 |      98438 |
| u             | EAFS          | no     | 3 |       98439 |     198438 |
|               | NOT USED      | no     | 4 |          -  |         -  |
|               | NOT USED      | no     | 5 |          -  |         -  |
| recover       | NON FS        | no     | 6 |      214439 |     214448 |
| hd0a          | WHOLE DISK    | no     | 7 |           0 |     214869 |
+---------------+---------------+--------+---+-------------+------------+
214449 1K blocks for divisions, 420 1K blocks reserved for the system
```

For this example, the names of the filesystems (**root**, **man**, **u**) are in bold. The root filesystem was initialized during installation, so that leaves **man** and **u**.

> The filesystems, **man** and **u**, were defined during a fully configurable install. **man** will store online manual pages. **u** will hold user files and directories.

2) From your screen, record any names other than: *root swap recover hd0a*
   Those four divisions are created by default for every installation.

   Any other named divisions could be filesystems that need to be initialized.

3-11

Essential SCO System Administration

3) Exit **divvy**.
   In response to: "Enter your choice or q to quit"   Type **q** and press ENTER
                        "Please enter your choice"   Type **e** and press ENTER

4) If you have filesystems to initialize, run: **mkdev fs**
   Otherwise you are done with this exercise.

   For each uninitialized filesystem, perform steps 5, 6, and 7 below.

5) Select "1" (type **1** and press ENTER) to add a new filesystem.

6) Determine the directory where the filesystem will be mounted.
   Normally, this would be an empty or new (not yet created) directory.

   In the above example, the following choices would have been used:

Name	Device Name	Mount Dir	Status
u	/dev/u	/u	new directory
man	/dev/man	/usr/man	existing directory

7) When requested, supply the following information:

   - for device name: enter the filesystem name, preceded by **/dev** (e.g. **/dev/u**)
   - for directory: use the directory name you have selected.
   - in response to:
         "When entering multi-user mode"   select: Always mount
         "Do you want to allow users to mount ..."   select: no

8) When all filesystems are done, exit: Type **q** and press ENTER

Configuring Basic System Services

SCO applications rely on the basic operating system services for their function. Most are configured automatically. These include:

| memory management | process scheduling | console I/O | disk I/O |

Configuring some of the other services requires a little planning and preparation. These include:

- terminal I/O   *[see Chapter 5 for details]*
- modem communications   *[see Chapter 5 for details]*
- print spooling   *[see Chapter 5 for details]*

Chapter 3   Overview of System Administration

We'll consider setting up a default printer here.

Quick Recipe SR3.3   **Configuring A Default Printer**

1. Run: **mkdev lp**

2. Go to the following menu: *Configure ⇨ Add*
   This displays a setup form.

3. Fill in the form as follows: *[leave fields not mentioned blank]*

   Printer name   enter any single-word name
   Use printer interface   select *Existing*
   Name of Interface   press F3 to display a window of choices,
                             select an interface, then press ENTER

   ☞ | Use ***standard*** (or ***postscript***, if applicable) if your printer is not found. |

   Connection   select *Direct*
   Device Name   enter the name of the printer port

   ☞ | Parallel ports are: **/dev/lp**[012]. Serial ports are usually: **/dev/tty**?[a-z] |

   Device   select *Hardwired*

4. Press F10 to transmit the completed form.
5. Press ESC to return to the main menu, then go to: *Schedule*
6. From this menu, select:

   Begin   to start the print service
   Enable   to activate the printer
   Accept   to open the queue for that printer

   ☞ | When asked for destinations, enter the printer name, then press F10 |

7. Press ESC to return to the main menu, then go to: *Configure ⇨ Default*
8. Enter the printer name, then press ENTER
9. Exit printer setup: press F2

3-13

Essential SCO System Administration

Installing Supplemental Software and Applications

Supplemental (or layered) software is designed to extend the capabilities of the OS. Such software includes:

Table 3-3:	Supplemental Applications and Software
MPX	symmetric multiple processor support
Merge	DOS and Windows application support
XSight	X11-based graphical user interface (GUI) support
AHS	advanced hardware supplement (network and graphics devices)
TCP/IP	network applications support
NFS	network filesystems support
IPX/SPX	Novell network client support
LAN Manager	networked DOS and OS/2 desktop support
Widget-Server	intelligent software agent support
[OEM-supplied]	(e.g. machine-dependent hardware & configuration support)
[Third-party]	(e.g. transaction processing, special hardware support, special filesystem support, administration & help tools)

Application software is typically designed for end-user or system administrator productivity. This includes software like:

word processing	desktop publishing	spreadsheet
data base	accounting	system management
network management	business graphics	image processing
data entry	document management	project management

To install most software designed for SCO UNIX, use the **custom**(ADM) utility.

 Some generic UNIX applications expect the OAMPKG package to be installed. This is the standard USL installation package.

Quick Recipe SR3.4   **Installing SCO Software**

1. Run: **custom**
2. From the initial menu, select: *Install*
   This displays a window of products.

3. From the display window, select: *A New Product*
   Follow the displayed instructions to install the application.

3-14

Chapter 3 Overview of System Administration

Configuring Security

Traditionally, security on UNIX systems has been taken for granted. Today, with hefty servers handling huge volumes of sensitive information, neglecting security can be hazardous to your system (and your career).

The key security configuration tasks are summarized below.

> - confirm or adjust base security level
> - secure root login and console access
> - customize default security parameters (predefined per level):
>   - login/password restrictions
>   - base user resource access (subsystem) authorizations
>   - base process-level (kernel) authorizations

SCO UNIX has four default security levels (*high*, *improved*, *traditional*, *low*). Each enforces its own predefined security parameters. You may also define new security levels customized to the specific needs of your system and environment.

The most important security parameters are listed below:

Table 3-4:	SCO Trusted Security Parameters	
SCO Security Parameter		**Author Recommendations**
[logins]		
maximum attempts before locking account		keep defaults
maximum attempts before locking terminal		keep defaults
[passwords]		
minimum days between changes		7 days
whether user can choose own password		yes
whether user can run generator		no (please!)
whether obvious passwords refused		yes
whether password required to login		yes!!
whether single-user password required		yes!!
[authorizations]		
kernel	(process privileges)	***chown***, ***execsuid*** [only]
subsystem	(user resource access capabilities)	***queryspace***, ***printqueue*** [only]

> *You are strongly encouraged to at least confirm and (hopefully) customize the security controls on your system **before** adding and configuring users.*

Essential SCO System Administration

> In **sysadmsh**, to inspect or customize:
> login parameters   Accounts ⇨ Defaults ⇨ Logins
> password parameters   Accounts ⇨ Defaults ⇨ Passwords
> authorizations   Accounts ⇨ Defaults ⇨ Authorizations
> *[Details of security configuration are addressed in Chapter 5.]*

Customizing the Kernel

By now, you know that the SCO UNIX kernel controls all activity on the system. As system administrator, you can customize various aspects of kernel behavior. Key parameters you may want to adjust immediately after installation include:

Table 3-5:   Key Kernel Parameters for New Installs

Parameter	Default	Min/Max	Controls or Configures
ETRUNC	0	0/1	when 1, truncates EAFS filenames to 255 chars
NGROUPS	8	0/16	maximum group memberships per user
ULIMIT	2097152	2048/4194303	maximum size (512-byte blocks) of user files
TBLNK	0	0/32767	screen-saver (seconds before blanking screen)
NSPTTYS	16	1/256	number of pseudo-terminals
NODE			the system name

> Pseudo-terminals are I/O resources used by the **mouse** and **mscreen** (serial multiscreen) drivers. Two or three should be allocated per user. Some layered system products (e.g. SCO XSight, SCO TCP/IP) automatically increase the number of pseudo-terminals. By default, 8 are created.

Quick Recipe SR3.5   **Changing Kernel Parameters**

1. Determine the desired parameter and value (e.g. NSPTTYS 24)
2. Change directory to: **/etc/conf/bin**
3. Run **idtune**, with parameter and value on the command line, for example:

   ./idtune NSPTTYS 24

   Repeat steps 1-3 for each parameter to be changed.

> *Important!* Changes to kernel parameters take effect only after the kernel is relinked and the system rebooted.

> In **sysadmsh**, an alternate way to set kernel parameters is to go to:
> System ➪ Configure ➪ Kernel ➪ Parameters

Quick Recipe SR3.6   Relinking the Kernel

1. Run **sysadmsh** and go to: System ➪ Configure ➪ Kernel ➪ Rebuild
2. Exit **sysadmsh**, then reboot the system: **init 6**

Configuring User Accounts

Users – whether they log in locally or remotely (via either modem or network connection), users provide your biggest challenge.

Here's an overview of the planning and implementation needed to support them.

- determine the data access groups (for files and executables)
- select or define user working environments (especially shells)
- determine user space requirements
- specify user home directories and/or filesystems
- (on networks) specify local system ranges for user and group IDs
- create user accounts
- customize user account attributes
- customize user working environments

As you see, there is more to adding users than simply creating accounts. Let's briefly consider each of the tasks listed above. *[User account considerations are addressed in detail in Chapter 5].*

Determining Groups

Groups and users work together. For example, you can group users by department, project, or function. The basic premise is to restrict access of private data (e.g. department calendars, project reports) to group members only. Groups are a powerful aspect of SCO UNIX security.

Essential SCO System Administration

> Before creating users, determine which groups are needed on your system. Then use SR3.7 to add the group names and group id numbers (GIDs) to the `/etc/group`. User assignment to groups occurs later.

Quick Recipe SR3.7   **Adding Groups**

Restriction: Must perform in single-user mode to avoid C2 security problems

1. Inspect the group file: **pg /etc/group**
2. Choose unique names for the groups to be added (3–8 characters/name)
   Assign a unique, unused group ID number (100 - 60000) to each group.
3. Edit **/etc/group**.
   For each group add a line as follows:

   group_name **::** *group_id* **:**   (e.g. **accounts::100:**)

> *Do not insert any spaces in your lines*. If so, you may be sorry.

☞ In **sysadmsh**, you can define groups automatically when adding user accounts.

Selecting User Shells

It's a prompt, it's a menu, it's ... the user's *login environment*. The login environment may be a menu, a graphical window, or a command line prompt. It may even place the user directly into an application.

The starting point for engineering your users' login environments is any of the system shells. Shells help users communicate with the operating system. On SCO systems these include:

Table 3-6:	SCO System Shells
Shell	**Function**
sh*(C)*	the standard UNIX command line interpreter (Bourne shell)
csh*(C)*	an improved command line interpreter (C-shell)
ksh*(C)*	an interpreter combining best of **sh** and **csh** (Korn shell)
scosh*(C)*	a menu-oriented user environment like **sysadmsh** (SCO shell)

Chapter 3 Overview of System Administration

> Not only does the SCO shell shield users from the terrors of the command line, but it also provides a friendly text editor. [Bye, **vi**!]

> Before creating users, determine which shells to use. You may want to customize the *login template* for each selected shell *[see below]*.

Table 3-7:	SCO System Shell Login Templates	
Shell	**Login Template(s)**	
sh	/usr/lib/mkuser/sh/profile	
csh	/usr/lib/mkuser/csh/login	/usr/lib/mkuser/csh/cshrc
ksh	/usr/lib/mkuser/ksh/profile	/usr/lib/mkuser/ksh/kshrc
scosh	*[see SR3.8 below]*	

[Consult Chapter 5 for details on customizing these files].

Quick Recipe SR3.8   Customizing the SCO Shell Template

1. Run the SCO shell in administrative mode: **scosh desktop -a**
2. Select: *Utility*
3. From this screen, configure SCO shell system-wide defaults as follows:

master list of applications	select	*Master Apps*
master list of system utilities	select	*Master Utils*
the default displayed applications	select	*Default Apps*
the default displayed utilities	select	*Default Utils*
the accessible printers	select	*Printers*
default screen (desktop) layout	select	*Set DeskPref*
default desktop colors	select	*Default Colr*

   > You may need to select *Quit* to exit some screens.

4. Exit the SCO shell

3-19

Essential SCO System Administration

Determining User Space Requirements

Users literally consume disk space. Among other things, they lavish it on:
- private data files and binaries
- current and backup application documents
- application-related environment files
- incoming and archived electronic mail
- personal copies of remote files

A good starting point for disk space allocation is 20MB per user. Use this figure to determine how to distribute user directories across your disk (or disks).

> Sadly, in SCO you cannot impose a *disk quota* (the amount of disk space a user can fill). Yet, you can place users on a separate filesystem, even a "one user" filesystem. The size of the filesystem is the upper limit on user disk space (for files in home directories).

Specifying User Home Directories

Home directories are where users stash their private files. By default, they are created in **/usr** on the root filesystem. Because the system may crash if **/dev/root** (the *root filesystem*) gets too full, it may be wise to keep home directories off of it.

> Select one or more parent directories to hold user home directories. Designate one as the default, the others as alternates. *[See SR3.9].*

Quick Recipe SR3.9 　　　　　　　　　　　**Situating User Home Directories**

Prerequisite: 　　　　　　　　Some knowledge of **vi**　　(sorry)

1. In **sysadmsh**, go to: 　　　*System ⇨ Configure ⇨ Defaults ⇨ Home*
   This places you in the vi editor.
   You will be editing two files. The first is: 　**/etc/default/authsh**
2. In **authsh**, find the line beginning with: 　HOME_DIR=
   Change the directory name to the right of "=".
   This the default parent home directory.
   Type **ZZ** to save the **authsh** file.
3. The next file is: 　　　　　　　　　　　　　**/usr/lib/mkuser/homepaths**.
   To edit it: 　　　　　　　　　　type **:n** and press ENTER

Chapter 3   Overview of System Administration

4. Edit **homepaths** as appropriate to add the default and alternate parent home directories. Lines have the following structure:

    directory **::** *comment*   (e.g. **/u::default home directory**)

    Type **ZZ** to save **homepaths** and exit **vi**.
5. Exit **sysadmsh**.

> ### User ID Ranges
>
> Many networks stipulate that user IDs (UIDs) be unique throughout the network. This is especially critical for TCP/IP, whose access security depends upon this assumption. One way to assure this is to assign a unique range of UIDs to each system. On SCO systems UIDs may range from 200 to 60000. Select a range for your system within those limits.
>
> The local UID range is specified in **/etc/default/authsh**, the first file edited in exercise SR3.9.

> ### About User Mailboxes
>
> By default, user mailboxes are maintained in **/usr/spool/mail** (on the root filesystem). This is far from ideal! If you want to change where mailboxes are located, you should do it *before* creating any users. *[Consult SR5.15 to configure mailboxes in user home directories].*

Creating User Accounts

Preparation complete, we're ready to create user accounts. The various types of accounts are listed below:

- personal accounts
- visitation accounts   (e.g. demo, games, visitor)
- administrative accounts   (e.g. backup, shutdown)
- remote system login accounts   (via **uucp**)

Personal accounts are, by far, the most common. *[Consult Chapter 5 for details on other types of accounts].*

Essential SCO System Administration

Use the checklist below to verify that you are ready to create your user accounts.

Table 3-8:   User Account Creation Checklist

☐ user groups defined
☐ shell login templates customized
☐ parent home directory and alternates configured
☐ user ID (UID) range selected
☐ basic account profile defined for each user
  ☐ the account name (8 characters maximum)
  ☐ the user's full name
  ☐ the unique user ID (UID) *[see digression below]*
  ☐ the user's default group name (and GID)
  ☐ list of other groups to which the user belongs
  ☐ the full pathname of the assigned shell
  ☐ the full pathname of the home directory
  ☐ an appropriate new user (or initial) password

☞   You can use **sysadmsh** to create user accounts interactively. Users created in **sysadmsh** are assigned UIDs automatically. Unfortunately, creating lots of users that way can be painfully slow and tedious. A much faster way is to use **addxusers***(ADM)*. *[See SR3.10 for details]*.

✆   *[New System Administrators]*

You might prefer to create user accounts with **sysadmsh**. If so, go to:

Accounts ⇨ User ⇨ Create

Quick Recipe SR3.10   **Creating User Accounts**

Prerequisite: Should understand the structure of standard UNIX password files.

1. Prepare a text file with the format of a generic UNIX password file:

    account **:** *password* **:** *uid* **:** *gid* **:** *comment* **:** *home_dir* **:** *login_shell*

    Add your new users as entries to this file, one per line, as in the example below.

    ronj::212:60:Ron Jackson:/u/ronj:/bin/ksh

☞   If desired, insert a captured encrypted password into each password field.
[See SR3.10b for details on capturing a password]

2. Save the file as: **/tmp/indiv**   (or any convenient name)

Chapter 3 Overview of System Administration

3. Manually create the home directories for all defined user accounts.

4. Run **addxusers***(ADM)* as follows:

    addxusers -v -t individual /tmp/indiv 2>&1 | tee -a /tmp/errs

✈ | Both standard output and errors will be logged to **/tmp/errs** |

This command adds the user accounts to the system, making the relevant entries in the SCO C2 protected password database.

☞ | To customize individual accounts (e.g. to add multiple groups) use **sysadmsh**, and go to: *Accounts* ⇨ *User* ⇨ *Examine* ⇨ *Identity*. |

<u>Quick Recipe SR3.10b</u>   **Capturing an Encrypted Password**

1. Change directory to **/etc**:   **cd /etc**
2. Backup the **d_passwd** file: **cp d_passwd d_passwd-**
3. Overwrite **d_passwd** with '**dummy::**':   **echo dummy:: > d_passwd**
4. Run: **passwd -m dummy**
   At the prompt enter a preselected password.
5. Copy **d_passwd** to **/tmp**:   **cp d_passwd /tmp**
   Restore original **d_passwd**:   **mv d_passwd- d_passwd**
6. Display the captured password: **cat /tmp/d_passwd**
   Your output should roughly resemble this:

   ```
   dummy:Crde4kMTpdN32:
   ```

   encrypted password ↗

Use your encrypted password where needed.

Customizing User Accounts

Most user account attributes can be modified or customized. Each user's login environment can be customized as well. *[Consult chapter 5 for details of account customization].*

Essential SCO System Administration

Backing Up the System

Now that the initial configuration is complete, it would be a shame to lose all of your hard work. For insurance, you'll want to back everything up.

Quick Recipe SR3.11   **Backing Up Your System**

Prerequisite: Must have configured a default backup device *[see SR2.8 for details]*.

1. From **sysadmsh**, go to: *Backup ▷ Create ▷ Unscheduled*
   This displays the backup form.
2. Fill in the form as follows:

   Filesystem to archive   press F3 to display a window of choices
                            select a filesystem, then press ENTER

   ☞ | Minimally, back up **/dev/root** and **/dev/u** (if listed) |

   Media   press F3 for choices; select media to be used

   ☞ | Choices include: floppy (drive 0 or 1)
                           HP DAT (partition 0 or 1)
                           SCSI (tape 0 or 1)
                           mini-cartridge (for Irwin)
                           ECC cartridge (for QIC tape) |

   ☞ | *Please make sure that your media is loaded before completing the form!* |

   Block size   keep the displayed size
   Volume size   if blank, enter the media size in KB (not MB)
   Format a floppy   if using floppies, select as needed

3. Press F10 (or ENTER) to start the backup.
4. When the backup completes, check it for readability as follows:
      press ESC (to return to Backup menu), then select: *Integrity*

   Repeat steps 2 (*Create ▷ Unscheduled*), 3, and 4 for the other filesystems.
5. Exit **sysadmsh**.

3-24

Chapter 3 Overview of System Administration

What to Do Next

Are you having fun yet? Well, you could consider your job done now that basic configuration is complete, but there are a few more tasks to be dispatched before you can grab your fishing gear and head for the lake. Some are listed below.

- configure scheduled backups
- customize installed applications
- customize system startup and shutdown
- continue to customize system services
- automate various administration tasks
- monitor logs generated by system services
- continue to monitor and improve security
- fine-tune user account configuration
- adjust tunable kernel parameters
- monitor and optimize system performance
- monitor and optimize system resource use
- generate periodic system reports
- configure additional disks and filesystems
- periodically free up disk space
- periodically reload/rebuild system from backups
- periodically update the system
- occasionally recover from major system faults
- troubleshoot print spooler configuration
- troubleshoot the hardware configuration
- troubleshoot the software configuration
- troubleshoot user problems
- assist and communicate with users

You can probably think of a few more tasks to add to this list. In any event, welcome to the fascinating world of SCO system administration!

Table 3-9:   **SCO UNIX Subsystems**

Print Spooler	Account Management	Kernel Link Kit
Filesystem	Process Management	System Monitoring
Login	Process Accounting	Memory Management
Authorization	Electronic Mail	Terminal Admin
Backup	UUCP	C2 Trusted Security
Cron	Hardware Config	Auditing
Custom/Fixperm	Run-level Initialization	Streams

Essential SCO System Administration

Table 3-10: **Summary of System Administration Tasks**

Task	Key Commands	Chapter Reference
Daily		
Perform daily backups	*Backup* ⇨ *Create* ⇨ *Scheduled*	[Chapter 5]
Monitor processes	**ps -ef**	[Chapter 6]
Check disk space	**df -v**	[Chapter 6]
Free disk space		[Chapter 6]
Check mail connections	**checkque** ∩ **cleanque**	[Chapter 6]
Monitor printer status	**lpstat -o -l**	[Chapter 5]
Check communications link	**uustat -m** ∩ **uustat -a**	[Chapter 6]
Monitor session idle time	**who -Hu**	[Chapter 4]
Maintain and monitor security	**authck -a**	[Chapter 4]
Weekly		
Check filesystem integrity	**fsck**	[Chapter 5]
Check print spool status report	**mail -u lp**	[Chapter 4]
Check and trim log files		[Chapter 4]
Generate weekly activity report	**sar -f /usr/adm/sa/**...	[Chapter 6]
Remove temporary files	**find /tmp /*/tmp -date** ...	[Chapter 6]
Generate disk utilization report	**quot**	[Chapter 4]
Monthly		
Perform full filesystem backup	*Backup* ⇨ *Create* ⇨ *Scheduled*	[Chapter 5]
Archive critical files	*Media* ⇨ *Archive*	[Chapter 5]
Retune system	*System* ⇨ *Configure* ⇨ *Kernel*	[Chapter 6]
Perform hardware maintenance		[Chapter 4]
Review and change passwords		[Chapter 6]
Occasionally		
Reload/upgrade system	**custom**	[Chapter 5]

Chapter 4

Looking Under the Hood

	Page
Introduction	4-4
Road Map	4-5
Determining the Status of Your Hardware	4-6
Inspecting the Hardware Configuration Report	4-7
Determining Hardware Device Files	4-8
Confirming Basic Peripheral Response	4-10
Testing Peripherals Attached to Serial or Parallel Ports	4-10
Testing Tape Devices	4-10
Testing Floppy and Hard Disk Devices	4-11
Verifying Hardware Response With System Services	4-11
Monitoring Your Software	4-14
Which Software Is Configured	4-14
Configuring the Remaining System Hardware	4-14
Monitoring System Status	4-16
General System Status	4-16
User Account Status	4-18
System Services Status	4-19
System Utilities Status	4-23
System Security Status	4-23
Checking Log Files	4-27
Hardware Diagnostic Notes	4-29

Essential SCO System Administration

Survival Recipes
                                                                                      Page

SR4.1:	Determining the Security Level	4-25
SR4.2:	Determining File Permission Integrity	4-25
SR4.3:	Identifying Idle Users	4-26
SR4.4:	Trimming Log Files	4-28

Titled Digressions

✈	Incorrect Hardware Configuration Reports	4-7
✈	SCSI Tape Drive Numbers	4-9
☞	Testing Modems	4-12
☞	Testing Mice with **usemouse**(C)	4-12
✈	Locating Serialized Binaries	4-14
✈	Determining Whether Trusted (C2) Security Is Configured	4-15
✈	Maximum Supported RAM	4-17
✈	Runaway Processes	4-20
✈	Supported Filesystem Types	4-21
✈	User Mailbox Location	4-23
✈	Listing SUID/SGID Files	4-24
✈	Generating a List of Configured Drivers and Devices	4-30
✈	Removing System Device Drivers	4-30
✈	System Relinked, But New Kernel Not Made Active	4-31
✈	Creating the Kernel Environment	4-31

Tables

4-1:	Device File Names For Supported Hardware	4-8
4-2:	Testing OS Hardware Services	4-12
4-3:	OS Hardware Services Summary	4-13
4-4:	Determining Installed Software and Version Levels	4-14
4-5:	Determining the Configured Software	4-15
4-6:	General System Information	4-16
4-7:	System Resources and Limits	4-17
4-8:	Device-Specific Limits	4-17
4-9:	User and Account Information	4-18
4-10:	User Account Creation Defaults	4-18
4-11:	User Resource Limits	4-18
4-12:	Individual User Status	4-19
4-13:	Print Spooler Status	4-19
4-14:	Job Scheduler Status	4-19

Chapter 4 Looking Under the Hood

Tables   [continued]

		Page
4-15:	Process Manager Status	4-20
4-16:	Filesystem Status	4-20
4-17:	Filesystem Backup Information	4-21
4-18:	File and Directory Archival Information	4-21
4-19:	Login Information	4-21
4-20:	Code, Character, and Screen Mapping Status	4-22
4-21:	Serial Port Support Information	4-22
4-22:	MMDF and SCO Mail Information	4-23
4-23:	Boot and Shutdown Information	4-23
4-24:	UUCP Status	4-24
4-25:	System Security Status	4-24
4-26:	SCO System Log Files	4-27
4-27:	Log Management Commands	4-28
4-28:	SCO Hardware Drivers Linked by Default	4-31
4-29:	Other Hardware Drivers Shipped with SCO Systems	4-31

Essential SCO System Administration

Introduction

> *Troy: What are you doing with that machine, Tina?*
>
> *Tina: What does it look like? I'm checking out the system that just arrived from the FCC (Friendly Computer Company).*
>
> *Troy: Oh yeah? Well, why don't you simply bring up some whiz-bang graphics that'll tell you everything you need to know on a single screen?*
>
> *Tina: I'll have you know, Einstein, that this is not some simple-minded one-horse system. It's UNIX. And what I need to know won't possibly fit on a single screen. Besides, I don't use the graphics.*
>
> *Troy: What!? Are you crazy!? Everybody needs graphics these days! Nobody would buy a computer without them.*
>
> *Tina: A little overdramatic aren't we, Shakespeare? Granted, graphics are nice, but they're useless on most of the terminals I'll use to access the system.*
>
> *Troy: Alright, ok, but how do you know what to ask the system? I could never remember all those niggly commands.*
>
> *Tina: Well, it takes some experience. Actually, there is a menu-based program that yields a lot of useful info, but I prefer entering the commands myself. That way I can access specific tools and command options not available through the menus. Also, knowing the commands, I can easily generate custom reports with shell scripts.*
>
> *Troy: You sure know your stuff, Tina! I'm really impressed.*
>
> *Tina: [sweetly] Well, coming from you, Troy dear, that means a lot. Thanks. So, have you learned to boot DOS yet?*

How is your system working? What hardware and software are configured? Who is using or attempting to access your system? Are all of your files accessible? You can answer these and many other questions with a few well-chosen SCO UNIX commands. Which commands, you say? This chapter surveys the most useful ones for assessing the state of your system.

Chapter 4   Looking Under The Hood

Road Map

> Although the target for this chapter is the experienced system administrator, new system administrators will greatly benefit from both the information and the structure.

This chapter offers a host of tools and strategies for assessing the state of your SCO system. This includes the status of system hardware, installed software, and system services.

Since most of the commands are presented in tables, without tutorial or in-depth explanation, administrators are encouraged to consult the (on-line) manual pages for detailed usage.

> Tools and strategies for configuring the system are the subject of Chapter 5. Troubleshooting is addressed in Chapter 6.

Essential Sections for All New Administrators

Determining the Status of Your Hardware
Monitoring System Status
Checking Log Files

Recommended Recipe: SR4.4: Trimming Log Files

Highly Recommended Topics for Experienced Administrators

Hardware Diagnostic Notes
SR4.3: Identifying Idle Users
✈   Locating Serialized Binaries
✈   Listing SUID/SGID Files

4-5

Essential SCO System Administration

Determining the Status of Your Hardware

Of course, you want to avoid system problems! Given that, your best defense is regular and thorough system inspections. And since nearly everything you do depends on hardware, it's a perfect place to start.

An effective hardware inspection attempts to confirm the following:
- that the installed hardware is configured
- that all configured hardware is recognized by the system
- that all hardware and peripherals properly respond to the OS

One recommended strategy follows.

> A. Inspect the hardware configuration report for hardware adapters and devices.
> B. Determine the device file names corresponding to attached peripherals.
> C. Poke peripherals with simple I/O commands to assess basic response.
> D. Invoke configured hardware services to confirm accurate response.

Inspecting the Hardware Configuration Report

The hardware configuration report (IICR, for short) lists configured hardware motherboard devices and adapters. It indicates:
- which devices are recognized by the OS
- the active configuration parameters assumed for those devices

A sample hardware configuration report follows:

```
device        address       vec   dma   comment
======        =======       ===   ===   =======
fpu           -             13    -     type=80387
serial        0x3f8-0x3ff   4     -     unit=0 type=Standard nports=1
serial        0x2f8-0x2ff   3     -     unit=1 type=Standard nports=1
floppy        0x3f2-0x3f7   6     2     unit=0 type=135ds18
console       -             -     -     unit=vga type=0 12 screens=68k
parallel      0x378-0x37a   7     -     unit=0
tape          0x300-0x304   5     1     type=everex/tandberg
disk          0x1f0-0x1f7   14    -     type=W0 unit=0 cyls=976 hds=15 secs=28
```

> To generate the hardware configuration report, enter: hwconfig -ch

4-6

Chapter 4 Looking Under the Hood

Unfortunately, the HCR doesn't tell you:
- which configured devices went unlisted because they did not respond
- which installed interface boards were ignored or undetected by the OS
- whether the displayed devices can actually respond
- whether the parameters displayed match the physical configuration
- anything about attached peripherals

So from the HCR, the only firm conclusions apply to devices *not* listed. These are summarized in the section "Hardware Diagnostic Notes".

> See table 3-2 for hardware configuration commands.
> From **sysadmsh** go to *System* ➪ *Hardware*.
>
> *[For further configuration guidance, consult Chapter 5].*

> To troubleshoot missing or inaccurate HCR information consult the section "Hardware Diagnostic Notes".

For the devices that *are* listed in the HCR, you may still need to:
- confirm that the device actually exists and was properly recognized *[see the note below]*.
- confirm that the device and any attached peripherals are accessible.

> **Incorrect Hardware Configuration Reports**
>
> Most instances of erroneous hardware configuration reports involve the SCO serial and parallel drivers. Proprietary adapters configured at the same base address as a supported serial or parallel device could confuse the driver. Before OS version 4.1, the serial driver tried to preconfigure the COM1 and COM2 by attempting to *autodetect* supported multiport adapters. The parallel driver tried similarly to preconfigure lp0, lp1, and lp2. Unfortunately, any installed device configured for the same base address as a supported serial or parallel adapter tended to fool the driver. As of OS version 4.1 this problem was remedied. Just one serial port was preconfigured, but only for a standard IBM serial adapter at COM1. No parallel ports were preconfigured.

Essential SCO System Administration

Determining Hardware Device File Names

You'll need to know the proper device file name in order to confirm access to a specific hardware device or peripheral. The tables below summarize the naming conventions for device files associated with supported system hardware:

 No device files exist for the floating point unit (FPU) or the SCSI adapters.

Table 4-1:   Device File Names For Supported Hardware

Device	File (in /dev)	Device	File (in /dev)
hard disk (raw interface)	rhd*	**parallel port**	[up to 2 parallel devices; only 1 of lp0 or lp1]
(block interface)	hd*		
entire disk 1, raw	rhd00	(standard interface)	lp?
disk 1, partition 1	hd01	(reset on open)	lp?i
entire disk 2, raw	rhd10	(force polling)	lp?p
disk 2, partition 4	hd14	default parallel device	lp
entire disk 4, raw	rhd30	printer at LPT1	lp0
floppy disk (raw)	rfd*	printer at LPT2	lp2
(block)	fd*	printer port on mono adapter, force polling	lp1p
[drive N link] (raw)	rfd0, rdf1		
(block)	fd0, fd1	{tape}	
link to floppy 1, raw	rfd0	**QIC-02/36 tape**	[up to 2 QIC-02/36 tape drives]
floppy 1, 3.5" HD, raw	rfd0135ds18	(status)	xct0, xct1
link to floppy 2, block	fd1	(data: rewind)	rct0, rct1
floppy 2, 5.25" HD, block	fd196ds15	(data: no rewind)	nrct0, nrct1
floppy 3, 3.5" HD, block	fd2135ds18	(data: error correction)	erct0, erct1
floppy 1, density unknown	install	drive 1 data	rct0
floppy 2, density unknown	install1	drive 2 data, no rewind	nrct1
serial port	tty*	drive 2 status	xct1
terminal @ COM1	tty1a	**QIC-40/80 tape**	[up to 2 Irwin drives or 1 floppy tape]
serial mouse @ COM2	tty2a		
modem @ COM2	tty2A	[Irwin] (status)	xmc0, xmc1
port 8, dumb card @ COM1	tty1h	(data)	rmc0, rmc1
modem port 3, dumb card @ COM2	tty2C	[floppy] (status)	xft0
for smart cards, consult installation notes		(data)	rft0
console (single user)	console	[default] (status)	xctmini
(multiuser)	tty01 -tty12	(data)	rctmini
default login screen	tty01	floppy tape drive data	rctmini, rft0
console multiscreen 10	tty10	Irwin drive 2 data	rmc1
serial console (COM1)	tty1a		

Chapter 4   Looking Under the Hood

Device	File (in /dev)	Device	File (in /dev)
SCSI tape [up to 4 SCSI tape devices]		**Compaq SCSI** [up to 6 Compaq tape or DAT devices]	
Exabyte tape			
(status)	xStp*	(status)	rmt/cst?x
(link to drive N data)	rStp*	(data: rewind)	rmt/cst?
(data, no rewind)	nrStp*	(data: no rewind)	rmt/cst?n
(data, unload, rewind)	urStp*	(data: immed return)	rmt/cst?i
(data, no unload, rewind)	nurStp*	(data: compression)	rmt/cst?c
drive 1 data	rStp0	(data: lo-dens. (150MB))	rmt/cst*-150
[links, if default system		drive 1 data, rewind	rmt/cst0
tape device:	rct0, xct0]	[links, if default system	
(cartridge tape default:	urStp0)	tape device: rct0, xct0]	
(Exabyte tape default:	nurStp0)	drive 2 data,	rmt/cst1cin
(9-track tape default:	nurStp0)	compression, immediate,	
(SCSI DAT default:	see below)	no rewind	
drive 2 data, no unload	nurStp1	drive 5 status	rmt/cst4x
drive 3 data, no rewind	nrStp2		
drive 4 status	xStp3	**CD-ROM** [up to 256 SCSI cdrom drives]	
		(raw interface)	rcd*
SCSI DAT see also *SCSI tape*		(block interface)	cd*
(link to partition 1 data)	rStp?.0	drive 1, block	cd0
	rStp?	drive 8, raw	rcd7
(link to partition 2 data)	rStp?.1		
drive 1, partition 1 data	rStp0,	**mice** (serial)	tty*
(DAT default: nurStp0.0)	rStp0.0	(bus)	mouse/bus?
drive 1, partition 2 data	rStp0.1	(keyboard)	mouse/kb0
(DAT default: nurStp0.1)		**video**	mono, cga
drive 2, partition 2 data,	nrStp1.1		ega, vga
no rewind			
drive 4, partition 2 status	xStp3.1	**real-time clock**	rtc
		CMOS RAM	cmos
SCSI 9-track see also *SCSI tape*			
drive 2 data,	nrhStp1	[For file names of third-party devices refer to the vendor's documentation]	
no rewind, high density			
drive 4 data,	urStp3		
unload, rewind, low density			

> ✈ **SCSI Tape Drive Numbers**
>
> Drive numbers for SCSI tape devices are determined by the order of devices in **/etc/conf/cf.d/mscsi**. Entries are placed in the **mscsi** file in the order of device configuration.   SCSI tape devices include: cartridge tape, DAT, 9-track, Exabyte tape, and 8mm.   For example, a DAT configured as drive 2 is the second SCSI *tape device* configured, not necessarily the second DAT drive.

Essential SCO System Administration

Confirming Basic Peripheral Response

Some hardware peripherals can be tested for basic response, even before any OS hardware services have been explicitly configured. These include:

- most peripherals attached to parallel or serial ports
- tape devices (QIC-02, QIC-40/80, SCSI)
- SCSI CD-ROM
- hard disk drives (ST506, IDE, ESDI, SCSI, IDA)

Testing Peripherals Attached to Serial or Parallel Ports

Device	Test Command	Result If Connected
terminals	**date** > *device file*	terminal displays the date
printers	**date** > *device file*	printer prints the date [see note for postscript printers]
modems	**yes** > *terminal device*	modem status lights flash

    Examples: **date** > **/dev/tty1h**
                     yes > **/dev/tty2a**

☞ For postscript printers use the following command:
    date | /usr/spool/lp/bin/text2post > *device file*

☞ Test modems with the terminal device, *not* the modem control device (e.g. **tty1a** (not **tty1A**)).

Testing Tape Devices

Device	Test Command	Result If Connected
QIC-40/80, QIC-02, SCSI	**tape status** *status device*	reports 2-line device status

    Examples: **tape status /dev/xft0**
                     tape status /dev/xStp2
                     tape status /dev/xStp3.1

Testing Floppy and Hard Disk Devices

Device	Test Command	Result If Connected
floppy drive	**hd** *floppy device*	reads & displays raw data bytes
hard disk	**hd** *physical disk device*	reads & displays raw data bytes

Examples: **hd /dev/rinstall**
               hd /dev/rfd196ds15
               hd /dev/rhd10

☞   Once **hd** starts displaying raw data from the device, you should abort.

Verifying Hardware Response With System Services

The last step in confirming proper hardware function is to invoke an appropriate OS hardware services. These services are often the only way to access devices with proprietary adapters. They also let you thoroughly exercise the device to expose any potential problems.

☞   Some OS hardware services need to be explicitly configured before they can be used with a specific device. These are listed below:

    terminal I/O   print spooling   modem I/O
    mouse I/O   network I/O   CD-ROM filesystem

[Consult Chapter 5 for configuration details].

Table 4-2 lists some of commands used to confirm proper device response through the hardware services.

Essential SCO System Administration

Table 4-2: Testing OS Hardware Services

Hardware	Test Command	Successful Result
hard disk	**fdisk -p** *disk device*	displays disk partition table
	dparam *disk device*	outputs a row of disk parameters
floppy disk	**dtype /dev/install**	reports type of floppy or archive format
	tar cvf *device dir*	archives files in directory dir to floppy
console	**setcolor**	displays screen colors
printer	**lpstat -v**	lists printer devices by name
	**date	lp -d***printer*	date/time output on named printer
modem	**cu -l***modem port* **dir**	starts conversation with modem
	[see modem note below]	
terminal	**who -ul**	reports status of all terminals
	enable *device*	displays login prompt on device
mouse	**usemouse**	the cursor echoes mouse movements
	[see mouse note below]	
tape	**tar cvf** *device dir*	archives files in directory dir to tape
	tar tvf *device*	lists a table of the archived files
cd-rom	**df -v** *device*	displays filesystem stats for cd-rom
	mount *device*	no complaints from mount command
SCSI bus	*[not accessible via OS services]*	
network card	*[consult your network product manual]*	

Testing Modems

The **cu** command specified above lets you converse directly with a previously configured modem. Use the terminal port name (e.g. **tty2a**, *not* **tty2A**) to specify the modem. Example: **cu -ltty2a dir**
Once **cu** returns the "CONNECTED" message, you could issue the following Hayes-compatible commands:

at	modem responds "OK"
atm1	turns on modem speaker
atdt	modem prepares to dial (dial tone audible)
press ENTER	aborts dialing; modem responds "NO CARRIER"
~. ENTER	typing ~. and pressing ENTER terminates **cu**

If the modem doesn't respond initially, try: **ate1q0**

Testing Mice with usemouse(C)

The **usemouse**(C) command actually launches a subshell to track the mouse movements and button presses. To terminate **usemouse**, use the **exit** command to terminate the subshell.

Chapter 4 Looking Under the Hood

Table 4-3 OS Hardware Services

Hardware	Associated Service	Controlling Software
hard disks	physical volume management	hd driver
	disk layout management	dk driver
	partition management	ROM BIOS
disk devices	filesystem management	kernel filesystem subsystem
	disk buffer management	
RAM	memory management	mm driver
	ramdisk management	ram driver
console monitor	monitor screen mapping	**mapscrn**(M)
	console multiscreens	cn (console) driver
	video display management	da (display adapter) driver
	ANSI screen management	cn driver
keyboard devices	scancode processing	**mapkey**(M)
	function key processing	**mapstr**(M)
	keystroke buffering	kernel
terminals	terminal multiscreens	**mscreen**(M)
terminal devices	login detection	**getty**(M)
	virtual terminal manager	mpt, spt drivers (master, slave)
	I/O code mapping	**mapchan**(M)
	canonical input processing	tty kernel subsystem
	input preprocessing	tty subsystem
	output postprocessing	tty subsystem
modems	modem control	sio (serial) driver
	data flow control	
	uucp device management	**uucp**(C), **cu**(C)
mice	event management	evld (mouse) driver
printers	print spooling	**lpsched**(ADM)
	output filtering	**lpsched**(ADM)
	output postprocessing	tty subsystem
tape devices	tape device control	*tape drivers*
	filesystem backup/restore	**cpio**(C)
parallel ports	parallel device control	pa (parallel) driver
PC speaker	sound generation	kernel ioctls

4-13

Essential SCO System Administration

Monitoring Your Software

Inspecting software is like checking your shirts for moth holes. Unless you are at risk it's something you do only occasionally. As far as software goes, you'll probably want to determine:

- which software is installed
- which components of your installed software are installed
- the version levels of the installed software
- which of the installed software needs to be configured
- the amount of disk space the software occupies
- the software serial numbers

Table 4-4:	Installed Software and Version Levels
Information Desired	**Command(s)**
list of installed software (includes version levels)	**swconfig**
list of installed components	**swconfig -p**
comprehensive status of components (including size on the disk)	**custom** (↪ *List*)
operating system version level	**uname -X**
software serial numbers	**getserno** *binary file*

> **Locating Serialized Binaries**
>
> When a software package is serialized, only selected binary files are imprinted with the serial number. The names of these binaries are listed in the package-specific file in the **/etc/perms** directory. The following commands should yield the required binaries:
>
>   **cd /etc/perms**
>   **grep "^#ser="** *product package file*

Which Software Is Configured?

Before determining which software is configured, you might want to know what *needs* to be configured. Yes? Good! Let's create a list.

- SCO UNIX hardware services
- SCO UNIX user account management
- SCO UNIX filesystems
- SCO UNIX system services

Chapter 4   Looking Under the Hood

Well, that looks pretty inclusive to me. Few SCO software products can be used effectively without some configuration.

Now we can consider the first question – Which software is configured? To answer, you can run a few exploratory probes. The results will indicate whether or not a specific software component or service is configured. Here goes.

Table 4-5:   Determining the Configured Software

Software Component	Configuration Test	Result If Configured
Hardware Services		
print spooling	**lpstat -rp**	lists configured printers
terminal support	**who -ul**	lists users and login ttys
terminal multiscreens	**grep $TERM /etc/mscreen**	finds terminal type in list
virtual terminals	**mkdev ptty** (⇨ *3*)	reports # of virtual ttys
mouse support	**mkdev mouse** (⇨ *1*)	lists configured mice
modem support	**uuinstall** (⇨ *3* ⇨ *1*)	lists modem devices
Port-Specific Services		
I/O code mapping	**mapchan -d** *device*	displays channel map
scan code support	**mapkey -d <** *device*	displays device key map
function key mapping	**mapstr -d <** *device*	displays Fn-key mapping
local printing	**date	lprint**	prints on local printer
mouse I/O	**usemouse**	cursor follows mouse
terminal type support	**clear ; tput cup 24 0**	puts cursor at lower left
System Services		
DOS filesystem support	**mount /dev/hd0d**	proceeds w/o complaint
job scheduler	**ps -e	grep cron**	finds cron daemon
system accounting	**who -A**	displays accounting info
system event auditing	**auditcmd -c**	reports auditing enabled
dialup password security	**l /etc/dialups**	a non-empty file exists
C2 security	[see C2 note below]	

Determining Whether Trusted (C2) Security Is Configured

Although there are a few ways to discern the security level, a quick way to check whether a C2 trusted level is configured is to run the command below:

        grep "tcbpw:" /etc/auth/system/default

If **grep** is successful, C2 security (*high* or *improved*) is configured.

4-15

Essential SCO System Administration

Monitoring System Status

Monitoring system status is just as critical as checking the hardware. Although there are hundreds of system attributes to track, only a few are vital to your system's health. Occasionally, you'll want to inquire about certain attributes simply for reference or verification.

The tables and notes below are designed to help effectively sample your system's status in order to take appropriate preventative measures to keep it healthy. *[Chapter 6 discusses strategies for maintaining healthy systems].*

The main system areas you should monitor include:

- general system status
- user account status
- system services status
- system utilities status
- system security status

Hardware and software status are addressed in the preceding sections.

Monitoring General System Status

General system status includes general information and system resource status.

Table 4-6:	General System Information
Information Desired	**Effective Command**
system name	**uname**
time of last reboot	**who -b**
	**who -a	grep "new time"**
current run-level	**who -r**
startup/error log	**pg /usr/adm/messages**

Reboot information often indicates the date of the last system modification. Booting to single-user mode provides the best opportunity to monitor key system parameters and make appropriate adjustments without user obstruction.

4-16

Chapter 4   Looking Under the Hood

Table 4-7:   System Resources and Limits

Information Desired	**Effective Command**
mounted filesystems	**mount**
available filesystems	**mkdev fs** (➪ *2* ➪ *q*)
free disk space	**dfspace	tail -1**
(percentage)	**df -v**
disk buffers	**sysdef	grep NBUFS**
	cd /etc/conf/cf.d ; ./configure -y MAXBUF
serial driver queue size	**cd /etc/conf/cf.d ; ./configure -y TTHOG**
terminal input buffers	**sysdef	grep NCLIST**
tape buffer size	**cd /etc/conf/cf.d ; ./configure -y CTBUF**
configured RAM (MB)	**dd bs=1000k < /dev/mem > /dev/null**
(bytes)	**memsize**
free RAM (4K units)	**sar -r 1**
max/free swap (0.5K units)	**swap -l**
free login ports	**who -l**
current/max open inodes	**sar -v 1**
current/max open files	**sar -v 1**
current/max processes	**sar -v 1**
process region table size	**sysdef	grep NREGION**

Maximum Supported RAM

SCO supports a maximum of 512MB of installed RAM. To fully utilize this much RAM, at least as much swap should be allocated. The swap space does not need to be contiguous and can span multiple disks. [See **swap***(ADM)*].

Table 4-8:   Device-Specific Limits

Information Desired	**Effective Command**
disk data capacity	**(set `dparam** *raw device*`
(MB	**expr $1 * $2 * $8 / 2048**
& total tracks)	**expr $1 * $2)**
hard disk partition sizes	**fdisk** *device* (➪ *1* ➪ *q*)
floppy data capacity (KB)	**dd bs=1k < /dev/install > /dev/null**

Hard disk partition sizes are in tracks. In the **dparam***(ADM)* command above:

   $1 = $ *cylinders* $2 = $ *heads* $8 = $ *sectors/track*

dparam expects a raw disk device (e.g. **/dev/rhd00**) as its argument.

4-17

Essential SCO System Administration

Monitoring User Account Status

User account status includes various types of user and account statistics.

Table 4-9:	User and Account Information
Information Desired	**Effective Command**
list of system accounts	**cut -d: -f1 /etc/passwd**
	sysadmsh (*Accounts* ⇨ *User* ⇨ *Examine* **<F3>**)
list of login users	**grep "sh$" /etc/passwd	cut -d: -f1**
who is logged in	**who -q**
	finger
where users are logged in	**who -f**
what users are doing	**w**
record of past logins	**who -a /etc/wtmp**
disk usage per user	**quot**
user home directories	**cut -d: -f1,6 /etc/passwd**
user home directory size	**du -s** *home directory*

Table 4-10:	User Account Creation Defaults
Information Desired	**Effective Command**
default parent home directory	**grep DIR= /etc/default/authsh**
parent home directory choices	**pg /usr/lib/mkuser/homepaths**
default login group	**grep GROUP= /etc/default/authsh**
default login shell	**grep SHELL= /etc/default/authsh**
default supplemental groups	**grep GROUPS= /etc/default/authsh**
system UID ranges	**grep UID /etc/default/authsh**
system GID ranges	**grep GID /etc/default/authsh**

Table 4-11:	User Resource Limits
Information Desired	**Effective Command**
maximum user file size	**ulimit**
max file size (specific user)	**su** *account* **-c ulimit**
max processes per user	**sysdef	grep MAXUP**

Chapter 4   Looking Under the Hood

Table 4-12:	Individual User Status
Information Desired	**Effective Command**
[applies below]	**sysadmsh** (*Accounts* ⇨ *User* ⇨ *Examine* <*user*> ...
UIG, GID, login shell, home dir	⇨ *Identity*)
account lock status	⇨ *Logins*)
password aging status	⇨ *Expiration*)
password status	⇨ *Password*)
system authorizations	⇨ *Privileges*)
raw account profile	**ap -dg** *user*
general user info	**finger** *user*

Monitoring Hardware Services Status

This section lists commands to monitor the following hardware services:

print spooler	job scheduler	process manager
filesystem	filesystem backup	file/directory archival
login	serial port services	I/O and character mapping

Table 4-13:	Print Spooler Status
Information Desired	**Effective Command**
scheduler status	**lpstat -r**
queue of print jobs	**lpstat -o**
printer device files	**lpstat -v**
printer status	**lpstat -p**
detailed printer status	**lpstat -p -l**
default printer	**lpstat -d**
printer class info	**lpstat -c**
detailed printer info	**lpstat -s**
available printer interfaces	**lf /usr/spool/lp/model**
active printer interfaces	**lf /usr/spool/lp/admins/lp/interfaces**

Table 4-14:	Job Scheduler Status
Information Desired	**Effective Command**
queue of deferred jobs	**at -l**
list of root's periodic jobs	**crontab -l**
list of all periodic jobs	**(cd /usr/spool/cron/crontabs**
	for i in * ; do crontab -u $i -l ; done)
list of authorized users	**cat /usr/lib/cron/cron.allow**

Essential SCO System Administration

Table 4-15:	Process Manager Status
Information Desired	**Effective Command**
table of current processes	**ps -ef**
(more detailed)	**ps -el**
process table size	**sysdef	grep NPROC**
processes ready to run	**ps -el	grep R	cut -c5-6,15-19,79-**
processes on a processor	**ps -el	grep O	cut -c5-6,15-19,79-**
most active processes	**ps -af**
process runtimes	**ps -e**
user processes	**whodo**
process run-queue status	**sar -q 5 5**
process launch script	**pg /etc/initscript**
potential runaway processes	**ps -ef** *[see note below]*

Runaway Processes

Runaway processes waste CPU bandwidth. They can exhibit tight looping, polling, or other antisocial system behavior. To spot runaway processes, run **ps -ef**. Potential runaways have values greater than 10 in the "C" column and times longer than 0:20 (20 minutes) in the "TIME" column.

Table 4-16:	Filesystem Status
Information Desired	**Effective Command**
filesystem configuration	**divvy** *filesystem device on partition*
(on active partition)	**divvy**
active filesystems (w/ mount points)	**mount**
defined filesystems	**mkdev fs** (⇨ *2* ⇨ *q*)
filesystem size and free space	**dfspace** *device* or **df -v** *device*
filesystem inodes	**df -i** *device*
filesystem consistency	**fsck -n** *device*
filesystem type	**fstyp** *device*
filesystem file list	**ncheck** *device*
(w/o duplicate links)	**ff** *device*
filesystem directory list	**find** *mount point* **-mount -type d -print**
list of regular files	**find** *mount point* **-mount -type f -print**
list of symbolic links	**find** *mount point* **-mount -type l -print**
multiply linked inodes	**ff -i2 -l** *device*
filesystem containing named file	**devnm** *file*
file size (in characters)	**l** *file*
file size (0.5KB units)	**ls -s** *file*
directory size (0.5KB units)	**du -fs** *directory*
processes using a filesystem	**fuser -u** *device*

4-20

Chapter 4   Looking Under the Hood

Supported Filesystem Types

Supported filesystem types in SCO include:
- EAFS   Extended ACER fast filesystem (default)
- AFS   old ACER fast filesystem (SCO UNIX v2.x)
- S51K   ATT UNIX 1K filesystem (SVR3)
- HS   High-Sierra CD-ROM filesystem
- DOS   MS-DOS filesystem
- NFS   Network Filesystem
- XENIX XENIX filesystem

Table 4-17:   **Filesystem Backup Information**

Information Desired	Effective Command
filesystem backup schedule	**tail /usr/lib/sysadmin/schedule**
current day into schedule (for given filesystem)	**cat /usr/lib/sysadmin/last/r***** *[where *** is filesystem name]*
default backup device	**grep \\^media /usr/lib/sysadmin/schedule**
available backup devices (for unscheduled backup)	**sysadmsh** (*Backups* ⇨ *Create* ⇨ *Unscheduled* **<F3> … <F2>**)
filesystems awaiting backup	**cd /usr/lib/sysadmin ;** **./fsphoto** (⇨ *p* ⇨ *p*)

Table 4-18:   **File and Directory Archival Information**

Information Desired	Effective Command
default tar device	**tail -1 /etc/default/tar**
available tar devices	**tar**
type of floppy archive	**dtype /dev/install**
type of tape archive	**dtype** *device*

Archive types include: tar, cpio, UNIX filesystem, MS-DOS filesystem.

Table 4-19:   **Login Information**

Information Desired	Effective Command
default login environment	**pg /etc/default/login**
login shell startup scripts	**pg /etc/profile /etc/cshrc**
postlogin message	**cat /etc/motd**
prelogin message	**cat /etc/issue**
default login prompt	**(grep "^m" /etc/gettydefs | cut -d\\# -f4)**
override tty for root	**grep OVERRIDE= /etc/default/login**
restricted console	**grep CONSOLE= /etc/default/login**

Essential SCO System Administration

> The *override tty* is the sole login port opened by the system keeps in the event of a security problem (e.g. root account lockout or corrupted password files). The *restricted console*, if defined, is the sole system device on which the root user can login. The full device file name must be specified.

Table 4-20:   Code, Character, & Screen Mapping Information

Information Desired	Effective Command
available i/o code maps	**lf /usr/lib/mapchan**
default scan code map	**pg /usr/lib/keyboard/keys**
available scan code maps	**lf /usr/lib/keyboard**
scan code configuration	**pg /etc/default/mapkey**
default monitor screen map	**pg /usr/lib/console/screens**
available screen maps	**lf /usr/lib/console**

Table 4-21:   Serial Port Support Information

Information Desired	Effective Command
master serial port setup	**pg /etc/conf/init.d/sio**
current port setup	**uuinstall 4** (⇨ *1*) [**q** to exit]
port attributes database	**pg /etc/gettydefs**
active port attributes	**stty -a <** *terminal device*
terminfo database source	**pg /usr/lib/terminfo/terminfo.src**
term type assignments	**pg /etc/ttytype**
current modem setup	**uuinstall 3** (⇨ *1*) [**q** to exit]
defined modem dialers	**pg /usr/lib/uucp/Dialers**
	lf /usr/lib/uucp/dial*
"atdial" modem scripts	**lf /etc/default/atd***

Chapter 4 Looking Under the Hood

Monitoring System Utilities

This section lists commands to monitor the following system utilities:

| mmdf and SCO mail | boot and shutdown | uucp |

Table 4-22: **MMDF & SCO Mail Information**

Information Desired	Effective Command
control file consistency	/usr/mmdf/bin/checkup -p -v7
delivery queue status	/usr/mmdf/bin/checkque
lost deliveries	l /usr/spool/mmdf/lock/home/msg
address reachability	/usr/mmdf/bin/checkaddr -w *mail address*
location of local mailboxes	*[see note below]*
control file for SCO mail	pg /usr/lib/mail/mailrc

User Mailbox Location

The **mmdf***(ADM)* configuration determines the location of user mailboxes. The default location is **/usr/spool/mail**. This can be overridden in **/usr/mmdf/mmdftailor** with the MDLVRDIR variable. If MDLVRDIR is "" (null), then each user's home directory is used. Similarly, the variable MMBXNAME overrides the default mailbox name, normally the user name.

Table 4-23: **Boot and Shutdown Information**

Information Desired	Effective Command
default boot device	grep DEFBOOTSTR= /etc/default/boot
default run-level	grep DEFAULT_LEVEL= /etc/default/boot *[default is 2]*
default startup script	pg /etc/rc2
run-level 2 startup tasks	ls /etc/rc2.d/[KS]*
shutdown tasks	ls /etc/rc0.d/[KS]*
autoboot enabled?	grep AUTOBOOT= /etc/default/boot
autoboot timeout	grep TIMEOUT= /etc/default/boot *[default is 60 seconds]*
panic boot enabled?	grep PANICBOOT= /etc/default/boot
master process launch table	pg /etc/inittab

Tasks in the **rc*X*.d** directories have names starting with **K** or **S**. **K** tasks run first. They "klean up" after software running at the old run-level. **S** tasks "start" or initialize software running at the new run-level.

4-23

Essential SCO System Administration

Table 4-24:	UUCP Status
Information Desired	**Effective Command**
defined comm ports	**uuinstall 3** (⇨ 1) [**q** to exit]
recognized remote sites	**uuinstall 2** (⇨ 1) [**q** to exit]
modem info & setup	*[see "Serial Port Support" above]*
site access permissions	**pg /usr/lib/uucp/Permissions**
control file consistency	**/usr/lib/uucp/uucheck -v -x5	pg**
site access status	**uustat -m**
(w/ queued job count)	**uustat -q**
pending jobs in queue	**uustat -a**
connectivity to site	**/usr/lib/uucp/uutry -r -x9** *site*

Monitoring System Security

The key aspects of SCO system security to monitor are listed below.

Table 4-25:	System Security Status
Information Desired	**Effective Command**
current security level	*[see SR4.1 below]*
TCB password status	**authck -pv**
TCB file status	**integrity -e**
TCB terminal status	**authck -tv**
TCB subsystem status	**authck -sv**
default TCB user profile	**pg /etc/auth/system/default**
password file consistency	**pwck** (**/etc/passwd**)
groups file consistency	**grpck** (**/etc/group**)
su (switch user) attempts	**grep SU /usr/adm/sulog**
SUID/SGID files	**ncheck -s** *[see the box below]*
recently changed files	**find / -mount -ctime -2 -print**
file permission integrity	*[see SR4.2 below]*
idle user logins	*[see SR4.3 below]*

> **Listing SUID/SGID Files**
>
> In the event that **ncheck***(ADM)* fails with an error, use the following command to list SUID/SGID files:
>
> **find / \(-perm -4000 -o -perm -2000 \) -print**

Chapter 4   Looking Under the Hood

Quick Recipe SR4.1   **Determining the Security Level**

SCO UNIX does not provide a convenient way to determine the current security level. Key attributes of the four predefined security levels are listed in the table below. This recipe supplies a strategy to determine which level is in force.

1. Run: **l /etc/shadow**
   If not found, then stop. *Low* is your security level.
2. Run: **grep REUSEID /etc/default/login**
   if REUSEID=YES, then stop. *Traditional* is your security level.
3. Run: **grep SECLUID /etc/conf/cf.d/stune**
   If SECLUID is 1, then stop. *High* is your security level.
   Otherwise, your security level is *Improved*.

security level	default umask	shadow file?	LUID check?	delete users?	password master
high	0077	yes	yes	no	TCB
improved	0027	yes	no	no	TCB
traditional	0022	yes	no	yes	UNIX
low	0022	no	no	yes	UNIX

Quick Recipe SR4.2   **Determining File Permission Integrity**

The files that control system file permissions reside in **/etc/perms**. Each file corresponds to a software package. **fixperm**(ADM) checks and repairs permissions.

1. Run: **cd /**
            find /etc/perms -print | fgrep -v bundle | xargs fixperm -n
   It generates a list of alleged inconsistencies that you should redirect to a file.
2. Analyze as follows:
   - ignore most "not an empty file" warnings; as systems get used, files grow.
   - scan the "file not found" messages for any files not removed by choice.
   - heed any "not linked to" messages; these should almost always be fixed.
   - note all "incorrect mode" and "incorrect uid/gid" messages *[see box below]*.

   ☞ > Often, files that are cited with "incorrect" modes/uids have been modified by the TCB software. If you have *high* or *improved* security, you'll need to restore TCB integrity after fixing problems with **fixperm**.

3. To fix the reported problems, run the command line in (1) without the "**-n**" flag. To restore TCB integrity, run: **fixmog -v**

Essential SCO System Administration

Quick Recipe SR4.3 **Identifying Idle User Logins**

Idle logins give unauthorized users an opportunity to compromise your system.

1. Run: **who -uH**

   Under "Idle", note any values larger than 0:30 (30 minutes). These indicate associated terminal ports are potential security holes.

2. Run: **w**

   Check to see if users are running **lock**(C). If not, the terminal may be unattended *and* unprotected. As administrator, you may need to take appropriate action.

☞ You can use **idleout**(ADM) to automatically terminate idle logins. Be aware that idle root logins will also be terminated. To protect root logins from being logged out, edit the file **/usr/bin/idleout**, as follows:

a) Find the line: **who -u > $TMPFILE**
b) Change to: **who -u | grep -v "^root " > $TMPFILE**

Checking Log Files

They say that beauty is more than skin deep. This must be the case with log files.

Many SCO utilities and most application software generate background records called *log files* (or *logs*). These files supposedly contain useful information for tracking, accounting, tuning, and debugging. More often than not, though, they simply consume valuable disk space. And do they grow! Log files are a lot like cost overruns on construction projects. They grow much faster than you expect.

Since they constantly grow, the best way to manage log files is to periodically inspect them, then trim. When time is short, just trim. *[See SR4.4 to trim log files].*

Even if every log file contained valuable system information (fortunately, most don't), you simply wouldn't have time to inspect them all. There are too many.

Table 4-26 lists some of the log files you might encounter.

Table 4-26:		SCO System Log Files	
Software	**Log File(s)**	**Log Contents**	**Check**
kernel	/usr/adm/messages	system start-up messages	weekly
accounting	/usr/adm/pacct	process accounting info	weekly
login	/etc/wtmp	user logins and logouts	weekly
sulogin	/usr/adm/*sulog	each use of the **su** command	weekly
audit	/tcb/audittmp/*	compressed **audit** files	daily
cron	/usr/lib/cron/*log	each use of **at** and **cron**	weekly
uucp	/usr/spool/uucp/.Old/*	old **uucp** log and admin files	monthly
	/usr/spool/uucp/.Log/*/*	job records by remote site	monthly
lp spooler	/usr/spool/mail/lp	spooler error messages	weekly
	/usr/spool/lp/logs/*	spooler & spooled job records	weekly
	/usr/spool/lp/temp/A-2	spooled printer errors	weekly
volcopy	/etc/log/*filesave.log	**volcopy** transfer messages	monthly
sar	/usr/adm/sa/sa*	daily **sar** data files	weekly
	/usr/adm/sa/sar*	daily **sar** report files	weekly
streams	/usr/adm/streams/error.*	streams errors	weekly
autoboot	/etc/bootlog	autoboot records	monthly
mmdf	/usr/mmdf/log/*.log	**mmdf** log files	weekly
custom	/usr/lib/custom/history	record of **custom** tasks	monthly
spell	/usr/lib/spell/spellhist	record of **spell** tasks	monthly
ksh	home dirs/.sh_history	**ksh** command history files	weekly
link kit	/etc/conf/cf.d/conflog	link error log	not needed

Essential SCO System Administration

Table 4-27:	Log Management Commands		
System Software	**Log Mgmt Command**	**Disable Logging?**	**Disable Procedure**
cron	./logchecker	yes	CRONLOG=NO in /etc/default/cron
autoboot	*none*	yes	AUTOBOOT=NO in /etc/default/boot
sulogin	/etc/cleanup	yes	no SULOG= in /etc/default/su
login	/etc/cleanup	no	
volcopy	/etc/cleanup	?	
accounting	./ckpacct	yes	run /usr/lib/acct/accton with no file
streams	strclean	yes	don't launch strerr*[ADM]*
uucp	uulog ./uudemon.clean	?	

> Most of the log file management commands are shell scripts run as **cron** jobs. Commands listed as *./command* are located in the software's lib directory (e.g. **/usr/lib/cron**, **/usr/lib/acct**, **/usr/lib/uucp**)

Quick Recipe SR4.4   Trimming Log Files

Trimming helps to manage quickly growing log files. It removes older data from the from the start of the file. The more drastic truncation option clears the file, but retains original ownership and permissions.

1. Identify a log file that you would like to trim (i.e. **/etc/bootlog**)

2. Determine whether you have enough disk space to trim or truncate.
   Run: **ls -s** *log file*
                                                           df

   The **ls** command above reports file size in 512-byte blocks. **df** reports free disk space in 512-byte blocks. To trim, you should at least to be able to copy the file.

3. Determine whether the log file is text or data. Run: **file** *log file*

4. Trim or truncate as appropriate.

   [To trim text]   run: **tail** *-200 log file > temp file*
                           cat *temp file > log file*

   [To trim data]   run: **dd if=***log file* **bs=256w skip=***N > temp file*
                           cat *temp file > log file*

   [To truncate]   run: **cp /dev/null** *log file*

> The **dd** option, **bs=***N***w**, specifies record size in words (2 bytes/word). The **skip=***N* option indicates how many records to skip before copying.

Chapter 4   Looking Under the Hood

Hardware Diagnostic Notes

> This section presents some strategies to resolve problem with unreported devices in the hardware configuration report (HCR).

When a device goes unreported in the hardware configuration report, one of the following cases may apply.

> A.   The device is not installed.
> B.   The device is not responding or is malfunctioning.
> C.   The configured device parameters differ from the physical parameters.
> D.   The system motherboard supports only 10 bits of I/O addressing.
> E.   The device driver was not linked into the kernel.
> F.   The configured device parameters overlap with those of another device.
> G.   The kernel was relinked with the device driver, but was not made active.

Determining (A) is simply a matter of checking whether the relevant adapter is installed and properly seated.

Determining (B) may require you to:
- check for adapter LED activity when the system is powered up.
- run the hardware diagnostics for the device (under MS-DOS)

Determining (C) may require you to:
- consult the vendor's installation guide to check the physical configuration
- run the hardware configuration program for the device (under MS-DOS) to determine the physical configuration

Determining (D) may require you to check just before the hardware configuration table in **/usr/adm/messages** for the message "10 bits of I/O addressing". If the device has a base I/O address higher than 0x3FF, the device won't be recognized when only 10 bits of I/O addressing are supported.

Determining (E) may require you to generate a list of configured device drivers *[see the box below]*. If the driver concerned is not listed, it wasn't configured.

4-29

Essential SCO System Administration

> **Generating a List of Configured Drivers and Devices**
>
> The directory **/etc/conf/sdevice.d** contains files for each driver that is linked into the kernel. Most files have a single entry for the driver itself. Some driver files (e.g. sio, pa) may have several entries, depending upon the number of concurrent adapters the driver supports. To generate a list of configured drivers and adapters, enter the commands below.
>
>   **cd /etc/conf/sdevice.d**
>   **grep -h Y * | pg**
>
> Each displayed line has 10 values, the most relevant being:
>
>   1) the driver name
>   6) the IRQ (interrupt vector)
>   7) the base I/O address
>   9) the starting controller RAM address
>
> *[Consult **sdevice**(F) for more details]*

Determining (F) may require you to:

- check for device parameter conflicts in **/etc/conf/sdevice.d** *[see the preceding box].*
- check your system log for device parameter conflicts with devices configured for non-SCO OSs (e.g. MS-DOS).

To resolve a parameter conflict with a system driver, you may need to either remove the driver or change the device parameters.

> **Removing System Device Drivers**
>
> There are several standard system drivers that can be removed from the SCO system in the event of a device conflict. Be aware, though that some of the drivers may be required for the kernel to link. To list the required system drivers, enter the commands below:
>
>   **cd /etc/conf/cf.d**
>   **cut -f1,3 mdevice | grep "[^A-z].*r"**
>
> *[Consult **mdevice**(F) to interpret the various fields].*
>
> To remove a system driver, edit the relevant file in **/etc/conf/device.d**. Change the second field from "Y" to "N". To effect the change, you must relink the kernel and reboot.

Determining (G) may require you to check for the existence of **/etc/conf/cf.d/unix**. If so, you will need to manually install the new kernel and rebuild the device environment *[see the box below].*

4-30

Chapter 4   Looking Under the Hood

System Relinked, But New Kernel Not Made Active

Sometimes a system administrator will create a new kernel linking new device drivers, yet choose to not overwrite the existing kernel. In such a case, you will need to run the following commands, then reboot the system:

    mv   /unix   /unix.old
    mv   /etc/conf/cf.d/unix   /
    touch   /etc/.new_unix
    /etc/conf/bin/idmkenv

Creating the Kernel Environment

Towards the end of a normal kernel relink, you are asked to rebuild the environment. This is fairly important to do. Among other things, it updates **/dev** with the device files associated with the configured drivers.

If, for some reason, you need to rebuild the kernel environment, enter the commands below.

    touch   /etc/.new_unix
    /etc/conf/bin/idmkenv

Table 4-28:	SCO Hardware Drivers Linked by Default
parallel	pa
serial	sio
SCSI tape driver	Stp
hard disk drivers	wd, wd0, wd1
floppy	fd
video adapters	mono, cga, ega, vga
console	cn
floating point	fp

Table 4-29:	Other Selected Hardware Drivers Shipped with SCO Systems
hard disk drivers	omni, esdi
SCSI adapters	ad, eiad, spad, wdha, wdex, fdha, tmcha, dpt, sumo, hf
SCSI peripherals	Sdsk, Srom
tape adapters	ct (QIC-02), ft (QIC-40/80), ir (Irwin mini)
mouse drivers	busmouse, kbmouse
proprietary	esc (Olivetti SCSI), cpqs (Compaq SCSI tape)
	ida1, ida2, ida3, ida4, ida5 (Compaq Disk Array)

Chapter 5

Configuring Your System

	Page
Introduction	5-8
Road Map	5-9
Hardware Adapter Configuration	5-10
Brief Overview of SCSI	5-16
Hardware Adapter Configuration Notes	5-19
Hard Disk Controller Configuration	5-19
SCSI Adapter Configuration	5-19
SCSI Peripheral Configuration	5-20
Serial Adapter Configuration Notes	5-21
Dumb Serial Adapters	5-21
Intelligent Serial Adapters	5-22
QIC Tape Controller Configuration Notes	5-22
Hardware Configured by Default	5-23
Hardware Configured for SCO UNIX Installation	5-24
The Device Driver Configuration Process	5-25
Device File Creation	5-26
Device Major and Minor Numbers	5-26
Recommended CMOS Configuration	5-27
Configuring Hardware Peripherals	5-30
Hard Disk Configuration	5-30
Disk Geometry and Partitions	5-31
Defining Disk Partitions	5-33
Bad Disk Track Remapping	5-34
Defining Divisions, Creating Filesystems	5-34
Printer Configuration	5-36
Printer Configuration Tips	5-38
Dialup Printer Configuration	5-40
Network Printer Configuration	5-42

Essential SCO System Administration

	Page
Configuring Serial Terminals	5-43
Setting Terminal Speed and Characteristics	5-44
Line Attributes	5-45
Applying the Line Attributes	5-45
Terminal Type	5-46
Enabling Terminal Logins	5-47
Configuring Local Printers	5-48
Serial Device Cabling	5-50
Configuring Modems	5-52
Initial Physical Modem Configuration	5-53
Modem Line Attributes	5-56
Configuring the Modem Dialer Software	5-57
Registering the Modem for Dial-Out	5-60
Testing the Modem Connection	5-61
Configuring Tape Devices	5-63
Configuring CD-ROM Devices	5-67
Configuring Mice	5-68

Configuring Hardware Services   5-70

Filesystem Configuration and Mounting	5-70
Specifying Filesystem Mount Points	5-71
Specifying Filesystem Mount Attributes	5-72
General Filesystem Configuration	5-74
Initializing Filesystem Data	5-78
Configuring Symbolic Links	5-79
Filesystem Optimization	5-80
Configuring Filesystem Backup	5-83
Scheduled Filesystem Backup	5-84
Unscheduled Filesystem Backup	5-86
Unattended Filesystem Backups	5-87
Verifying Filesystem Backups	5-88
Configuring The Print Spooler Service	5-91
Print Spooler Configuration Tips	5-93
Configuring Outbound Modem Dialing	5-96
Defining a Remote Site	5-96
Connecting to the Remote Site	5-99
Configuring Scancode-Mode Terminals	5-99
Configuring Terminal Multiscreens	5-100
Configuring Console Color, Cursor, and Characters	5-101

Chapter 5   Configuring Your System

	Page
Configuring System Services	5-102
Configuring System Security	5-102
Trusted Security States	5-103
Security Tips and Recommendations	5-105
Security Monitoring Configuration	5-106
System Access Security	5-107
Protected Subsystem Security	5-108
Discretionary Access Control (DAC)	5-108
Configuring Groups	5-110
Configuring SUID and SGID Files	5-112
Configuring Privileged System Access	5-114
Creating Administrative Users	5-116
Configuring Processes	5-117
Configuring the Scheduled Job Daemon, Cron	5-119
Configuring the Default User Account Environment	5-120
Review of User Account Creation	5-124
Configuring the Kernel	5-124

Survival Recipes

SR5.1	Selecting and Configuring a Modem Dialer	5-41
SR5.2	Loading Modem Codes into NVRAM	5-56
SR5.4	Moving a Directory Tree to a New Filesystem	5-78
SR5.5	Determining Disk Blocks/Cylinder	5-82
SR5.6	Budget Backup Verify	5-89
SR5.7	Positioning a Multiple Filesystem Backup	5-90
SR5.8	Logging Attempts to Use su(C)	5-107
SR5.9	Preparing to Identify Suspicious SUID/SGID Files	5-107
SR5.10	Setting System File Permissions	5-111
SR5.11	Making Commands Executable by asroot(ADM)	5-115
SR5.12	Restricting root logins to the console	5-115
SR5.13	Designating a Backup Administrative User	5-116
SR5.14	Submitting Jobs with Crontab	5-120
SR5.15	Configuring User Mailbox in the Home Directory	5-121
SR5.16	Enabling Hashpling	5-123

Concept Demonstrations

SD5.1	Supplemental Groups	5-110
SD5.2	Using SUID and SGID	5-113
SD5.3	Crontab Entries	5-119

Essential SCO System Administration

Technical Backgrounders

		Page
SB5.1	SCSI Cabling and Termination	5-17
SB5.2	Filesystem Structure	5-75
SB5.3	Structure of an SCO System Inode	5-76
SB5.4	Block Versus Character Device Files	5-77
SB5.5	How the Print Service Works	5-91
SB5.6	Introduction to Processes	5-117
SB5.7	How Processes are Initiated	5-118

Procedures and Strategies

Configuring Hardware Adapters	5-11
Configuring a Dial-up Printer	5-40
Configuring a Network Printer	5-42
Configuring a Local Printer	5-48
Internal Modem Configuration Rationale	5-55
Backup Verification Strategies	5-89
Preparing a Terminal for Scancode Mode	5-99
Configuring Terminal Multiscreens	5-100

Titled Digressions

✈	Adapter ROM Conflicts	5-12
☞	Unexpected IRQ Conflicts	5-13
✈	COM3 and COM4	5-14
ℂ	"10 Bits of I/O Address Decoding"	5-14
✈	Segment Addressing	5-15
✈	Fundamental SCSI Operation	5-18
✈	SCSI Master Configuration File	5-21
✈	Keystrokes and the Standard Line Discipline	5-22
☞	Linking the SCO System Kernel	5-25
☞	Major and Minor Numbers for Key System Devices	5-26
☞	When the Primary Hard Disk Is SCSI	5-27
✈	BIOS Extensions	5-28
✈	Shadowing Adapter ROM	5-29
☞	Disk Device Names	5-31
✈	Disk Geometry Spoofing	5-31
✈	Maximum Disk Size	5-31
ℂ	Using Partitions for Data Backup	5-33
✈	Managing Large Disks with Filesystems	5-35

Chapter 5   Configuring Your System

Page

Titled Digressions   [continued]

✈	User-Specified Print Options	5-36
✈	Hardware Handshaking	5-39
☞	Printer Dial Names vs. Phone Numbers	5-40
✈	Scancode Terminal Configuration	5-44
✈	Baud Rate and Transmission Speed	5-44
✈	High-Speed Serial Ports	5-52
☞	Shielded Cabling for Modems	5-53
✈	Atdial... Configuration Secrets	5-59
✈	QIC ECC	5-65
✈	SCSI ECC	5-65
✈	Tape setblk Option	5-66
✈	Notes on Selected Filesystem Attributes	5-73
✈	Maximum File Size (on EAFS filesystems)	5-78
✈	Symbolic Links to Directories	5-79
☞	Tape Backup Labels	5-85
✈	Multiple Volume Backups	5-85
✈	Procedure for Unscheduled Filesystem Backup	5-86
✈	User-requested Forms and Content Types	5-95
✈	SCO Dialer Serial Port Speed Problems	5-97
✈	Supporting Lower Speed Modem Connections	5-98
✈	Pseudo-terminals	5-100
ℭ	Scancode Terminals and mscreen(C)	5-101
✈	Setting Console Cursor Size	5-101
✈	Trusted Security	5-102
☞	Selecting Effective Passwords	5-106
✈	Proper Use of su(C)	5-106
✈	Kernel Authorizations	5-108
☞	Setting File Permission Bits	5-109
✈	The Sticky Bit	5-109
☞	How umask(C) Works	5-109
✈	System File Permissions	5-110
✈	Links and Security	5-111
☞	The Group "Owner" of a File	5-112
✈	SUID, SGID, and the Effective UID (EUID)	5-112
✈	The LUID	5-114
☞	Where to Locate User Home Directories?	5-121
☞	Where to Locate User Mailboxes?	5-121
✈	Configuring SCO Shell as Login Shell	5-123
✈	Executable Shell Scripts	5-123

Essential SCO System Administration

Terminology

		Page
✎ What's What:	Hardware Adapter Configuration	5-11
✎ What's What:	CMOS Configuration	5-28
✎ What's What:	Printer Configuration	5-37
✎ What's What:	Serial Device Cabling	5-51
✎ What's What:	Modem Configuration	5-53
✎ What's What:	Filesystem Mounting	5-70
✎ What's What:	General Filesystem Configuration	5-74
✎ What's What:	Filesystem Optimization	5-80
✎ What's What:	Print Spooler Configuration	5-92
✎ What's What:	Trusted Security	5-103
✎ What's What:	Trusted Security Technical Features	5-104

Tables

5-1:	Default IRQs Assigned to Hardware Under SCO	5-13
5-2:	Default I/O Port Addresses Assigned Under SCO	5-14
5-3:	Default DMA Channels Assigned Under SCO	5-15
5-4:	Conventional Address Assignments in DOS High Memory	5-15
5-5:	Supported SCSI Adapter Types	5-20
5-6:	Supported QIC-02/36 Controllers	5-23
5-7:	SCO Hardware Configured by Default	5-23
5-8:	Hardware-related System Configuration Files	5-24
5-9:	Recommended CMOS System Settings	5-28
5-10:	Key Printer Interface Models	5-38
5-11:	Default Configuration Values in Interface Model "standard"	5-39
5-12:	Standalone Commands for Configuring Printers	5-43
5-13:	Terminal Configuration Summary	5-47
5-14:	Key EIA-232-D (RS-232-C) Connector Assignments	5-51
5-15:	Internal Modem Configuration Checklist	5-54
5-16:	Modem Dialer Comparison Chart	5-57
5-17:	Modem Configuration Summary	5-62
5-18:	Special Tape Devices	5-64
5-19:	Key tape (C) Configuration Options	5-65
5-20:	Other Configurable Tape Parameters	5-66
5-21:	CD-ROM Configuration Options to mount(ADM)	5-67
5-22:	Summary of Files Used for Mouse Configuration	5-69
5-23:	Filesystem Mount Attributes	5-73
5-24:	SCO System File Types	5-77
5-25:	Default Filesystem Creation Parameters	5-81

Chapter 5   Configuring Your System

Page

Tables   [continued]

5-26:	Filesystem Creation Limits	5-81
5-27:	Three Reasons to Perform Periodic Filesystem Backups	5-83
5-28:	Relevant Files in the Scheduled Backup Facility	5-85
5-29:	Some Third-Party Tape Backup Products	5-88
5-30:	General Spooler Configuration	5-93
5-31:	Print Request Configuration	5-94
5-32:	Printer Alert Configuration	5-94
5-33:	User Options Supported by lp(C)	5-95
5-34:	Scancode-related Commands	5-99
5-35:	Scancode-related Files	5-99
5-36:	Comparison of Trusted Security Levels	5-104
5-37:	Guidelines for a Trusted System	5-105
5-38:	Required Authorizations For Subsystem Administration	5-108
5-39:	Recommendations For File and Directory Permissions	5-110
5-40:	Protected Subsystem Design Criteria	5-112
5-41:	User IDs and Privileged Applications	5-114
5-42:	Comparison of Methods Used to Grant Root Access	5-114
5-43:	Configuring Key TCB Components	5-116
5-44:	Recommended User Account Defaults	5-121
5-45:	Configuring User Account Defaults	5-122
5-46:	New Account Profiles	5-122
5-47:	Kernel Tuning Tools	5-124
5-48:	Summary of SCO Tunable Kernel Parameters	5-125

Diagrams

Hard Disk Partition Structure	5-32
Structure of the UNIX Partition	5-32
Serial Device Cabling	5-50
File Permission Bits	5-108

Essential SCO System Administration

Introduction

> *John and Heather were quite excited. The mail-order peripherals for their 486-based SCO system had just arrived. They'd been waiting to upgrade for some time, but could not afford the prices being charged by local dealers.*
>
> *John was reeling off the list of new toys – cordless bus mouse, 28,800 baud fax/modem, PostScript laser printer, 16-bit color scanner, 586MB SCSI disk, dual CD-ROM, DAT drive, and SCSI-2 adapter board. Heather had started opening boxes and was skimming the installation guides when reality hit. "Holy cow! We'd better call the dealer to configure all this!" After glancing at the manuals himself, John agreed. They called the dealer.*
>
> *"Well, no, some of the stuff we didn't buy from you... What!? Why that's robbery! Oh, you'll finance the first $2000. Ummm, we'll get back to you on that." Click! "Well, Heather, it looks like we're on our own. At least, we can use SCO SOS if we really get stuck." Always supportive and understanding, Heather vented, "You just **had** to order by mail, didn't you?!" John ardently hoped that 1994 was a vintage year for the bottle he was about to open.*

Don't fret too much about the plight of John and Heather. As it turns out, hardware configuration under SCO UNIX is fairly straightforward. Once your hardware is installed, you'll find that SCO provides a host of powerful tools for configuring it. After that, you simply adjust your existing system configuration (especially user access) to best utilize the new resources.

This chapter presents the basic tools, skills, and knowledge to enable you to successfully install and configure your SCO UNIX-based system.

By the way, John and Heather were able to install the hardware and configure their system, all by the next day. They did dial up the SCO SOS (support online service) once, only to discover that the problem was simply a missing parameter.

Chapter 5   Configuring Your System

Road Map

This chapter is suitable for all system administrators.

This chapter offers tools and strategies to effectively configure and structure your base SCO system. This includes hardware, installed system software, and system services. Although you could conceivably work your way sequentially through the chapter, the structure is designed to help you comfortably jump to specific topics of interest.

System maintenance and troubleshooting are addressed in Chapter 6. Initial system configuration is addressed in Chapter 3. This includes much of the user configuration planning.

Essential Sections for All New Administrators

    Hardware Adapter Configuration Notes
    Filesystem Configuration and Mounting
    Configuring Filesystem Backup
    Configuring System Security

Essential Recipes: SR5.6: Budget Backup Verify
Highly Recommended: Recommended CMOS Configuration

Recommended Topics for Experienced Administrators

    SR5.7:   Positioning a Multiple Filesystem Backup
    SR5.11:   Making Commands Executable by asroot(ADM)
    SR5.16:   Enabling Hashpling
    ✈ Managing Large Disks with Filesystems
    ✈ Atdial... Configuration Secrets
    Table 5-26: Filesystem Creation Limits
    Table 5-36: Comparison of Trusted Security Levels
    Table 5-48: Summary of SCO Tunable Kernel Parameters

Essential SCO System Administration

Hardware Adapter Configuration

> *John:*   *IRQs, base addrs, DMA!! Who thinks up all this stuff?!*
>
> *Susan:*   *C'mon, calm down, John. There must be a simple way that all this fits together. Hmm, let's start by figuring out what an IRQ is, and whether we need any.*

> *This section addresses hardware adapter configuration (e.g. ISA bus cards). Consult the next section to configure peripherals (e.g. printers, modems, terminals).*

Hardware adapters are typically the boards that plug into the board slots on your computer's motherboard. In some cases, though, several adapters may reside on a single *multifunction board*. For example, many disk controller boards also host serial and parallel adapters.

The job of each adapter is to mediate data and control messages between the CPU and a specific type of hardware device (e.g. a serial port). Adapters are often called *controllers*.

There are four key pieces of information you need to know when installing a hardware adapter on SCO systems. These are:

- the hardware's default IRQ *
- the hardware's base I/O address *
- the DMA channel (if any) that the hardware uses *
- the current configuration of your existing hardware (e.g. IRQ, base address, DMA channel) *as documented in your log!*

       * and whether it can be reset

> In some cases, you may also be asked for the adapter's controller RAM address. This is usually only necessary for adapters such as video cards, network interface cards, and caching disk controllers.

5-10

Chapter 5 Configuring Your System

> **What's What: Hardware Adapter Configuration**
>
> An ***IRQ*** (interrupt request) is like an inbound phone line to a small switchboard. Each hardware adapter needs its own line in order to clearly signal the CPU. The kernel determines who's calling by the number of the line (the IRQ).
>
> A ***base address*** is like a short stack of in/out trays at an office mail stop. The kernel uses an adapter's base address for small data (8–32 bits) transfers. So that no adapter receives another's data, the base addresses must be unique.
>
> A ***DMA*** (direct memory addressing) ***channel*** is like a package courier. The channel handles bulk data (kilobyte) transfers between system RAM and a hardware device.
>
> ***Controller RAM*** is like a personal data bank for certain very busy adapters. Video adapters, for example, need it to keep track of the bits that display on the screen. A special attribute of controller memory is that the CPU can access it, too.

The hardware adapter configuration process involves several stages.

> A. manually adjusting physical device parameters to avoid conflicts
> B. insuring that the appropriate hardware driver is (or will be) linked into the SCO kernel
> C. configuring the driver with the physical device parameters
> D. relinking the modified driver into the kernel
> E. attaching and configuring peripherals
> F. configuring applicable hardware services

A strategy I recommend for configuring new adapter hardware is as follows.

Configuring Hardware Adapters

1. From your system log, tabulate the IRQs, DMA channels, and base addresses allocated to existing hardware. Note that some of these values may be reserved by default *[see Tables 5-1, 5-2, 5-3]*.

> Although you can derive much configuration information from the HCR, be aware that devices configured exclusively for other OSs (e.g. MS-DOS) may not be listed. Typical devices include hand-held scanners, sound cards, and synchronous datacomm controllers (e.g. IRMA boards).

5-11

Essential SCO System Administration

> To generate the HCR, run: **hwconfig -c -h**

2. Adjust the configuration of the to-be-installed device to use unallocated values for IRQ, base address, and (if applicable) DMA. Configuration parameters are most commonly reset by flipping DIP switches on the adapter.

> Some devices are software-configurable only. The vendor's hardware documentation must indicate this and should either include the software or specify how to procure it. Since most vendors provide hardware tools specifically for DOS, you may well need to reboot under MS-DOS to reconfigure the device.

3. If it is not possible to avoid a parameter conflict with existing hardware, you will need to adjust the relevant settings of an already installed device. Be sure to update your log with any changes.

4. Since it is often difficult to know which controller RAM addresses are in use, you should next perform a test boot under MS-DOS. If the DOS **config.sys** file is configured to preload the relevant device drivers, DOS will either abort or hang if any conflicts exist.

> Although starting and ending controller RAM addresses are two of the device fields in **/etc/conf/cf.d/sdevice**, they are typically left empty. In any event, they are not reported by the HCR. *[See sdevice(F) for file format].*

> **Adapter ROM Conflicts**
>
> Beware of possible conflicts with the ROM addresses of other adapters. Such conflicts can cause installed hardware to fail or not be recognized. Though not a common problem, adapter ROM conflict can arise when multiple devices such as graphics adapters, SCSI adapters, caching disk controllers, and proprietary hardware boards are installed. ***You should definitely note the ROM addresses of all installed adapters in your system log!***

> Windows 3.x provides a tool named **msd**, which is quite good at identifying allocated controller RAM and ROM. *[Some default ROM and controller address allocations are listed in Table 5-4].*

5. Run the applicable SCO UNIX command *[see table 3-2]* to configure and link the relevant hardware driver (or drivers). Consult the *SCO Open Systems Software Hardware Configuration Guide* for detailed configuration instructions. *[See the*

Chapter 5 Configuring Your System

section "Hardware Adapter Configuration Notes" below for special notes and warnings about specific adapters].

6. Reboot the system under SCO UNIX to activate the new driver(s). Generate a hardware configuration report to verify the installation.

7. If you encounter difficulties, consult the troubleshooting section of this chapter for specific suggestions, recipes, and hints.

Table 5-1:   Default IRQs Assigned to Hardware Under SCO

IRQ	Device
0*	CMOS clock
1*	console keyboard
2**	*unassigned* [maps to IRQ9]
3	serial COM2 [not installed by default, but enabled on the motherboard]
4	serial COM1 [not installed by default, but enabled on the motherboard]
5	second parallel port (**/dev/lp2**) [assigned only if installed]
6*	floppy disk/tape controller (**/dev/fd0**, **/dev/fd1**, **/dev/rctmini**)
7	main parallel port (**/dev/lp0** or **/dev/lp1**) [assigned only if installed]
8*	real-time clock (RTC)
9*	*not used* [linked to IRQ2]
10	*unassigned*
11	*unassigned*
12	*unassigned* [sometimes used for keyboard mice]
13*	floating-point unit (FPU)
14	primary ST506 or IDE hard disk controller [assigned only if installed]
15	secondary ST506 or IDE hard disk controller [assigned only if installed]

  * these interrupts are reserved and cannot be used
  ** used in certain video modes by some graphics cards

Unexpected IRQ Conflicts

IRQ and base address conflicts may occur with COM1 and COM2 even when these interfaces are not configured into the kernel. This is because they can be active at the hardware level on the motherboard. To eliminate these conflicts, you must disable one or both ports on the motherboard.

IRQ2 is used by some graphics cards in certain video modes for video graphics retrace. In that case, IRQ2 should not be used. Consult the *SCO Open Systems Software Hardware Configuration Guide* for known boards using this IRQ.

5-13

Essential SCO System Administration

> **COM3 and COM4**
>
> COM3 and COM4 are not typically usable on SCO UNIX systems, since they share IRQs with COM1 and COM2. Also, the base addresses for COM3 and COM4 may vary among vendors.

Table 5-2:   Default I/O Port Addresses Assigned Under SCO

Address Range	Assigned Device
0x000-0x01F *	primary DMA controller
0x020-0x03F *	master interrupt controller
0x040-0x05F *	clock/timer
0x060-0x06F *	keyboard controller
0x070-0x07F *	non-maskable interrupt (NMI) register
0x080-0x09F *	DMA page register
0x0A0-0x0BF *	slave interrupt controller
0x0F0-0x0FF *	math co-processor
0x170-0x177	secondary ST506 or IDE hard disk controller
0x1F0-0x1F7	primary ST506 or IDE hard disk controller
0x23C-0x23F	bus mouse
0x278-0x27F	second parallel port (**/dev/lp2**)
0x2F8-0x2FF	COM2 (secondary serial port, **/dev/tty2**?)
0x378-0x37F	primary parallel port (**/dev/lp0**)
0x3BC-0x3BF	monochrome adapter/printer port (**/dev/lp1**)
0x3F0-0x3F7 *	floppy driver
0x3F8-0x3FF	COM1 (primary serial port, **/dev/tty1**?)

* I/O port address range is reserved

> The range of supported I/O port addresses is 0x0000 – 0xFFFF (16 bits). Typical port addresses fall in the range 0x0100 – 0x03FF.

> **"10 Bits of I/O Address Decoding"**
>
> When this message appears during system boot, it indicates that system hardware is limited to 10-bit I/O addresses (0x100 - 0x3FF). Hardware with I/O addresses above 0x3FF should not be installed on these systems.

Chapter 5 Configuring Your System

Table 5-3: Default DMA Channels Assigned Under SCO

Channel	Device
0	*unassigned*
1	*unassigned*
2	floppy controller
3	*unassigned*
4	*[reserved by the system]*
5	*unassigned*
6	*unassigned*
7	*unassigned*

Table 5-4: Conventional Address Assignments in the (DOS) High Memory Area

Address Range	Purpose
A0000-BFFFF	reserved for graphics adapter RAM (128K)
C0000-C8000	conventionally assigned to graphics adapter ROM (32K)
C8000-EFFFF	available for miscellaneous adapter RAM and ROM (160K)
F0000-FFFFF	reserved for system ROM (ROM-BIOS, startup ROM, diagnostic ROM, hard disk ROM)

Segment Addressing

Most ROM and adapter (controller) RAM are configured with *segment addresses* instead byte addresses. Since segments are always 16-byte multiples, segment addresses simply drop the last digit of the byte address.

    segment address: 0x1FFF   <=>   byte address: 0x1FFF0

Essential SCO System Administration

Brief Overview of SCSI

SCSI (small computer systems interface) is an enormously popular standard for interfacing high-speed peripherals. Technically, SCSI is a collection of high-speed data lines (a *bus*) linked to an intelligent controller/adapter which interfaces with your system. *By the way, it's pronounced "scuzzy".*

SCSI hosts a wide range of peripherals, including:

CD-ROM   optical disks   hard disks   tape drives   DAT drives   printers

The beauty of SCSI is that once the adapter is installed, a SCSI peripheral can be attached with a standard SCSI cable. Additional peripherals can be attached in a daisy chain. The SCSI bus runs through the cables.

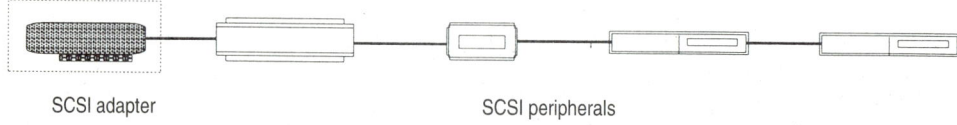

SCSI adapter   SCSI peripherals

> The original SCSI specification was poorly defined; and many SCSI-1 devices and adapters were incompatible. Then came SCSI-2. It provided high interoperability and improved device I/O and control. SCSI-2 adapters support SCSI-1 devices, but not vice versa.

Each device sharing the SCSI bus must have a unique target ID number. SCSI target IDs range from 0–7 (7 is typically reserved for the adapter, 0 for the first hard disk).

The logical unit number (LUN) is a secondary identifier. It differentiates peripherals that share a controller. In that case, the peripherals would hang directly off the controller, not the SCSI bus.

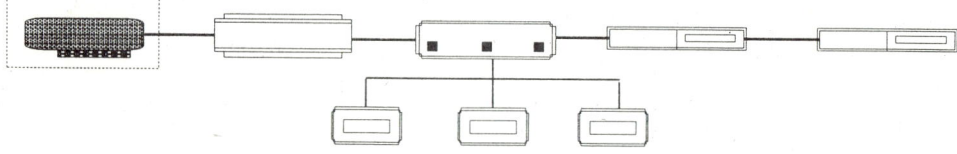

Three Peripherals Sharing a Controller

5-16

Chapter 5 Configuring Your System

Most SCSI peripherals have built-in controllers. For them the LUN is typically 0. Peripherals sharing a controller must have unique LUNs in the range 1–7 (LUN 0 is usually reserved for the controller).

> Standalone SCSI controllers (bridge adapters) are not supported by SCO.

Quick Backgrounder SB5.1   **SCSI Cabling and Termination**

An understanding of the way that SCSI peripherals are attached to the adapter and to each other is vital to successful SCSI configuration.

> Warning! Although the information in this backgrounder is important, it may be a bit technical for some. To make matters worse, there are no helpful illustrations. Please accept my apologies.

SCSI peripherals can be connected to the adapter using an internal cable or a series of external cables. The internal cable connects internal SCSI peripherals. External cables connect external SCSI peripherals.

The internal cable connects to a ribbon cable interface on the SCSI adapter, inside the system chassis. The initial external cable connects to a special port on the adapter board, at the back of the system chassis (where peripherals are usually attached). The internal cable is only required if internal SCSI peripherals are to be attached. External cables are, likewise, only required if external SCSI peripherals are to be attached.

Internal SCSI peripherals are installed inside the computer chassis. The most common type of internal SCSI peripherals are hard disks and CD-ROMs. The internal cable is usually a ribbon cable with one or more drop branches to support multiple peripherals. The last internal peripheral terminates the cable. Think of internal SCSI peripherals as leaves hanging from a common branch, with a final leaf at the end. The SCSI bus branches to reach each internal peripheral.

External SCSI peripherals differ in the respect that the SCSI bus runs through the peripheral, rather than branching to reach it. Multiple external peripherals are connected in a physical daisy chain. Each external peripheral has input and output ports for SCSI cables. The output of one peripheral connects to the input of the next peripheral. The last external peripheral has no output. Because of the extra sophistication, external SCSI peripherals tend cost a bit more than internal peripherals.

Although there are many detailed SCSI specifications to learn (if you're so inclined), the one key fact to remember is that *the SCSI bus must be properly terminated*.

When internal and external cables are connected, the SCSI bus concludes at the last peripheral at the end of each cable. When only one cable is connected (either an internal or external cable) to the adapter, the other end of the SCSI bus concludes at the adapter. The device where the bus concludes must be *terminated*.

Many SCSI adapters and peripherals can be configured for termination with DIP switches. Others require special *terminating resistors* to be in place and properly seated. To summarize:

- Make sure that the device (peripheral or adapter) at each end of the SCSI bus is properly terminated per the vendor's installation instructions.
- When both external and internal peripherals are attached, make sure that the adapter is *not* terminated.
- Ensure that no other devices are terminated.

> Since terminating resistors are quite device-specific, make sure that they come with the peripherals that require them. They are rarely available separately.

Fundamental SCSI Operation

Effectively, the SCSI bus is a chain of connected peripherals. The control signals and data pass along the bus for every peripheral in the chain to see and process. Fortunately, chaos is avoided, since each data or control message is addressed to a specific target ID and LUN. That uniquely identifies the receiving peripheral.

To prevent messages from reflecting off the end of the bus, and echoing back to cause real confusion, the bus must be terminated at each end. Only the ends must be terminated, otherwise the bus could not propagate to all the attached peripherals.

Chapter 5   Configuring Your System

Hardware Adapter Configuration Notes

The following topics are considered here:

- hard disk controller configuration
- SCSI adapter configuration
- serial adapter configuration
- QIC-02/36 tape controller configuration

Hard Disk Controller Configuration

The following disk controller types and combinations are supported:

- one to two ST506-compatible controllers (WD-1xxx, MFM, IDE, ESDI) *[each controlling up to 2 hard disks]*
- one or more SCSI adapters *[each controlling up to 7 hard disks]*
- one to two ST506-compatible controllers *[non-SCSI root disk]*, and one or more SCSI adapters
- one to six Compaq EISA IDA controllers *[each with 1 or 2 IDA disks]*

 You cannot add an ST506/ESDI controller to a system with a SCSI root disk.

When configuring a disk, the system asks you to supply the number of the controller to which to attach it. Disk controllers are numbered by type (ST506, SCSI, IDA) in the order configured.

SCSI Adapter Configuration

SCO UNIX supports multiple SCSI adapters, but typically no more than two of the same type. In some cases, only one SCSI adapter of a specific type can be included in the adapter mix. Ultimately, though, the maximum number of adapters supported by your machine is limited by the available IRQs.

 The **mdevice***(F)* file in **/etc/conf/cf.d** specifies the minimum and maximum adapters supported per SCSI type. *[See table 5-5 for a list of supported types]*. To determine the minimum/maximum for a specific adapter type, run:

cut -f1,7,8 /etc/conf/cf.d/mdevice | fgrep *adapter type*

5-19

Essential SCO System Administration

Table 5-5: Supported SCSI Adapter Types	
Type	**Corresponding Adapter Model(s)**
ad	Adaptec 154x, 154x emulation, 164x
ciha	386/486 CBUS SCSI
dpt	DPT PM2012, PM2011, PM2201
eiad	Adaptec 174x
esc	Olivetti ESC-1
fdha	Future Domain adapters [1800 chip] (e.g. TMC-16xx, MCS-600/700)
hf	IBM hard file
spad	Adaptec 152x
sumo	Storage Plus SCSI-AT
tmcha	Future Domain adapters [950 chip] (e.g. TMC-8xx)
wdex	Future Domain/Western Digital 7000EX
wdha	Future Domain/Western Digital 7000

SCSI adapters are usually configured as a result of configuring a SCSI peripheral into the system. There may be special configuration considerations for certain adapters. *[Consult the* SCO Open Systems Software Hardware Configuration Guide *for detailed instructions on configuring specific SCSI adapters.]*

SCSI Peripheral Configuration

When configuring a SCSI peripheral, the system first asks you for the host adapter type *[see Table 5-5]*.

> When the system asks you for the host adapter type during SCSI device configuration, you can enter **h** to view a list of types.

Once you've selected the adapter type, the system determines whether any adapters of that type are already configured. If so, it asks you to indicate which adapter of the given type is the one you intend to use.

> To select the first (or only) adapter of that type, enter 0. To select the second configured adapter of that type, enter 1.

Chapter 5 Configuring Your System

If a new adapter is indicated the system will request the following configuration parameters:

- the interrupt vector (IRQ) for the adapter
- the starting (base) I/O address for the adapter
- the ending I/O address for the adapter
- the starting controller memory (RAM) address
- the ending controller memory (RAM) address

> You'll need to relink the kernel and reboot to effect any adapter configuration changes. Most SCO hardware configuration procedures offer you the chance to do this before exiting.

Finally, the system asks you for the SCSI target ID and LUN for the device. This completes the configuration.

> **SCSI Master Configuration File**
>
> The system records all configured SCSI devices in **/etc/conf/cf.d/mscsi**. The order of the devices in this file, determines the device number by type. Types include: *Srom* (CD-ROM), *Sdsk* (disk), *Stp* (tape).

Serial Adapter Configuration Notes

Serial adapters come in various flavors:

- built-in serial ports (IBM-type COM ports)
- serial ports on multifunction cards (IBM-type COM ports)
- dumb multiport cards
- intelligent serial cards

> Most serial adapters can be set for COM1 or COM2. To avoid interrupt conflicts, adapters enabling COM3 or COM4 must not use IRQ3 or IRQ4.

Dumb Serial Adapters

The first three can be considered together as *dumb serial adapters*. Dumb adapters are actually fairly sophisticated. They are "dumb" only in the sense that they do not offload keyboard interrupt and line-edit processing from the kernel.

Dumb serial adapters are configured with: **mkdev serial**

Essential SCO System Administration

> **Keystrokes and the Standard Line Discipline**
>
> Normally, every single terminal keystroke (or input character) sends an interrupt to the kernel. The serial driver is then called to process the keystroke (or character) and queue it for input to a waiting process. Standard *line discipline* is to queue all input keystrokes and characters until a newline character, NL (normally generated by pressing the ENTER key), is received. The newline character informs the driver to pass the queued input (the input line) to the process. Imagine how much performance is degraded by heavy incoming modem data on a dumb serial port!

Intelligent Serial Adapters

Intelligent serial adapters are different. By processing keystrokes and interrupts on-board, they free the kernel for other tasks. In so doing, many of these cards can support hundreds of terminals (many times more than dumb adapters).

Since they bypass the standard serial driver (sio), intelligent cards are installed with their own proprietary drivers. *[Consult the vendor's documentation for installation instructions].*

> Due to the system impact, 16 terminals are the maximum recommended limit per dumb serial adapter. In contrast, some intelligent adapters can support over 256 terminals without adversely affecting system performance.

QIC Tape Controller Configuration Notes

The following tape controller combinations are supported:
- one QIC-02/36 controller
- up to two Irwin mini-cartridge controllers
- up to two QIC-40/80 floppy tape controllers
- up to four SCSI tape devices
- one QIC-02/36 controller, one Irwin or QIC-40/80 controller, and up to four SCSI tape devices

Both QIC tape controllers and SCSI tapes are configured using: **mkdev tape**

> From **sysadmsh**, proceed to: *System ⇨ Hardware ⇨ Tape*

Chapter 5   Configuring Your System

Table 5-6:   Supported QIC-02/36 Controller Types

ISA		Microchannel	
1	Archive/Conner	1	Mountain
3	Wangtek	2	IBM 6157
4	Emerald	3	Everex/Archive/Tandberg
5	Mountain	4	Tecmar/Wangtek
6	Tecmar		
7	Everex/Tandberg		

Match your controller with one of the supported types above. For most controllers, configuration is straightforward. Simply supply the values below:

controller type	DMA channel	interrupt	base address

Typically, the default values suggested by the configuration utility suffice. But you are strongly advised to consult the *SCO Open Systems Software Hardware Configuration Guide* for model-specific configuration values.

> To configure QIC-40, QIC-80, or SCSI tape devices, see the section "Configuring Hardware Peripherals".

Hardware Configured by Default

Fortunately, some hardware is configured for you. These, invariably, are devices whose configuration is recorded in the system's CMOS memory *[see the section "Recommended CMOS Configuration" for details]*. Representative "auto-configured" devices are included in Table 5-7.

Table 5-7:   SCO UNIX Hardware Configured by Default

Controllers	**Peripherals**
master disk controller	primary hard disk (**/dev/hd00**)
floppy controller	floppy drives 0 and 1 (**/dev/fd0**, **/dev/fd1**)
graphics adapter	console display (**/dev/console**, **/dev/tty01**)
keyboard controller	console keyboard (**/dev/console**, **/dev/tty01**)
math coprocessor	

5-23

Essential SCO System Administration

> The primary hard disk is configured during SCO UNIX installation.

Hardware Configured for SCO UNIX Installation

To maximize ease of installation, SCO preconfigures most of the devices useful for installing software into the installation kernel. These include:

- most standard ST506 and ESDI hard disks
- all supported SCSI adapters
- all supported QIC-02/36 tape controllers
- CD-ROM drives
- SCSI cartridge tape devices

> Although most of these devices are preconfigured with default values *[see "Preparing to Install" in Chapter 2]*, most configuration parameters can be overridden at the boot prompt *[see **boot**(HW)]*. The boot-time loadable driver (btld) facility allows nonstandard devices to be used as well.

Upon completion of the installation, virtually all hardware is deconfigured and all associated drivers are unlinked. The two exceptions are:

- the disk controller for the root hard disk
- the tape controller *[when the installation medium is tape]*

This seemingly thoughtless response actually does benefit you. In particular, it:

- reduces configuration parameter conflict when adding new devices
- makes the kernel much smaller and much faster to load
- enables you to reconfigure devices with nondefault parameters

Chapter 5   Configuring Your System

The Device Driver Configuration Process

Configured device drivers are incorporated right into the SCO UNIX kernel. The more drivers that are configured, the larger the kernel becomes.

The process of rebuilding the kernel is called *linking*. The link procedure compiles relevant data from several system configuration files into one large executable file – the new kernel. It is activated when the system next boots.

Linking the SCO System Kernel

Use the following commands to manually relink the kernel:

    cd   /etc/conf/cf.d
    ./link_unix

From **sysadmsh**, select *System* ⇨ *Configure* ⇨ *Kernel* (⇨ *Rebuild*)

Table 5-8:	Hardware-related System Configuration Files (in /etc/conf/cf.d)	
File	**Purpose**	**Reference**
mdevice	device driver module descriptions	**mdevice**(F)
sdevice	local device configuration file	**sdevice**(F)
mvdevice	master video driver configuration file	**mvdevice**(F)
mscsi	master SCSI device configuration file	**mscsi**(F)
mtune	master kernel configuration file	**mtune**(F)
stune	kernel configuration override file	**stune**(F)

A number of kernel configuration parameters in the **mtune** and **stune** files directly affect the function of many hardware devices and drivers.

Device File Creation

A key part of the driver configuration process is the creation of *device nodes*. Nodes are device files created under **/dev**.

By design, each driver specifies the device nodes to be created in a file in the directory **/etc/conf/node.d**. The file bears the name of the driver. In practice, though, most device files for required system drivers are hard-coded during system installation. Those device files are specified in **/etc/perms/rtsmd**.

5-25

Essential SCO System Administration

Device nodes enable UNIX processes to access specific devices. The device file header (the inode) contains two key values: the device *major number* and *minor number*.

Device Major and Minor Numbers

In the device file listing below, note the two values indicated as *major number* and *minor number*. Those values work together to identify a specific device.

```
brw-rw-rw-   7 bin    bin      2, 60   Aug 10 21:18  /dev/fd0
                                /     \
                        major number   minor number
```

 By convention, **/dev/fd0** accesses the first floppy drive on SCO systems.

The *major number* references the controlling device driver. The kernel uses that number to lookup the actual driver in the master driver table, **mdevice**(F).

Typically, the *minor number* specifies a particular device under the control of that driver. Actually the minor number is a bit pattern of specific interest to the controlling driver. Each driver has total freedom to interpret the minor number.

 For example, the minor number for floppy devices is interpreted as follows:

```
                         Bits
   7        6      5      4      3      2        1      0
(not used)         floppy density       ss/ds    drive number
```

Minor number 60 indicates: 135tpi (18 sectors/track), double-sided, drive 0 [consult **fd**(HW) for details of the bit representation].

Major and Minor Numbers for Key System Devices

- high-density 3.5" floppy on drive 0   (2, 60)
- high-density 3.5" floppy on drive 1   (2, 61)
- high-density 5.25" floppy on drive 0   (2, 52)
- high-density 5.25" floppy on drive 1   (2, 53)
- hard disk root filesystem   (1, 40)
- memory dump device   (1, 41)
- **/dev/u** filesystem   (1, 42)

Chapter 5   Configuring Your System

Recommended CMOS Configuration

 Caution! Although the configuration recommendations included here are very important, much of the terminology will be quite technical (and mystical). Be assured that the relevant terms will be explained.

Like adapter configuration, CMOS configuration is critical for hardware function. CMOS is a special chunk of battery-maintained memory (typically less than 64 bytes) that retains the system hardware profile. The CMOS is responsible for the hardware devices that are configured by default.

 The ROM-BIOS is responsible for reading and updating the CMOS when you initialize your computer. You potentially modify CMOS information each time you update the configuration screen on your PC.

Typical CMOS memories contain the following relevant information:
- which disk devices to initialize
- the expected attributes of those devices (e.g. heads, tracks, sectors/track)
- which on-board serial and parallel interfaces to initialize
- the expected configuration of those devices
- the time and date from the motherboard's real-time clock chip
- the base video adapter mode (e.g. VGA)
- whether a math co-processor is detected
- the amount of base memory (up to 640 KB) installed
- the system processing speed (in MHz)
- which system optimizations to perform (including shadow RAM, shadow ROM, caching, et cetera)

 When the Primary Hard Disk Is SCSI

When the primary hard disk is attached to a SCSI adapter, you must:
- tell the CMOS that zero hard disks are attached,
- enable the BIOS on the SCSI adapter hosting the hard disk,
- disable the BIOSs on all other SCSI adapters.

The ROM-BIOS normally checks the CMOS for disks attached to standard (i.e. IDE, ESDI) disk controllers. When none are found, the ROM-BIOS then passes control to the first SCSI adapter whose BIOS is enabled.

Once control passes to the SCSI adapter ROM, the SCSI disk will be initialized, and the system can boot from that disk.

Essential SCO System Administration

> **BIOS Extensions**
>
> BIOS extensions are automatically supported by the main motherboard ROM-BIOS. After executing its own startup code, the ROM-BIOS then searches the high memory area (0xC0000 - 0xDF800) for BIOS extensions. Each BIOS extension that is found will be instructed to run its start-up code.
>
> BIOS extensions are identified by a special byte signature (0x55AA). They must start on a 2K boundary (i.e. the ROM address must be a multiple of 0x800).

Of most interest to us are the system optimizations. Some of the standard optimizations used with MS-DOS can impede the operation of SCO systems. The recommended CMOS values are summarized in Table 5-9.

Table 5-9: Recommended CMOS System Settings

Option	Setting
shadow ROM	disabled
shadow RAM	disabled
memory cache	enabled
cache shadow ROM	disabled

> **What's What: CMOS Configuration**
>
> The CMOS optimizations, for the most part, employ the normally inaccessible system RAM between 640K and 1024K (1MB) to speed up selected system functions. The most important of these are defined below.
>
> *Shadow ROM* has an effect similar to the speed dialing feature on your telephone. It copies the ROM-BIOS from slower ROM (or EPROM) to faster RAM. This makes it faster to perform BIOS calls. Unfortunately, since SCO only access the ROM-BIOS during the boot phase, this optimization has no benefit.
>
> *Shadow RAM* is a little like having an extra room in your house created from all of the floor space concealed by furniture. Effectively, it remaps the memory area between 640K and 1MB to a location above the traditional 1MB MS-DOS memory barrier. This is fine for DOS systems, which normally must operate within the 0 - 640K range, but it creates havoc on UNIX systems, which assume unrestricted use of the memory above 1MB. By the way, shadow RAM and shadow ROM are mutually exclusive. Shadow RAM is also called *remapped memory*.

5-28

Chapter 5   Configuring Your System

Memory cache is sort of like the speed dialing feature on your telephone. It enables the system to move selected chunks of system RAM (DRAM memory) into faster SRAM. SRAM is about 3-4 times faster than DRAM, but is a lot more expensive. The complex logic that determines which chunks of memory get *cached* is programmed into the processor chip.

Cache shadow RAM (or ROM) is a feature that depends on shadow ROM being enabled. Enabling this feature allows you to waste part of the precious cache on ROM code that SCO never uses.

Shadowing Adapter ROM

Many hardware adapters also offer the option of moving slower ROM into faster RAM. As with shadowing the ROM-BIOS on the motherboard, this option should be disabled.

Essential SCO System Administration

Configuring Hardware Peripherals

John: Susan! I thought you'd finished that configuration stuff by now. So, why doesn't this modem work? No beep, no flash, nothing!!

*Susan: John, modems do **not** beep. And I **have** finished the configuration. I'm simply waiting for you. Besides, if you'd attached the proper cable, you wouldn't need so much duct tape.*

Finally, your adapters are installed, and all device conflicts resolved. Now you can actually configure some working devices – your peripherals. This section gives you the key information you need to ready your peripherals for use.

The following peripherals are addressed:

> hard disks   printers   serial terminals   modems   tape   mice   CD-ROM

Hard Disk Configuration

Yikes! Your system has been running out of space, and you can no longer open your mailbox! It just might be time to free up disk space or add another disk.

The main steps involved are:

> 1. properly connecting the new disk to an installed disk controller
> 2. verifying the hard disk geometry (e.g. cylinders, tracks, sectors/track)
> 3. partitioning the disk (**fdisk**)
> 4. inspecting and mapping bad disk tracks (**badtrk**)
> 5. allocating filesystems and divisions (**divvy**)

> *You need to verify and configure the logical (remapped) disk geometry!*

> If you are reconfiguring an installed disk, ensure that you reliably back-up its contents. If simply reconfiguring divisions on a single partition, only that partition needs to be backed up. If you are resizing a partition, everything must be backed up. Resizing a partition resets the tables.

One SCO UNIX command does virtually everything for you: **mkdev hd**

Chapter 5 Configuring Your System

> From **sysadmsh**, go to: System ⇨ Hardware (⇨ Hard Disk)

FYI, here are the standalone commands for performing the steps above:

- verifying disk parameters: **dparam** *raw disk device*
- partitioning the disk: **fdisk -f** *disk device*
- mapping bad disk tracks: **badtrk -f** *raw disk partition*
- defining divisions: **divvy** *-m 1 disk partition*

Disk Device Names

Disk device names are simple and consistent. The first disk device, disk 0, is **hd00**, the second is **hd10**. This is followed by **hd20**, **hd30**, **hd40**, ...

Disk partition names are similar. The first is **hd*x*1**, followed by **hd*x*2**, **hd*x*3**, and **hd*x*4**. For example, **hd13** is partition 3 on the second disk. Four partitions are allowed per disk. Partition numbers are as displayed by **fdisk**.

Disk Geometry and Partitions

Forbidding as it sounds, hard disk geometry is actually quite useful to know. Disk geometry lets you efficiently configure your hard disk. The **dparam***(ADM)* command displays the relevant disk geometry parameters as follows:

   *cylinders   heads   *   *   *   landing zone sectors/track*

Parameters labeled "*" are hardware-specific *[consult **dparam**(ADM)]*. Of the rest, only *cylinders*, *heads*, and *sectors/track* are useful for configuration.

Disk Geometry Spoofing

Most modern disk controllers translate the actual physical disk geometry to a logical geometry. This lets the BIOS see it as a disk with "legal" parameters. Luckily, controller translation is usually transparent to the SCO UNIX kernel.

Maximum Disk Size

The maximum supported disk size is 1 terabyte (2^{40} bytes), but due to the limit of 2GB (2^{31} bytes) per division, the maximum usable space is 56GB.

Hard Disk Partition Structure

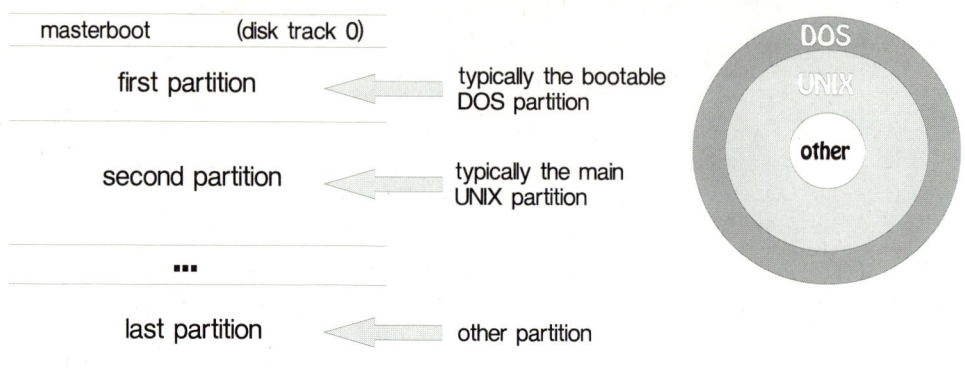

masterboot (disk track 0)	
first partition	⇐ typically the bootable DOS partition
second partition	⇐ typically the main UNIX partition
...	
last partition	⇐ other partition

 Not all partitions need to be bootable. For example, the "last" partition above could be an extended DOS partition or an extra UNIX filesystem partition.

Structure of the UNIX Partition

sectors	
2	boot 0
40	boot 1
2	divvy table
8	bad track table
???	alias tracks area
*	divvy division 0
	...
*	divvy division N

⎫ reserved ⇒

 Alias tracks are where bad disk tracks are remapped. The size of this area is determined at configuration. Some space is wasted, since the alias tracks must start on a cylinder boundary. Up to 8 divisions can follow the alias tracks.

Chapter 5   Configuring Your System

tool	unit	computation
fdisk	tracks	cylinders * heads
divvy	physical blocks	unit = 1024 bytes
dfspace	megabytes (MB)	cylinders * heads * sectors/track / 2048
others	virtual blocks, sectors	unit = 512 bytes

hard disks are configured in different units, depending on the tool

Defining Disk Partitions

The primary job of disk partitions is to separate the various OSs contending for the same disk. Each partition is associated with exactly one operating system.

Typically, partitions are used to hold an entire bootable OS distribution (or at least as much as will fit). But partitions have other uses, including:

- extended DOS partitions for DOS virtual disks (e.g. E:, F:)
- extra UNIX filesystems (since only 6 can be defined on the boot partition)
- raw space for data backup

> **Using Partitions for Data Backup**
>
> Beware of using raw partitions for data backup. If you do so, you will not be protected by the SCO UNIX badtracking scheme. When writing directly to a partition device, the badtrack table (and the remapped tracks) can be overwritten. The recommended way to use a partition for backup is to create a single division, then write to that division. You can use the following command to create a single division:
>
>   **divvy -m1** *disk partition device*

Use **fdisk***(ADM)* to define, inspect, and realign partitions. Just keep in mind the following "Rules of Partition":

> A. Partitions like to start on cylinder boundaries.
>   [the starting track should be divisible by the number of heads]
> B. The active partition is the one that will boot.
>   [you can still boot DOS when the active partition is SCO UNIX]
> C. Back up all files on a partition before resizing.
>   [data will be lost when a partition is resized]
> D. Partition numbers are almost *never* related to physical order on the disk.

Bad Disk Track Remapping

Unfortunately, no disk is perfect. Unto each disk some bad tracks must fall. SCO UNIX provides a bad-tracking scheme and the **badtrk**(ADM) utility to keep your systems running when the disk gets rough.

> The SCO UNIX badtracking scheme does not apply to IDA or SCSI disks. Many SCSI disks support ***automatic write/read remapping***, which enables the controller to remap tracks at the firmware level. In some cases, SCSI disks ship with this feature disabled. If so, run **scsibadblk**(ADM) to reenable it. The utility also supports manual remapping (and scanning) on SCSI disks.

Although you can map bad tracks encountered during system operation, you do risk possible data corruption or blocked disk access (the system repeatedly tries to read or write a bad sector). The best defense is to run **badtrk** at disk configuration, then afterward every 3 months (as marginal tracks get worse).

> Most disks provide a flaw map indicating bad (or marginal) tracks. Entries from the flaw map should be entered after manually scanning the disk.
>
> NOTE: The disk flaw map may be unusable for controllers formatted for alternate modes such as *translation*, *mapping*, or *63-sector*. In those cases, rely solely upon the disk scan to report logical sectors for bad tracks.

Be sure to allocate sufficient space for bad tracks. The system suggests a default number of tracks to allocate when **badtrk** is run. Allocate at least this number.

> ***Never ever*** allocate zero (0) bad tracks! Once you fix that number, you must reinstall the OS to change it. *[The alias track area starts and ends on a cylinder boundary. Allocating 0 tracks leaves no alias track area at all]*

Defining Divisions, Creating Filesystems

The final disk configuration step is defining divisions and creating filesystems. As you might expect, there are a few key things to know in order to effectively configure your system.

> ***Divisions*** are a convenient way to divide up a partition among different data uses (e.g. raw data, backup, virtual memory, files). ***Filesystems*** are divisions that have been specially formatted for storing and retrieving files.

Chapter 5 Configuring Your System

The **divvy**(ADM) utility creates divisions and filesystems.

> The **mkdev hd** utility prepares to invoke **divvy** by asking whether or not you want block by block control over the partition configuration. Respond "yes".

Following is a sample configuration that Susan has just defined with **divvy** for a new hard disk. All that remains is for Susan to tell **divvy** to commit this configuration on the disk (sample command to use: **divvy -m5** /**dev**/**hd11**).

```
+-----------+------------+--------+---+-------------+------------+
| Name      | Type       | New FS | # | First Block | Last Block |
+-----------+------------+--------+---+-------------+------------+
| man       | EAFS       | yes    | 0 |           0 |       9997 |
| util      | EAFS       | yes    | 1 |        9998 |      69997 |
| tmp       | EAFS       | yes    | 2 |       69998 |     109997 |
| dskhog    | EAFS       | yes    | 3 |      109998 |     159997 |
| backup    | NON FS     | no     | 4 |      159998 |     323762 |
|           | NOT USED   | no     | 5 |          -  |         -  |
|           | NOT USED   | no     | 6 |          -  |         -  |
| d1047all  | WHOLE DISK | no     | 7 |           0 |     324631 |
+-----------+------------+--------+---+-------------+------------+
323763 1K blocks for divisions, 868 1K blocks reserved for system
```

> Although **divvy** shows the reserved area following the division, exactly the opposite is true. [FYI, the reserved area above has 31 alias tracks (14K each)].

> Susan is preparing to move the online manual pages (**/usr/man/***) to their own filesystem, **/dev/man**. She's created a separate **/dev/tmp** filesystem to offload **/tmp** from the crowded **/dev/root** filesystem. She has also set aside a raw division (**/dev/backup**) for quick filesystem backups. This will be convenient for reconfiguring other filesystems or partitions without the need for tape.

Once this configuration is installed, the filesystems will be formatted, and the following device nodes created in /**dev**:   **man**, **util**, **tmp**, **dskhog**, **backup**.

> **Managing Large Disks with Filesystems**
>
> Multiple filesystems are the way to manage hard disks (or disk arrays) over 2GB. The effective limits are 2GB per filesystem and 28 filesystems per disk. Many controllers can depict an array of disks as a single large disk to the OS.

So concludes actual disk configuration. What remains is for the filesystem service to be configured for multiuser use. *[For further filesystem configuration see "Configuring Hardware Services"]*.

Essential SCO System Administration

Printer Configuration

SCO UNIX doesn't simply support printing, it provides a full-fledged print service. Some of the features offered by this service include:

- scheduling print jobs for specific printers
- spooling to local, system, dialup, and network printers
- converting raw print data into forms acceptable to specific printers
- managing the mounting of special forms or printwheels on printers
- tracking and managing the status of printers and print jobs
- processing user-specified options to customize printing
- alerting users and administrators to printer problems

Although the SCO UNIX print service supports many powerful features, most users will find that only a small subset applies to their daily printing needs. It is upon those features that this section and the print services section (following later) will focus.

> **User-Specified Print Options**
>
> For many printers, users are able to specify print options such as no banner and character pitch. Some also support variable line pitch, page width & length, and page orientation (e.g. landscape or portrait). Users typically specify these options on the **lp** command line using **-o** or **-y**. The specific options supported depend upon the ***printer interface***, the available ***filters***, and the capabilities of the printer itself.

This section describes the essential steps required to prepare a specific printer for basic use with the print service. Further aspects of print service configuration are addressed in "Hardware Services Configuration", below.

Configuring a printer for basic use with the print service involves the following:

> 1. connecting the printer to an appropriate serial or parallel port
> 2. ensuring that the proper cable is used to support printer datacomm. *[see "Serial Device Cabling" later in this chapter]*
> 3. confirming the physical connection to the printer *[see Chapter 4]*
> 4. specifying appropriate spooler attributes for the printer *[see box below]*
> 5. specifying an optional type for the printer
> 6. enabling the printer for printing
> 7. opening the printer queue to accept print jobs

5-36

Chapter 5 Configuring Your System

> **Spooler Attributes for Printers**
> - a name (up to 14 characters) for the printer
> - a brief comment pertaining to the printer *[optional]*
> - an interface model for the printer
> - a class to which the printer belongs *[optional]*
> - whether the printer is directly connected or dialup
> - the device name (or dial info) to reach the printer
> - whether to print banners identifying print jobs

> **What's What: Printer Configuration**
>
> A *printer interface* is effectively a language translator. It translates data and printing instructions from users into a form that the printer can use. In DOS, it would be called a *printer driver*. Technically, interfaces are shell scripts that convert print requests into suitable datastreams for target printers. Interface models reside in **/usr/spool/lp/model**. Typically, each configured printer accesses its own copy of a selected interface model. This copy can be customized as needed.
>
> A *class* is effectively a taxi stand for selected printers. Technically, it is a named list of printers. A print request sent to a class (instead of a printer) prints on the first available printer in the class. A configured printer can be associated with multiple classes.
>
> The *printer type* indicates a printer's capabilities (e.g. variable fonts, character sets, landscape mode). It is an entry into the terminfo printer database, which fully defines the capabilities of a specific model of printer. Some printer interfaces (e.g. **standard**) perform lookups on the printer type to process user-supplied print options. If no type is specified, the default type, "unknown" (which defines no print capabilities), is used.
>
> A *print filter* is the translation component of a printer interface. For example, the print filter, **text2post**, translates ascii text into postscript code (for postscript printers). Another key function of the filter is to detect and report printer faults. The default filter, **lp.cat**, reports simple printer faults, but does not perform any data translation.

> The specific interfaces in use reside in **/usr/spool/lp/admins/lp/interfaces**. Each interface file bears the name of its associated printer.
>
> Names of supported printer types can be found in the uncompiled source file, **/usr/lib/terminfo/terminfo.lp**. *[Consult **terminfo**(M) for a description of the various printer capabilities.]*
>
> Supplied print filters (e.g. **lp.cat** and **text2post**) reside in **/usr/spool/lp/bin**.

Essential SCO System Administration

Table 5-10:	Key Printer Interface Models
Interface	**Printers Supported**
* standard	standard printers (supports variable cpi, lpi, width, length)
* dosmodel	standard printers as above, but no formfeeds between files
postscript	postscript printers
network	remote printing over UUCP or ethernet
network.ps	remote postscript printing over UUCP or ethernet
epson	Epson-compatible printers
HPLaserJet	HP PCL V -compatible laser printers
proprinter	IBM Proprinter XL
* HPDeskJet500,	
* HPDeskJetPlus	HP DeskJet500, DeskJetPlus, ThinkJet, or QuietJet printers
* - supports the printer type	

As with disks, one command does virtually everything for you: **mkdev lp**

☞ From **sysadmsh** proceed to: *Printers*

From this point, use the following selections to perform printer configuration

Configure ⇨ Add	define printer's spooler attributes
Configure ⇨ Parameters	define printer's type
Schedule ⇨ Accept	open printer's job queue to accept print requests
Schedule ⇨ Enable	enable printing at the printer

Printer Configuration Tips

Following are suggestions for configuring various types of printer connection. Except for remote printing, most involve the use of the **standard** interface model. In many cases, the selected interface will need to be customized. If so, changes should be made to the interface copy bearing the name of the printer. As noted earlier, these are located in **/usr/spool/lp/admins/lp/interfaces**.

Chapter 5 Configuring Your System

Table 5-12:	Standalone Commands for Configuring Printers
• linking a printer name to a device	**lpadmin -p** *printer* **-v** *device file*
• entering a comment for a printer	**lpadmin -p** *printer* **-D** *"comment"*
• linking printer to an interface model	**lpadmin -p** *printer* **-m** *interface*
• adding printer to a class	**lpadmin -p** *printer* **-c** *class*
• linking printer to remote connection	**lpadmin -p** *printer* **-U** *dial info*
• initialize a printer	**echo** *"printer init codes"* **>** *device*
• enabling printer	**enable** *printer*
• disabling printer	**disable** *printer*
• open destination to requests	**/usr/lib/accept** *printer* <u>or</u> *class*
• close destination to requests	**/usr/lib/reject** *printer* <u>or</u> *class*

> If using hardware handshaking for a serial printer, you must use the modem control device (e.g. **/dev/tty2A**) instead of the terminal device (e.g. **/dev/tty2a**).

This completes basic printer configuration. This readies the printer for further configuration into the overall print spooler service. *[For spooler configuration details see "Configuring Hardware Services"].*

Configuring Serial Terminals

Strangers to the DOS world, terminals are old companions to UNIX. They offer an inexpensive way to share a powerful system among multiple users.

Properly configuring a serial terminal enables terminal users to log in and communicate with the system. Here are the relevant steps:

1. connecting the terminal to an available serial port
2. ensuring that the proper cable is used for terminal datacomm
   [see "Serial Device Cabling" below]
3. setting the terminal speed (baud rate)
4. determining appropriate line characteristics from **/etc/gettydefs**
5. indicating the line characteristics in **/etc/inittab**
6. confirming the physical connection *[see Chapter 4]*
7. determining an appropriate terminal type from the **terminfo** database
8. indicating the terminal type in **/etc/ttytype**
9. enabling logins on the terminal
10. updating the permanent serial port database, **/etc/conf/init.d/sio**

Essential SCO System Administration

Scancode Terminal Configuration

Scancode terminals (or terminals with a scancode mode) process keystrokes like PC keyboards. Unlike ASCII keystrokes, each scancode key transmits one code when depressed, and another when released. These codes are mapped by the system into ASCII keystrokes or special functions (e.g. ALT, CTRL, or function keys). The default key mapping can be overridden for individual terminals.

Setting Terminal Speed and Characteristics

Face it, we're speed addicts! Even our terminals must run ever faster. Actually, pursuing speed is fine, as long as you honor the "Rules of Serial Engagement":

  A. SCO UNIX serial lines are configured for 9600 baud by default.
  B. Exceed 9600 baud with the standard SCO UNIX serial driver at your peril.
  C. Dumb hardware (e.g. slow UARTs) thwart high-speed processing.
  D. Intelligent serial drivers are required for reliable high-speed support.
  E. Most humans cannot read faster than 9600 baud (*net* 960 cps) anyway.

Baud Rate and Transmission Speed

Baud is a data communications term indicating the maximum rate of signal changes on a line. Unencoded transmissions, like those used for terminals, transmit one bit per baud (encoded techniques such as V.32 for modems can transmit 4 or more bits per baud). Normal terminal communication transmits 2 extra bits (1 start bit & 1 stop bit) per 8 data bits. In this case, the net data transmission rate is 80% of the baud rate.

Initially, set the terminal's physical configuration as follows (you can increase the speed later):

   9600 baud, 8 data bits, 1 stop bit, no parity, full duplex, data to modem port

Chapter 5   Configuring Your System

Line Attributes

Line attributes are datacomm features of interest to serial devices like terminals. They include things like baud rate, data bits, parity, echo, and CR-to-NL translation. And, where there are line attributes, **getty** is close behind.

The **getty** program is responsible for keeping terminals in line. It maintains a database of line attributes in **/etc/gettydefs**.

Below is a sample entry from the **gettydefs** database:

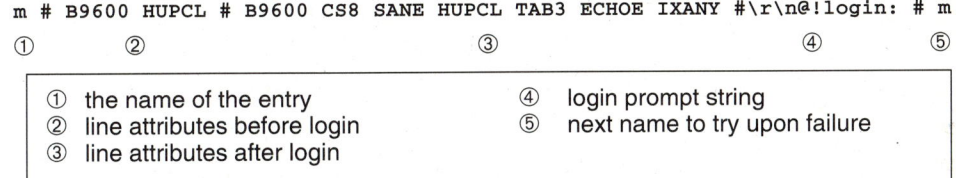

```
m # B9600 HUPCL # B9600 CS8 SANE HUPCL TAB3 ECHOE IXANY #\r\n@!login: # m
①        ②                    ③                               ④              ⑤
```

① the name of the entry
② line attributes before login
③ line attributes after login
④ login prompt string
⑤ next name to try upon failure

The key attributes you need to note are the entry name (in this case "m") and the baud rate (e.g. B9600). Use the "m" entry for now. *[For more info on **gettydefs** consult **gettydefs(F)** and **termio(M)**].*

☞ If your terminal is set for scancode mode, use the "sc_m" entry instead.

✈ **gettydefs** has entries for other baud rates (e.g. B19200, B38400), as well. These can be specified later in the configuration.

Applying the Line Attributes

To apply the selected attributes to the terminal, you must modify the process initialization table, **/etc/inittab**.

In the sample **inittab** section below, note the entry titled (beginning with) "Se1a".

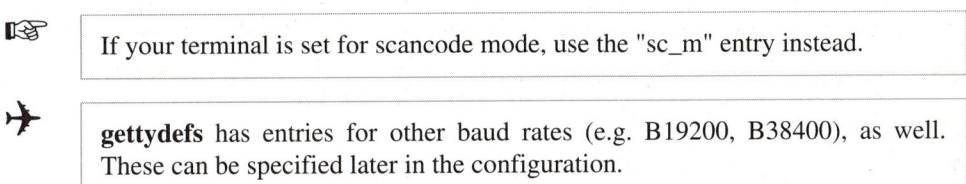

```
co:2345:respawn:/etc/getty tty01 sc_m
Se1A:23:off:/etc/getty -t60 tty1A M
Se1a:23:off:/etc/getty tty1a m
Se2A:23:off:/etc/getty -t60 tty2A O
Se2a:23:off:/etc/getty tty2a o
 ①   ②   ③               ④        ⑤
```

① name of the entry (1-4 chars)
② applicable run-levels
③ port enabled state
④ login port watched by getty
⑤ line attributes code

5-45

That entry specifies line attributes associated with the "m" entry in **/etc/gettydefs**. On the rare occasion that you might need to add some new entries (e.g. "**tty1b**" and "**tty1B**"), you would simply insert new lines into the **inittab** file. Usually, though, this is performed automatically during serial adapter configuration.

> Serial port **inittab** entries are typically added in pairs. One entry is for modem control; the other is for a standard terminal port. The modem control entry applies to devices that use hardware flow control (e.g. modems, certain printers). The names of **inittab** entries are arbitrary, but must not conflict.

> At this point you may want to confirm the physical connection to the terminal. After verifying the connection, you are free to increase the terminal speed to the desired value.

Terminal Type

If only there were as many flavors of ice cream as there are types of terminals. Over 800 terminal types are defined in the SCO UNIX **terminfo** database alone?

The directory **/usr/lib/terminfo** holds the SCO UNIX database of terminal types. Although each individual type has its own compiled file (in one of the single-character subdirectories), there is one master file that has all the information you need - **/usr/lib/terminfo/terminfo.src**.

Peruse that file to locate the most appropriate type for your terminal. Entries begin with lines like the samples below. Use the first name (e.g. "ansi", "vt100") as the terminal type. *[See **terminfo(M)** for details on interpreting terminfo entries]*

```
ansi|ansic|ansi80x25|Ansi standard console,
    ...
vt100|vt100-am|dec vt100 (w/advanced video),
    ...
```

To indicate the terminal type to the system, you must edit **/etc/ttytype**. This file contains lines like those below:

```
ansi       console
unknown    tty1a
unknown    tty2a
```

Chapter 5 Configuring Your System

For example, to change the type of **tty2a** (above) to "vt100", you'd simply replace "unknown", the default type assigned to new terminal ports.

> Be very careful to introduce no spaces into this file! A single TAB character separates the terminal type and the port name.

Enabling Terminal Logins

Now you're ready to enable the port for logins. The command is: **enable** *port*

If successful, you'll see the login prompt appear on the terminal.

> Enabling a port updates the port's entry in **/etc/inittab**. The new state will be "respawn". A new login will be spawned after the current user logs out.

Finally, to ensure that your changes will persist after the next boot, duplicate your **inittab** changes in **/etc/conf/init.d/sio**.

Table 5-13:	Terminal Configuration Summary
• select serial line attributes	scan /etc/gettydefs
• assign serial line attributes	edit /etc/inittab
• select terminal type	view /usr/lib/terminfo/terminfo.src
• assign terminal type	edit /etc/ttytype
• update permanent port file	edit /etc/conf/init.d/sio
• enable terminal port	**enable** *device port*
• disable terminal port	**disable** *device port*
• test terminal	**yes** > *device file*
• report active line attributes	**stty -a** < *device file*
• verify **gettydefs** structure	**getty -c**

> *Device port* refers to the base device name (e.g. **tty1a**). *Device file* refers to the full pathname (e.g. **/dev/tty1a**).

Essential SCO System Administration

Configuring Local Printers

Local printers hang off of terminals. Unlike system printers, which connect to system serial or parallel ports, a local printer connects directly to a special data port at the back of a terminal. Specific control codes are used to redirect system output from the terminal screen to the printer, and vice-versa.

The logged-on terminal user usually has exclusive access to the local printer.

> Unlike spooled printing, which uses the **lp**(C) command, local printing uses **lprint**(C). Beware that local printing may not be configurable for all terminals [see following note]. And, although it is possible to configure a local printer for use with lp, the procedure is non-trivial *[consult the SCO SOS database for detailed instructions]*.

> By default, local printing is supported for just a few terminals; and only via the XENIX terminal capabilities database, **/etc/termcap**. For most terminal types, you must manually edit the **termcap** file to add the required functionality. Appropriate control codes need to be defined for the attributes *PN* (to start printing) and *PS* (to stop printing). [*PN* is also specified as *po* (*mc5* in **terminfo**), and *PS* as *pf* (*mc4* in **terminfo**)]. *[Consult the terminal vendor's reference documentation for the relevant control codes].*

The following steps apply to local printer configuration:

Configuring a Local Printer

1. Verify that the control codes to support local printing on your terminal(s) are defined in **/etc/termcap** *[see the above note]*.

   > A sample **termcap** entry with added *PN* and *PS* capabilities to support local printing (displayed in bold) is included in the box below.

2. Ensure that the host terminal is properly configured for user logins.
3. Connect the printer to a free data port (typically "AUX" or "PRINT") at the rear of the terminal.
4. Enter the terminal's internal configuration; and modify the attributes of the selected data port to match the relevant settings for the local printer (e.g. baud rate, parity, data bits, flow control)
5. Log out and login again to make your changes available to the shell.
6. Use the **lprint** command to print a file to your printer.

Chapter 5 Configuring Your System

Sample /etc/termcap Entry
```
# start of entry
# next line specifies terminal type
s5|si100|Simple 100|Simple Technologies si-100 terminal:\
:is=\Ez1\Ec1\Ej1\Ek0:\E\072:\
:cm=\E@%2X%2Y:co#80:li#24:\
:kd=^J:ku=^K:kl=^H:kr:^L:\
:k1=^A[1\r:k2=^A[2\r:k3=^A[3\r:k4=^A[4\r:k5=^A[5\r:\
:k6=^A[6\r:k7=^A[7\r:k8=^A[8\r:k9=^A[9\r:k0=^A[0\r:\
:cl=\Ee0:dc=\Ee2:ic=\Ee3\
:PN=\E>0:PS=\E>1:\
:am:bs:
# end of entry
```

- commented lines begin with '#'.
- individual capabilities begin with ':'.
- continued lines end with ':\'.
- entry ends with ':'.
- capability formats: *name = control string*
  name # numeric value
  name   [boolean]

Legend

\E	ESC key
\r	CR (carriage return)
^x	CTRL X (control x)
%…	cursor motion control
\0xx	octal character code
	(useful for ':')

*[Consult **termcap**(F) for details of **termcap** structure]*

5-49

Essential SCO System Administration

Serial Device Cabling

Terminal Cables

Terminal cables are easy; just three wires. The catch is whether your serial port is DCE or DTE. Most ports are DTE, but keep a breakout box (which pinpoints individual signals) handy, just in case. Some printers can use these cables, also.

Both 25-pin and 9-pin cable pin-outs are shown at the right. [See table 5-X for pin assignments].

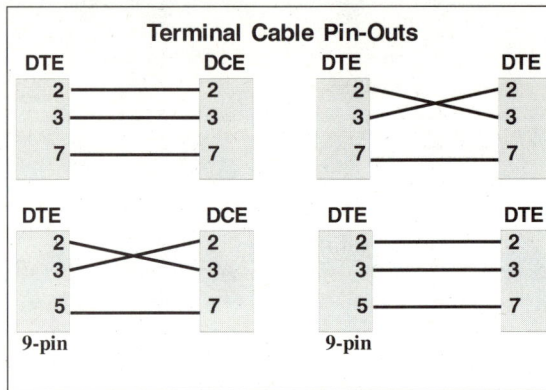

Printer Cables

Many printers require fine coordination with the system. Hardware handshaking lets the printer tell the system to moderate its output.

Cable pin-outs for the two most common types of hardware handshaking are shown at right.

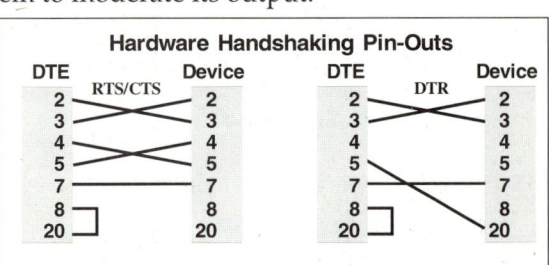

Modem Cables

Modem cables are also simple. Since modems are DCEs, a straight-through serial cable does the trick. Make sure that it is adequately shielded.

The minimum modem cable pin-outs are displayed at right.

Chapter 5 Configuring Your System

> **What's What: Serial Device Cabling**
>
> ***DCE*** (data communications equipment) and ***DTE*** (data terminal equipment) are inherited data communications terms. DCE's are typically devices like modems that talk directly to (or are part of) the telecommunications network. DTE's are typically end-user devices (like PC's or terminals) that connect to DCE's to access the network.
>
> ***EIA-232-D*** is a wiring specification for serial communications. Among other things, it defines a pin-numbering scheme for serial cable connections (25-pin or 9-pin). Each pin is assigned a specific datacomm function. Separate wires connect pins at each end of the cable. Some pins receive signals or data, while others transmit. This enables data transmission in both directions at the same time. *[See table 5-14 for a list of the key EIA-232-D pin assignments].*
>
> ***Hardware handshaking*** allows two devices to agree on the method of communication. Each device uses specific pins (wires) of a connecting cable to coordinate data transmission. For example, pin XX transmits the signal to postpone further data, while pin YY transmits the resume signal.

Table 5-14:   Key EIA-232-D (RS-232-C) Connector Assignments

25-Pin (DTE)	25-Pin (DCE)	9-Pin (DTE)	RS Name	EIA Name	Source	Description
2	3	3	TD	BA	DTE	Transmitted data
3	2	2	RD	BB	DCE	Received data
4	5	7	RTS	CA	DTE	Request to send
5	4	8	CTS	CB	DCE	Clear to send
6	20	6	DSR	CC	DCE	Dataset (DCE) ready
7	7	5	GD	AB		Signal ground
8	8	1	CD	CF	DCE	Carrier detect
15	17		?	DB	DCE	Transmit signal timing
17	15		?	DD	DTE	Receiver signal timing
20	6	4	DTR	CD	DTE	Data terminal ready
22	22	9	RI	?	DCE	Ring Indicator

Note that the serial data is transmitted over pins 2 and 3.

Essential SCO System Administration

Configuring Modems

Proc: *Hey! What is this? Where did these bits come from? This'll be the last time I ask **you** for a remote connection to Singapore!!*

Kernel: *Sorry process, I just follow instructions. But, off the record, we need some smarter input units [ie human operators]. The ones we have now seem quite defective. Any self-respecting kernel knows not to change baud rate in the middle of a data stream.*

Proc: *Yes, you're probably right. These units need some real intelligence to get their configurations right, especially modems.*

Kernel: *Alright, wise guy, what do you mean by "probably"?*

Was there life before modems? These days it's almost barbaric to be without bulletin boards, dialup sites, or online services. If only it were easier to get the devices to work. Defective "input units" indeed!

So that you can make life happier for the kernel and its friends, here are the key steps for configuring a modem:

```
   1. Connecting the modem to an available high-speed serial port
   2. Securing the proper shielded cable [see "Serial Device Cables" above]
   3. Initializing the modem's physical configuration
 * 4. Determining appropriate line attributes from /etc/gettydefs
 * 5. Indicating the line attributes in /etc/inittab
 * 6. Updating the permanent serial port database, /etc/conf/init.d/sio
   7. Testing the physical connection to the modem
   8. Selecting and customizing an appropriate modem dialer program
   9. Registering the modem as a uucp automatic calling device
  10. Testing the configured modem
          * only if modem is used for dial-in
```

High-Speed Serial Ports

The secret of speed is in the UART (universal asynchronous receiver/transmitter). Slow serial ports utilize the older 8250 chips. These were limited to 9600 baud (the speed generated by a 2400 baud modem w/ compression). Faster ports use the 16450 or 16550 chips. They can handle throughput up to 38400 baud, and higher when these chips are used on intelligent adapters. [Even higher rates can be sustained through bi-directional parallel ports (currently supported only by 3rd-party drivers)].

Chapter 5   Configuring Your System

> **Shielded Cabling for Modems**
>
> Although the quality of the signals over the telephone network may be beyond your control, you can minimize the *noise* (signal interference) between the modem and the serial port. This requires using a shielded cable to minimize any radio frequency (RF) interference. Such noise can severely corrupt incoming or outgoing modem signals, resulting in significant errors in your data. The probability of data loss is quite high in electronically noisy environments. RF interference can originate from televisions, radios, stereo equipment, most electronic devices, and even telephones.

Initial Physical Modem Configuration

> **Recommended Modem Features**
>
> - error-control   (V.42, MNP1, MNP2, MNP3 and/or MNP4)
> - high signalling speed (V.32 [9600 baud], V.32bis [14400 baud], or V.34 [28800 baud])
> - data compression   (V.42bis, MNP5, and/or MNP7)
> - hardware flow control (RTS/CTS)

> **What's What: Modem Configuration**
>
> *Modem* is short for <u>mo</u>dulate/<u>dem</u>odulate. Modems *modulate* binary data into analogue (audio) signals for transmission across a phone line. Conversely they *demodulate* analog signals back into binary data. Modern modulation techniques are able to encode several binary digits into a single bleep (waveform), thus enabling very high transmission speeds.
>
> *Carrier* is a little like the musical key used to tune instruments for a concert. Once the key is established, it serves as a reference for the highs and lows of the music to follow. Carrier is the reference signal used to modulate (and demodulate) data transmissions across a communications circuit.
>
> *Protocols* are rules describing how to represent, manipulate, and verify transmitted data between two parties. In this case, the parties are modems.
>
> *Error control* protocols provide insurance against transmission errors. Modems pass blocks of data back and forth like tennis balls. Anytime the data is bad, the receiving modem requests the sending modem to retransmit. Various methods are used to determine whether the data is bad. For example, ARQ-type protocols (e.g. MNP-3) add a *check code* based on the data transmitted. When the data arrives a new check code is generated. If the check codes don't match, a data error is assumed. Some protocols include the ability to correct a limited number of errors as well.

Essential SCO System Administration

> *Data compression* protocols (e.g. V42bis) can reduce the amount of data actually transmitted. The data is compressed on one end of the connection, then decompressed on the other end. The decompression codes are inserted into the data. Some methods can compress text data as much as 80%. Beware that already compressed data (e.g. Xmodem) may actually increase in transmitted size.
>
> *Flow control* lets a data receiving device say "hold it!". Hardware flow control uses dedicated wires to transmit the control signals between two devices. One example is RTS/CTS across an EIA-232-D line. Hardware flow control is especially useful when the transmitting device is much faster than the receiving device. Software flow control uses special codes inserted in to the data. On example is XON/XOFF. This is commonly used by serial printers to control the flow of data from the system.

The recommended internal configuration for your modem is listed below:

Table 5-15:   Internal Modem Configuration Checklist

- ❏ transmit and received data hardware flow control enabled
- ❏ software flow control disabled
- ❏ fixed serial port rate set (to modem)
- ❏ variable modem-to-modem connect speed
- ❏ error-control enabled w/ intelligent fallback to no error-control
- ❏ data compression set for auto enable/disable
- ❏ DSR (data set ready) controlled by modem
- ❏ CD (carrier detect) asserted only when carrier is present
- ❏ carrier detect timeout set to at least 90 seconds
- ❏ modem responds to DTR (data terminal ready) from computer
- ❏ verbal result codes enabled (especially "CONNECT" messages)
- ❏ modem local echo disabled
- ❏ speaker on until carrier detect
- ❏ automatic recognition of data format (8-bit or 7-bit)

These settings can be entered into the modem's configuration directly (e.g. by DIP switches), in NVRAM (non-volatile RAM), or in the initialization string in the selected modem dialing program (e.g. **atdial**...) *[see "Configuring the Modem Dialer Software" below].*

Chapter 5   Configuring Your System

Internal Modem Configuration Rationale

Unlike software flow control (e.g. XON/XOFF) *hardware flow control* cannot be misinterpreted as data (or vice-versa). Hardware flow control is also more efficient. *Software flow control* must be explicitly disabled, or it may be used as well.

A *fixed serial port* rate lets you comfortably receive compressed data, which may expand to several times its transmitted size. The fixed rate should be somewhat higher than the modem's top connect rate.

Variable connect speed lets the modems negotiate a suitable transmission rate, especially if they are different models. Poor line quality may make high-speed transmissions unsuitable for some connections. The alternative is to only accept connections at a fixed rate (e.g. 9600 baud), but this is not suitable for general outbound dialing.

Error control may be unneeded when the data quality is not critical, (e.g. remote logins not involving file transfers). *Automatic fallback* allows the modem to disable error control when not needed (e.g. with protocols like ZMODEM that use software error control)

Auto enable/disable data compression lets the modems determine whether or not data compression will be efficient.

It is only natural the *DSR* (data set ready) be controlled by the modem (the *data set*).

By detecting carrier (*CD*) normally, the modem connects only when another modem answers; and disconnects properly. To suitably handle long distance dialing and connection delays, a timeout of 90 seconds to wait for the carrier signal seems reasonable.

By responding to *DTR* (data terminal ready), the modem rightly lets the transmitting system determine when to start.

Verbal result codes allow the communications software to interpret and respond to actions taken by the modem. For example, if a modem establishes a 2400 baud connection with error control, it may report "CONNECT 2400 ARQ". The software can then respond appropriately; perhaps rejecting the connection as too slow.

Modem local echo is not needed, since it echoes data sent to the remote system.

Having the *speaker on until carrier detect* lets you detect whether or not the call is to a modem or a telephone. Once carrier is detected, the modems can safely take over.

Automatic recognition of data format (8-bit or 7-bit) minimizes potential data errors, especially when calling system in foreign countries or with older software.

Essential SCO System Administration

Quick Recipe SR5.2   **Loading Modem Codes into NVRAM**

Simple steps to preload modem initialization codes into modem NVRAM

1. Append this line to **Devices**:   **Direct** *tty1a* **- 9600 direct**

   Replace *tty1a* with the ***terminal port*** attached to the modem. You may need to replace 9600 with a more suitable speed for your modem.

2. Run: **cu -l** *tty1a* **dir**

   This connects you directly to the modem. Wait for the message "Connected" before entering the appropriate modem initialization codes.

3. Enter one or more lines of modem codes. The code to load the configuration to NVRAM must be the last one entered.

4. Verify your set-up. Enter the code to display the current configuration.

5. To exit **cu**:   press ENTER; type the 2 characters '**~.**'; then press ENTER.

Modem Line Attributes

This section is needed only if using the modem for dial-in (as well as dial-out).

Use the following **gettydefs** attributes for modem ports in your **inittab** file.

Fixed Port Rates		Variable Port Rates	
m	(9600 baud)	1	(300-1200-2400 baud)
n	(19200 baud)	2	(1200-2400-300 baud)
o	(38400 baud)	3	(2400-300-1200 baud)
l	(4800 baud)	6	(9600-4800-2400 baud)

For high-speed modems (9600 baud and above), fixed port rates are preferable. *[As mentioned before, be aware that some serial ports may not support data speeds over 9600 baud].*

As an example, the **inittab** line below sets the COM2 port speed to 38400 baud.

                         Se2A:2:off:/etc/getty -t60 tty2A o

As with serial terminals, update **/etc/inittab** and **/etc/conf/cf.d/init.d/sio**.

Chapter 5   Configuring Your System

Configuring the Modem Dialer Software

There are three supported types of modem dialers. They are:
- **atdial**... binary dialers (e.g. **atdialUSR**)
- **dial**... binary dialers (e.g. **dialHA24**)
- dialer strings in the **Dialers** file (e.g. "hayes2400")

> All the above files reside in **/usr/lib/uucp**. The source files for the dialer binaries reside there as well. The configurable components of the **atdial**... (and some **dial**...) dialers are in **/etc/default**.

Table 5-16:	Modem Dialer Comparison Chart	
Dialer	**Advantages**	**Disadvantages**
atdial...	readily configurable; reliable; no programming	tricky to configure properly
dial...	fast and reliable; some configurability w/o programming	full configuration requires programming; Development System must be installed
Dialer string	easiest to configure	lowest reliability; slowest

> With the exception of **dialHA96V**, the **dial**... config files only support an "STTY=..." entry. In **dialHA96V** you can also configure the modem initialization string by adding the line:
> **MDM_SETUP=***modem init string*

My preference is the **atdial**... dialers. They have the advantage of being compiled, and can be readily configured through configuration files (bearing the same name) in **/etc/default**.

A sample **atdial**... configuration file follows.

5-57

Essential SCO System Administration

```
*       @(#) generic atdial              RTC_NOCARR=NO CARRIER
*                                        RTC_ERROR=ERROR
MDM_SETUP=old modem init string          RTC_NOTONE=NO DIALTONE
MDM_OPTION=                              RTC_BUSY=BUSY
MDM_DIALCMD=ATDT                         RTC_NOANS=NO ANSWER
MDM_ESCAPE=+++                           RTC_300=not used
MDM_HANGUP=AT...                         RTC_1200=not used
MDM_RESET=ATZ                            RTC_2400=not used
MDM_DIALIN=AT...                         RTC_4800=not used
MDM_ATTN=AT                              RTC_9600=CONNECT
MDM_DSBLESC=ATS2=128                     RTC_19200=not used
RTC_OK=OK                                RTC_38400=not used
```

The above listing is for a Hayes-type modem set for a fixed serial port rate of 9600 baud. Note the line: RTC_9600=CONNECT

The modem config file should be changed as follows:

```
*       @(#) generic atdial              RTC_ERROR=ERROR
*                                        RTC_NOTONE=NO DIALTONE
MDM_SETUP=modified modem init string     RTC_BUSY=BUSY
MDM_OPTION=                              RTC_NOANS=NO ANSWER
MDM_DIALCMD=ATDT                       * RTC_300=CONNECT 300
MDM_ESCAPE=+++                         * RTC_1200=CONNECT 1200
MDM_HANGUP=AT...                       * RTC_2400=CONNECT 2400
MDM_RESET=ATZ                          * RTC_4800=CONNECT 4800
MDM_DIALIN=AT...                       * RTC_9600=not used
MDM_ATTN=AT                              RTC_19200=not used
MDM_DSBLESC=ATS2=128                   * RTC_38400=CONNECT
RTC_OK=OK                              * STTY=RTSFLOW CTSFLOW HUPCL
   RTC_NOCARR=NO CARRIER
```

lines indicated by ✶ *have been changed.*

These modifications let you fix your serial baud rate at 38400 whenever the connection rate ranges from 9600 - 38400 baud (this includes 12000 and 14400 baud). It also lets you reject connections slower than 9600 baud. *[See "atdial... configuration Secrets" below for details].*

5-58

Chapter 5 Configuring Your System

Note also in the listing that the line ("STTY=...") has been added. This line lets you specify additional stty settings (e.g. CTSFLOW, RTSFLOW, HUPCL). The most relevant atdial... STTY settings are summarized below.

CTSFLOW	modem-to-system hardware flow control
RTSFLOW	system-to-modem hardware flow control
ORTSFL	sets direction of flow control based on RTSFLOW and CTSFLOW
HUPCL	hangs up when last process closes the line
CLOCAL	assumes line has no modem control; ignores inbound modem signals

> Use these settings to turn on bidirectional flow control:
>   CTSFLOW RTSFLOW -ORTSFL -IXON -IXOFF HUPCL
> In a few cases, the settings below must be used instead:
>   -CTSFLOW -RTSFLOW ORTSFL -IXON -IXOFF HUPCL

> For hints on configuring other modem dialers, consult modem chapter in the *SCO UNIX Operating System System Administrator's Guide*.

Once you have selected and configured your modem dialer, you are ready to register the modem for dial-out use.

> **Atdial... Configuration Secrets**
>
> Based upon the values of the RTC_ strings in the configuration file, **atdial**... resets the serial port rate just before making the connection. It performs a string match against the verbal result code returned by the modem to determine which rate applies.
>
> Matches specific "CONNECT" strings (e.g. *"CONNECT 1200"*) to fix the serial port at the given RTC_ rate. The simple string, "CONNECT", is treated special. It matches any result code not matching a specific "CONNECT *xxxx*" message. <u>Take care to include only one simple "CONNECT", since atdial tries to match the lowest possible RTC_ string</u>. Consider the following examples, using the listing above:
>
> | modem result code | matching RTC_ line | resulting port rate |
> |---|---|---|
> | "CONNECT 1200" | RTC_1200=*CONNECT 1200* | 1200 baud |
> | "CONNECT 2400 ARQ" | RTC_2400=*CONNECT 2400* | 2400 baud |
> | "CONNECT 9600" | RTC_38400=*CONNECT* | 38400 baud |
> | "CONNECT 14400 ARQ" | RTC_38400=*CONNECT* | 38400 baud |
>
> Any modem connect rate from 9600 baud up, fixes the serial port rate at 38400 baud. Using the following dial-out command, you can refuse (as too slow) any connections below 9600 baud:
>
>   cu -s **9600-38400** *phone number*

Essential SCO System Administration

> **atdial**... (and the SCO serial driver) supports a maximum serial port rate of 38400 baud. While sufficient for 19200 baud connections, this will impede higher rates (e.g. 28800 baud). Users running third-party serial drivers (supporting 57600 baud and higher) have experienced much better success with higher modem connect rates by employing the dialer strings in **Dialers**.

Registering the Modem for Dial-Out

Register dial-out modems by adding an entry to **/usr/lib/uucp/Devices**. A typical **Devices** modem entry looks like:

> **ACU** **tty***XX* -   *speed*   *modem dialer*

              tty*XX*   is the serial modem port (e.g. tty2A)
              speed   is a single speed or a speed range

Examples are: ACU tty3A - 2400-9600 dialHA96V
                          ACU tty331 - 38400 atdialUSR \T

> Menu-oriented (e.g. **sysadmsh**) users can run: **uuinstall** (➪ *3* ➪ *2*)

> The speed range (e.g. 2400-9600) is the range of connect speeds that the administrator chooses to allow on a particular serial modem port. This is quite often a subset of the modem's full supported speed range. An optional '\T' terminating an entry indicates that dial token (alphabetic code) expansion can be applied to the dial-out phone number. Legal dial tokens are defined in **Dialcodes** (in **/usr/lib/uucp**). '\T' is the default for dialer binaries.

Add the following entry immediately after in order to connect directly to the modem. Such an entry is extremely useful for connection debugging. It can also be used to load configuration settings into the modem's NVRAM.

> **Direct** **tty***XY* -   *speed*   *direct*

              tty*XY*   is the serial ***terminal*** port (e.g. tty2a) !!
              speed   is a single speed (a range is less useful)

Below is an example of a properly configured pair of entries in **Devices**:

        ACU tty3A - 9600-14400 atdialUSR
        Direct tty3a - 9600 direct

Chapter 5 Configuring Your System

Testing the Modem Connection

Use a command like the one below to test the modem connection:

> **cu** **-s** *speed* **-l** *line* **-x** *test level* *phone number*

        speed   is the desired speed or speed range
        line   is the desired modem port (e.g. tty2A)
        test level is the desired level of debugging output
                        (range is 1-9; 9 provides the most detail)

> With the modem set for fixed serial port rate, the modem senses the serial port rate only once, when first opened. You must ensure that your terminal session speed does not get changed by the modem dialer. The consequences can be quite dire (i.e. unresponsive keyboard, unreadable screen). The best assurance is to use a dial procedure (e.g. **atdial**..., as configured in this section) that fixes the serial speed at a known rate. Set your login terminal session to that rate.

> The **cu** debugging level (enabled by the **-x** option) provides valuable information, such as modem result codes, attempted connect speed, and (in case of failure) diagnostic detail. It can even help identify problems with successful connections, such as character mismatches (e.g. 7-bit vrs. 8-bit) or timing problems (i.e. session running at 19200 baud, but port set at 9600).

For example, the command below provides maximum on-line debugging detail, while recording the session's output in the user file **connect.out**:

    cu **-s** 9600-19200 **-l** tty2A **-x**9 15553242 | **tee connect.out**

> With speed ranges, results may vary. Most modems attempt to connect at the highest possible speed. Some, though, may require one or more retries to negotiate an acceptable speed within the range.

Essential SCO System Administration

Table 5-17:	Modem Configuration Summary
• select modem dialer	inspect **/usr/lib/uucp**
• configure **atdial**… dialer	edit **/etc/default/atdial/**
• configure **dial**… dialer	edit **/usr/lib/uucp/dial/**.c; make
	edit **/etc/default/dial/**
• configure **Dialers** dialer	edit **/usr/lib/uucp/Dialers**
• add modem dial-out entry	**uuinstall** (⇨ 3 ⇨ 2) *or*
	edit **/usr/lib/uucp/Devices**
	insert "**ACU** *port* - *speed* **modem** *dialer*"
• add modem direct entry	**uuinstall** (⇨ 3 ⇨ 2) *or*
	edit **/usr/lib/uucp/Devices**
	insert "**Direct** *port* - *speed* **direct**"
• display modem configuration	**uuinstall** (⇨ 3 ⇨ 1)
• check modem configuration	**uuinstall** (⇨ 5)
• initialize modem NVRAM	**cu -l terminal port dir**
• test modem dial-out	**cu -s** *speed* **-l** *modem port* **-x9** *phonenum*
• dial out from modem	**cu -s** *speed* **-l** *modem port phonenum*
• disable modem port	**disable** *modem device port*
	disable *terminal device port*
• test physical connection	**yes** > *terminal device file*
• report active line attributes	**stty -a** < *modem device file*
• select modem line attributes	scan **/etc/gettydefs**
• assign modem line attributes	edit **/etc/inittab**
• update permanent port file	edit **/etc/conf/init.d/sio**
• verify **gettydefs** structure	**getty -c**

And so concludes basic modem configuration. *[Consult "Configuring Dial-Out Sites" in the next section for modem services configuration information].*

Chapter 5   Configuring Your System

Configuring Tape Devices

By virtue of their high capacity, portability, low cost, and relative quickness, tape devices are the backup tools of choice. SCO UNIX tape support is quite aggressive. Supported devices include:

- SCSI cartridge drives
- SCSI DAT drives
- SCSI 8mm (Exabyte) drives
- SCSI 9-track drives
- QIC-02/36 cartridge drives
- floppy tape drives
- Irwin mini drives

All the above devices can be configured using: **mkdev tape**

> From **sysadmsh**, go to: *System* ⇨ *Hardware* (⇨ *Tape*).

Specific notes follow.

> For configuration details for Irwin mini and Compaq SCSI tape drives, consult the *SCO Open Systems Software Hardware Configuration Guide*.

For QIC-02/36 controllers only the adapter board needs to be configured *[see "Hardware Adapter Configuration Notes"]*.

To configure QIC-40/80 drives, you'll first need to know whether your drive and floppy controller support the following:

extended length mode   (intelligence to write DC2120 tapes)
soft select   (intelligence to switch between floppy and tape i/o)
hard select   (switch-selectable tape drive number)

> The options above are selectable in the configuration dialogue. **Soft select** is the ability to use a floppy tape device concurrent with floppy disk I/O. Note that older drives may not support this feature. Additional configuration options are described in **tape**(HW).

To configure SCSI tape devices you'll need to know the following:

- the host adapter type   *[see table 5-5 for a list of types]*
- the number of the adapter of that type   (if multiple adapters installed)
- the SCSI target id

5-63

Essential SCO System Administration

> If this is the first device to be configured for that host adapter, you may be asked for the following:
> - interrupt vector
> - starting/ending I/O address
> - starting/ending controller memory address

> At boot, many host adapters expect to see a hard disk at target IDs 0 and 1. Target ID 7 is reserved for the adapter itself. Typically, IDs 2-6 are safe for SCSI tape devices. *[Consult the vendor's installation notes for details]*

> Currently no more than 4 SCSI tape devices can be configured.

After supplying the requested information, you may be asked to relink the kernel. Relinking updates the system with any adapter changes. For example, newly configured host adapters require a kernel relink before they can be used.

Once configuration is complete, use the commands below to test your tape drive:

    tape load *tape device*
    tape reten *tape device*
    tape erase *tape device*

> The **load** option only applies to DAT, Exabyte, and 9-track devices. The **reten** option retensions the tape, an essential function for all tape devices. The **erase** option intializes many tapes for writing, and tends to clean stray particles off of new tapes. It is essential for DAT tapes.

> Consult table 4-x for the names of specific tape devices. If configured as the default tape device, use **/dev/rct0**. The default device for QIC-40/80 and Irwin drives is **/dev/rctmini**.

Table 5-18		Special Tape Devices
Device	**Type**	**Description**
erct0	QIC-02	read/write with software ECC error correction
nrct0	QIC-02	multi-volume archival (no rewind)
nrStp0	SCSI	multi-volume archival (no rewind, no unload)
rhStp0	SCSI	high-density (for 9-track tape only)

Chapter 5   Configuring Your System

QIC ECC

For QIC-02 devices, **/dev/erct0** provides a high degree of error recovery. The 2/64 ECC scheme employed by the tape driver allows up to two 512-byte blocks out of each 64 to be bad, and the errors will be corrected. The ECC overhead is approximately 10%. For QIC-40/80 and Irwin drives, ECC is automatically employed by the drivers, so no special devices are required. ECC is also supported for SCSI devices, but you must manually create the appropriate device *[see the next box]*.

SCSI ECC

To enable ECC for SCSI (and QIC-02) tape devices, set bit 5 (add 32) in the device minor number. For example, to create corresponding ECC devices for **rStp0** (minor number 0) and **nrStp0** (minor number 8), use the following commands:

    cd /dev
    mknod erStp0 c *major* **32**   *[0 + 32]*
    mknod enrStp0 c *major* **40**   *[8 + 32]*
        major - applicable major number as displayed by: **ls -l rStp0**

For some applications (e.g. scheduled filesystem backup) you may want to link the ECC device to a standard device such as **rStp0**.

Table 5-19   Key tape(C) Configuration Options

Option	Affects	Function
status	all*	reports current tape status
reset	all*	resets controller and drive; clears errors
reten	all	retensions the tape media
load	SCSI	loads tape cartridge
unload	SCSI	unloads tape cartridge
format	QIC-40/80	formats floppy tape
rfm	QIC-02,SCSI	reads past the next (end of) file mark on the tape
wfm	QIC-02,SCSI	writes a file mark at the current tape position
partition	SCSI DAT	partitions HP DAT tape
setblk	SCSI	sets fixed or variable block size (for tapes > 150MB)

    * - except Irwin drives

Essential SCO System Administration

> **Tape setblk Option**
>
> The **setblk** option fixes the input and output tape block size. For example:
>
> > **tape -a 1024 setblk** *device*
>
> fixes the block size at 1KB (1024 bytes). With a parameter of 0, **setblk** supports variable block size, which is determined by the tape application (i.e. **cpio**, **tar**). Most tapes have a media default block size, which is used during tape initialization. The variable block size option lets tape applications override this default.

Table 5-20:		Other Configurable Tape Parameters			
Parameter	**File**	**Function**	**Device Type**	**Min/Max**	**Default**
CTBUFSIZE	①	static system tape buffer	QIC-02,SCSI	0/256	128
ft_minbufs	②	minimum 32K buffer request	QIC-40/80	2/20	3
ft_maxbufs	②	maximum 32K buffer request	QIC-40/80	2/20	8

① - tunable kernel parameter (**/etc/conf/cf.d/stune**)
② - source code variable (**/etc/conf/pack.d/ft/space.c**)

> The tunable kernel parameter, CTBUFSIZE, (static system tape buffer size) can be configured to either conserve memory or enhance streaming. The default size is: 128K. This only applies to QIC-02/36 and SCSI tapes. *[Consult **tape**(HW) for configuration options for QIC-40/80 controllers].*

Chapter 5   Configuring Your System

Configuring CD-ROM Devices

The growing popularity, and high capacity, high-speed, and low cost of CD-ROM devices makes them an essential tool for data and image management. SCO UNIX supports most SCSI CD-ROM drives.

CD-ROM devices are configured with: **mkdev cdrom**

> There is currently no way to configure CD-ROMs from **sysadmsh**

> In contrast to tape, up to 255 CD-ROM drives can be configured.

To be accessed, CD-ROMs must be mounted. Properly mounting a CD-ROM involves choosing appropriate options for the **mount**(ADM) command.

Table 5-21:	CD-ROM Configuration Options to mount(ADM)
Option	**Function**
-fHS	identifies mount device as a CD-ROM *[mandatory first option]*
lower	removes trailing dot from filenames; translates name to lowercase
nolower	translates filenames to uppercase
version	displays version numbers of files in the filename
novers	suppresses the file version number in filenames
showhidden	displays files with the hidden (MS-DOS) attribute set

The **mount** command for CD-ROMs has the following format:

    mount *options   device   mount point*
        options   are comma-separated options *[described above]*
        device   is **/dev/cd**X (where 0 denotes the first device,
                              1 denotes the second, and so on)
        mount point   is the access directory for files on the CD-ROM
                              [See "Configuring Filesystems" for mount details]

Some examples follow:

    mount -fHS,lower,noversion /dev/cd0 /mnt
    mount -fHS,nolower,showhidden /dev/cd1 /mnt2
    mount -fHS /dev/cd0 /mnt

> The option **-fHS** alone implies the defaults: **-fHS,nolower,noversion**

> The **mount** command is principally used to access hard disk filesystems. Under SCO UNIX, a CD-ROM disk is considered to be a single filesystem.

Essential SCO System Administration

Configuring Mice

Mice are the primary input devices for SCO Open Desktop. And yes, they can be configured for use with SCO UNIX. SCO supports serial, bus, and keyboard mice. The configuration command is: **mkdev mouse**

> From **sysadmsh**, go to: System ⇨ Hardware (⇨ Mouse)

You'll need to know the following:
- the mouse type
- the serial port to be used *[serial mice only]*
- the terminals to be associated with the mouse

For bus mice, you'll also be asked for:
- IRQ
- base address

> When configuring two mice of the same type, you must modify the **devices** and **ttys** files. Each mouse requires its own entry in **/usr/lib/event/devices**.

The mouse should be compatible with one of the following types:

serial mice	bus mice	keyboard mice
Logitech Serial Mouse	Logitech Bus Mouse	IBM PS2 Keyboard Mouse
Logitech MouseMan	Microsoft Bus Mouse	(low resolution)
Microsoft Serial Mouse	Olivetti Bus Mouse	(high resolution)
Mouse Systems PC Mouse		
Mouse Systems PC II Mouse		

Once you have configured the mouse, its use is automatic. Use the command below to test a configured mouse:

   usemouse -t vi -c "view /usr/lib/event/devices"

Verify the following behavior:
- The cursor follows the mouse.
- The left mouse button moves to the top of the file.
- The right mouse button moves to the bottom of the file.
- The middle mouse button deletes the character at the cursor.

> ☞ To exit **view**:   press ESC, type `:q!`, then press ENTER.
> To exit **usemouse**:   enter `exit`

Chapter 5 Configuring Your System

Table 5-22: Summary of Files Used for Mouse Configuration

File	Function
/usr/lib/event/devices	database of mouse entries; each entry specifies the type and the current configuration
/usr/lib/event/ttys	maps serial ports to mouse entries
/usr/lib/mouse/*	**usemouse** application-specific function files
/etc/conf/pack.d/kbmouse/space.c	sets polling and resolution for keyboard mice
/etc/conf/pack.d/busmouse/space.c	sets IRQ and base address for bus mice
/etc/conf/pack.d/sio/space.c	sets 16550 trigger level and FIFO size for serial mice

Essential SCO System Administration

Configuring Hardware Services

This section addresses the following hardware sevices:

- filesystem configuration and mounting
- configuring filesystem backup
- configuring the print spooler service
- configuring outbound modem dialing
- configuring scancode terminals
- configuring terminal multiscreens
- configuring console color and cursor

Filesystem Configuration and Mounting

You've long since configured your disk and subdivided it into filesystems. Just a few tasks remain to complete the configuration. Primarily, they concern making the filesystems ready to mount.

- Determine mount points for your filesystems
- Specify the mount attributes for each filesystem
- Configure the filesystems for mounting
- Verify the mount configuration

What's What: **Filesystem Mounting**

Mounting a filesystem effectively grafts it onto the system directory tree at a specific point. In fact, the system directory tree is itself the result of one or more filesystems grafted together. The converse operation, *unmounting*, effectively prunes a filesystem from the tree.

A *pathname* indicates the sequence of directories to search in order to reach the file. For example, the pathname, **etc/default/filsys**, indicates that the directory **etc** needs to be searched for a directory named **default**, which, in turn, will be searched for a file (or directory) named **filsys**. *Full pathnames* begin with the *root directory*, **/**, the root of the system directory tree (or *root directory tree*). They uniquely name files in the tree.

The *mount point* is the full pathname of the directory where a filesystem is mounted (grafted) onto the root directory tree.

5-70

Chapter 5   Configuring Your System

Specifying Filesystem Mount Points

Since the mount point determines the pathnames for the files on a filesystem, it must be chosen carefully. Here are a few useful rules to inform your choice.

> A.   The root filesystem is automatically mounted first, at **/**.
> B.   Filesystems are mounted in the order found in **/etc/filesys**.
> C.   Two filesystems cannot share the same mount point.
> D.   The mount point must be a valid directory (in the tree).
> E.   Directories can be explicitly created as mount points.
> F.   When possible, choose mount points on the root filesystem.
> G.   Typically, a mount point bears the name of its filesystem.
> H.   Use non-empty directories as mount points at your peril!

Using the example from the disk configuration section, we will design a viable table of mount points. Assume that the following divisions already exist:

Division	FS	Device Name	Mount Point	Purpose
root	yes	**/dev/root**	**/**	UNIX system files
u	yes	**/dev/u**	**/u**	user home directories
swap	no	**/dev/swap**	*not used*	*reserved* (memory management)
recover	no	**/dev/recover**	*not used*	*reserved* (disk management)

> Nonfilesystem divisions (e.g. **swap**) are not mounted and use no mount points.

Now we add the divisions from the configuration example earlier in the chapter:

Division	FS	Device Name	Mount Point	Purpose
man	yes	**/dev/man**	**/usr/man**	system on-line manuals
util	yes	**/dev/util**	???	as needed for system admin
tmp	yes	**/dev/tmp**	**/tmp**	system temporary files
dskhog	yes	**/dev/dskhog**	???	special user home directories
backup	no	**/dev/backup**	*not used*	as needed for filesystem admin

Notice that mount points are already specified for two of the new filesystems (**man** and **tmp**). Since they were created for specific system uses, these filesystems must be mounted at known system directories. We need to determine mount points for the other two filesystems (**util** and **dskhog**).

Applying rules E,F, and G above, we could assign the following mount points:

        util: **/util**   **dskhog**: **/dskhog**

Essential SCO System Administration

From a system perspective there's no real problem, but, frankly, which of your users could be happy with "dskhog" in their account pathname? Let's select an innocuous name like **/v**.

The final table looks like:

Filesystem	Device Name	Mount Point	Purpose
root	/dev/root	/	UNIX system files
u	/dev/u	/u	user home directories
man	/dev/man	/usr/man	system on-line manuals
util	/dev/util	/util	as needed for system admin
tmp	/dev/tmp	/tmp	system temporary files
dskhog	/dev/dskhog	/v	special user home directories

Specifying Filesystem Mount Attributes

A filesystem's mount attributes are specified in the file **/etc/default/filesys**. This file specifies how and when to make the defined filesystems available to users. It is accessed by the **mount** command when instructed to mount the filesystem.

SCO UNIX provides a command to ease the process of specifying filesystem mount attributes in **/etc/default/filesys**. The command is: **mkdev fs**

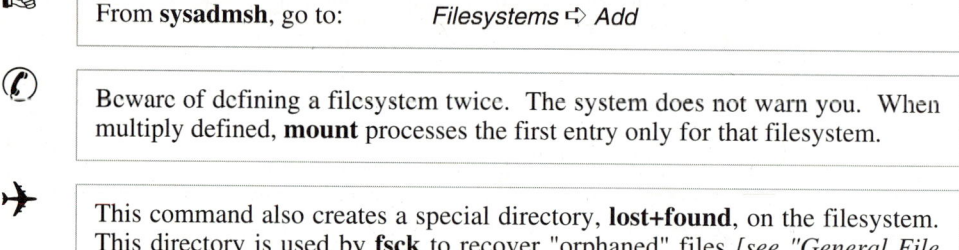

> From **sysadmsh**, go to: Filesystems ⇨ Add

> Beware of defining a filesystem twice. The system does not warn you. When multiply defined, **mount** processes the first entry only for that filesystem.

> This command also creates a special directory, **lost+found**, on the filesystem. This directory is used by **fsck** to recover "orphaned" files *[see "General File Configuration" for details]*.

The available filesystem mount attributes are defined in table 5-23 below.

Chapter 5 Configuring Your System

Table 5-23:   Filesystem Mount Attributes

Attribute	Status	Attribute Description
bdev	required ✓	filesystem block device
cdev	useful	filesystem character device
mountdir	required ✓	filesystem mount point
desc	optional	filesystem description
fstyp	optional	filesystem type
fsck	advised	filesystem cleaning clearance
fsckflags	advised	filesystem cleaning flags
mount	advised ✓	filesystem user mount clearance
rcmount	advised ✓	multiuser mode automatic mount clearance
mountflags	useful	mount command options
nfsopts	advised *	network filesystem mount options
passwd	useful	filesystem access password
prep	optional	prep command execute clearance
prepcmd	optional	command to run immediately before mount
init	optional	init command execute clearance
initcmd	optional	command to run directly after mount

✓ - set during **mkdev fs**
* - only for NFS network filesystems

Clearance is one of: *yes*, *no*, or *prompt*. "*yes*" grants permission. "*no*" denies permission. "*prompt*" prompts for 'yes' or 'no' at mount time.

Notes on Selected Filesystem Attributes

mount	*yes* clearance enables users to mount filesystem with **mnt**(C)
rcmount	*yes* clearance allows filesystem to be mounted automatically when entering multi-user mode
passwd	provides security on manually mounted filesystems; set with: **passwd -F**
prepcmd	applied after password check, but before mount; sample use: to check floppy filesystems for SUID (root) binaries
initcmd	applied after successful mount; sample use: to pause, allowing NFS filesystem to initialize

To verify the completed filesystem mount configuration, run the following:

   cd /
   mount device
   df -v
   umount device

Successful mounts appear in the **df -v** report.

5-73

Essential SCO System Administration

> It is a good idea to determine the maximum number of filesystems that can be mounted concurrently on your system. The kernel imposes a default limit of 8, which can be changed by redefining the tunable kernel parameter, NMOUNT. The new value becomes effective after you relink the kernel.

Besides mounting, there are other aspects of filesystems to configure, as well. These include: general filesystem configuration and filesystem optimization:

General Filesystem Configuration

Just a few more tasks stand between you and some hard-working filesystems.

- initializing filesystem data
- configuring hard links *[see "Configuring User Accounts"]*
- configuring symbolic links

The focus here is on configuring effective access to files on the filesystem. A basic understanding of filesystem structure will help you immensely.

> **What's What:**   **General Filesystem Configuration**
>
> A UNIX **filesystem** stores and manages *files*. There are several *file types* in UNIX, the most common of which hold user data.
>
> Disk data is accessed in **physical blocks**. The size of a physical block is 512 bytes. Every disk data transfer is a multiple of this size.
>
> File data is accessed in **logical blocks**. The size of a logical block varies by filesystem. The size is 1024 bytes (or two physical blocks) for EAFS and AFS filesystems. The system allocates logical blocks to growing files.
>
> An **inode** is a busy structure (within a filesystem) that manages a file's attributes. File attributes include: file size in bytes, permissions, links, and a list of the logical blocks currently allocated to it.
>
> A **file** is a package with three parts. These are: the inode (the header), a chain of logical data blocks (the contents), and a name. Multiple names may be bound to the inode with **links**. Links are entries in *directories*.
>
> A **directory** groups files. A directory is a table of links between file names and inode numbers. Directories may list other directories. The listed directories are called **subdirectories**. The SCO directory tree is assembled from many such levels of directories and subdirectories.

Chapter 5 Configuring Your System

> A *hard link* is a direct connection to an inode. It is simply a directory entry, or link. When two directory entries reference the same inode, the file is said to have two *links*. There is a limit of 1000 links to any file (or inode).
>
> A *symbolic link* is a connection to a pathname. It is a directory entry whose inode references a pathname rather than blocks of data. The pathname can be either a file or a directory. The pathname is only resolved when the link is referenced. There is no limit on the number of symbolic links to a pathname.
>
> The *superblock* is a special structure that manages a filesystem's attributes. These attributes include: the device, the filesystem size, the number of inodes, and the list of unallocated (free) logical blocks.

Quick Backgrounder SB5.2   **Filesystem Structure**

Although the specific details differ by filesystem type, nearly all have the following basic structure:

```
+---------------------+
|      (unused)       |
+---------------------+
|     Superblock      |
|        ...          |
+---------------------+
|     Inode List      |
+---------------------+
|                     |
|   Data Block Area   |
|                     |
+---------------------+
```

Filesystems have three main components:
- a *superblock* to keep track of filesystem attributes
- an *inode list* to keep track of file attributes
- a *data area* for file data blocks

Once configured, the sizes of these regions are fixed.

Each file is assigned exactly one inode from the inode list. The inode tracks the data, the file type, and other info. The system allocates blocks from the data block area to growing files, recording the block addresses in the inode.

The superblock tracks unallocated data blocks. Its size is determined by the filesystem type (512 bytes for EAFS).

Essential SCO System Administration

Quick Backgrounder SB5.3   Structure of an SCO System Inode

For those with a technical bent, here is the structure of an inode.

bits	field	abbr
4 bits	file type	
12 bits	access mode	md
16 bits	# of links	ln
16 bits	user id of owner	uid
16 bits	group id of preferred group	gid
32 bits	number of bytes in file	sz
24 bits	disk block address 0 *or* major / minor number	a0 / maj/min
...	...	...
24 bits	disk block address 10 ①	a10
24 bits	disk block address 11 ②	a11
24 bits	disk block address 12 ③	a12
8 bits	reserved (file generation #)	
32 bits	time file last opened	at
32 bits	time file last modified	mt
32 bits	time inode last changed	ct

① - indirect address
② - double-indirect address
③ - triple-indirect address

The file type determines the content of the *a0* field. If the type is device special file, the first two bytes of *a0* are interpreted as minor and major number, respectively. Otherwise *a0* is the address of the first assigned data block. If the type is symbolic link, then the first data block contains the target pathname.

Chapter 5   Configuring Your System

Table 5-24:		SCO System File Types	
	Symbol Used By		
Type	**ls -l**	**Type Bits**	**Description**
regular	-	0x8000	text, data, and executables
directory	d	0x4000	all directories
block special	b	0x6000 *	block interface device files
char special	c	0x2000 *	raw interface device files
named pipe	p	0x1000	named pipe (or FIFO)
symbolic link	l	0xA000	symbolic link
semaphore	s	0x5000	[XENIX only]
shared memory	m	0x5000	[XENIX only]
		* multiplex versions also supported	

 The twelve low-order bits in the type value hold the access permissions.

Quick Backgrounder SB5.4   **Block Versus Character Device Files**

The device file type - block special or character special, determines nature of the data transfer interface between the controlled device and a user process.

The interface (block or character) that is opened to a file determines how efficiently data is transfered. As you might expect, there are trade-offs between disk transfer efficiency for individual files and that of the overall system.

A character (or *raw*) special file provides direct access to a device. It can be quite efficient for large data transfers. Character special files do not restrict the amount of data transfered.

A block special file uses the system disk buffers to provide indirect but managed device access. Block special files enforce data transfers in logical blocks.

Data written to or read from block special files are cached in kernel buffers for subsequent transfer. This is the source of the term *buffered I/O*.

When a block special file is opened for reading, the system uses a read-ahead formula to preload logical disk blocks before they are requested. Thus the desired data is usually in RAM when a process needs it.

When a block special file is opened for writing (or update), the system puts the written blocks directly into kernel buffers. These buffers then wait to be flushed back to the disk. Two kernel parameters control when flushing occurs: NAUTOUP and BDFLUSHR.

5-77

Essential SCO System Administration

NAUTOUP specifies the age in seconds (default is 10) that a write buffer must attain before becoming eligible to be flushed. Every BDFLUSHR seconds (default is 30), the **bdflush** process seeks suitably aged (eligible) buffers to flush to disk.

> **Maximum File Size** (on EAFS filesystems)
>
> The maximum file size is 2^31 (2147483648) bytes or 2GB.

Initializing Filesystem Data

You can initialize a filesystem's data by either:

- mounting the filesystem, and copying an existing directory tree onto it.
  [see SR5.4 for an example]
- predefining the files and directories with a prototype
  [see mkfs(ADM) for details]
- loading the filesystem from a filesystem backup
  [see SR6.5 for details]

Quick Recipe SR5.4   **Moving a Directory Tree to a New Filesystem**

The example for this exercise is the online manual pages directory tree, **/usr/man**.

The online **man** pages can be conveniently moved to their own filesystem. This not only frees space on **/dev/root**, but also conserves backup resources. The **man** pages need to be backed up far less often than the root filesystem.

1. Reboot to single-user mode.
2. Mount the filesystem you've configured for this purpose.
   Run: **mount** *device file* **/mnt**

   Replace *device file* with your filesystem device.
3. Copy the source directory tree (e.g. **/usr/man**) to that filesystem
   Run: **copy -romv /usr/man /mnt**
4. Verify the copy with: **ls -lR /mnt | pg**
5. Unmount and remount your filesystem as follows:
   Run: **umount /mnt**
                  mount *device file* **/usr/man**
6. Use **man**(C) to verify that you can access the copied on-line manual pages.
7. Unmount your filesystem.

Chapter 5 Configuring Your System

8. Remove the **/usr/man** directory tree from **/dev/root**.
   Run: **cd /usr/man ; pwd**
                   rm -r .
9. Boot to multiuser mode and resume normal system operation.

Configuring Symbolic Links

Symbolic links provide transparent access to files and directories on other filesystems (including network filesystems). They can also "rewire" the directory structure of the host filesystem.

For example, to configure a symbolic link to a directory named **/remote/u2/thesarus**, run:

   ln -s /remote/u2/thesaurus synonyms

The subsequent command: **cd synonyms**
puts you directly in **/remote/u2/thesaurus**.

> The link is created even if **/remote/u2/thesaurus** does not exist. Symbolic links are resolved only when accessed.

> Beware of unexpected results using symbolic links to directories in the Bourne shell, **sh** *[see the next box]*. If possible, use **ksh**, instead.

> **Symbolic Links to Directories**
>
> The Bourne shell, **bin/sh**, follows symbolic links in only one direction. The Korn shell, **/bin/ksh**, follows them in both directions.
>
> Consider the following two examples, starting from **/u/alex**:
> Bourne shell: **cd synonyms ; pwd**   *[displays /remote/u2/thesaurus]*
>   **cd .. ; pwd**   *[displays /remote/u2]*
>
> Korn shell: **cd synonyms ; pwd**   *[displays /u/alex/synonyms]*
>   **cd .. ; pwd**   *[displays /u/alex]*
>
> The default **ksh**(C) behavior can be overridden with **cd -P**.

Essential SCO System Administration

Filesystem Optimization

 This section is quite technical (and optional for novice system administrators).

Many experienced SCO UNIX system administrators opt to manually configure (or rebuild) their filesystems. The main reasons are listed below.

- to optimize file access for specific disk characteristics [i.e. heads, sectors/track, physical interleave]
- to provide more inodes for devices files, symbolic links, or networking
- to maximize data capacity by reducing inode overhead (1.5% by default)
- to defragment existing filesystems

 The defaults used by **divvy**(ADM) to create filesystems are not always optimal for file and data access *[see table 5-25]*.

 What's What: **Filesystem Optimization**

A hard disk is essentially a rapidly rotating stack of magnetic platters *[see diagram 2-2]*. Special read/write *heads* move across the top and bottom face of each disk platter. Each head can read or write a complete physical block in one instant. The disk controller busily transfers physical blocks between the disk and the kernel. The controller is also must precisely position the disk heads.

The ***disk interleave*** describes a way to number the physical blocks on a disk's platters. Imagine dividing each platter into segments as if slicing an apple pie. You can then number the segments radially around the platter. The interleave defines the number of segments to skip before a assigning the next number. For example, a 1:1 interleave numbers contiguous segments, none are skipped. A 2:1 interleave skips every other segment. The numbering resulting from the interleave is called the ***logical block numbering***, ironically no relation to a logical block.

Low disk interleaves (e.g. 1:1) are ideal for controllers that respond quickly enough to read the next physical block as it rotates past the read/write head. Slower controllers require higher interleaves (e.g. 4:1). For instance, a 4:1 interleave assumes that three blocks will rotate past a stationary head before the controller is ready to process the "next" block. As long as the controller reads as slowly as it writes, that interleave ensures that the next logical block number will be right under the read/write head when the controller is ready. With an incorrect interleave, the controller may need to wait for another rotation before being positioned for the "next" block. According to the

Chapter 5 Configuring Your System

experts, efficient disk access must minimize both the time that the controller waits and the distance that the heads travel.

A *cluster* is a sequence of logical blocks that the filesystem provisionally allocates to a new or growing file. Once the file is closed, any unused blocks are returned to the filesystem. Ideally, each file should occupy contiguous clusters.

Disk *fragmentation* results when a file's data blocks are scattered about the disk, rather than in the interleave sequence. Initially every file occupies sequential blocks. Fragmentation begins when holes or gaps emerge in the list of unallocated blocks. This occurs naturally when files are removed, truncated, or extended. The disk controller must wait longer and the read/write heads must travel further to process a fragmented file.

To optimize a filesystem you'll need to know:

- the number of physical disk blocks/cylinder   *[see recipe SR5.6]*
- the filesystem device   *[e.g. /dev/man]*
- the filesystem type   **fstyp** *device*
- the filesystem size (physical blocks)   **df -v** *device*
- the desired interleave gap   *[see below]*

The gap is N for an N:1 interleave. For example, the gap is 2 for a 2:1 interleave. Note that many disk/controller combinations can use a gap of 1.

Table 5-25:   Default Filesystem Creation Parameters

- ratio of inodes to logical blocks: 1:4
- physical blocks assumed per cylinder: 400 (in **divvy** and **mkfs**)
- logical disk interleave   1:1 (in **divvy**)
                                            7:1 (in **mkfs**)
- cluster size: 32KB (32 logical blocks)

Table 5-26:   Filesystem Creation Limits

maximum supported physical blocks per cylinder: 1600
maximum cluster size: 32 blocks
minimum cluster size: 2 blocks
maximum number of filesystem inodes: 65488
maximum filesystem size: 2GB

Essential SCO System Administration

<u>Quick Recipe SR5.5</u>   **Determining Disk Blocks/Cylinder**

1. Determine the raw device name for the hard disk that will hold the filesystem. [for example: **/dev/rhd10**]

2. Run: **set `dparam /dev/rhd10`**

   Replace **rhd10** with the raw device name that applies to your disk. Remember to use reverse quotes (`).

3. Multiply the 2nd and 8th parameters to yield the blocks/cylinder.
   Run: **expr $2 * $8**

> When blocks/cylinder (BPC) exceeds 1600, use any multiple of the sectors/track (8th parameter of: **dparam** *raw disk device*) that divides BPC. This effectively divides the disk into *logical cylinders*.

New filesystems can be optimized with one of the commands below. This also applies to filesystems created by **divvy** that have yet to be populated.

> **mkfs -f** *type   filesystem device   blocks   gap blocks/cylinder*
> **mkfs -f** *type   filesystem device   blocks:inodes   gap blocks/cylinder*

For existing populated filesystems, follow the steps below:

> 1. Back up the filesystem onto a free disk division or a tape
>   *[see "Configuring Filesystem Backup"].*
> 2. Verify the backup.
> 3. Optimize the filesystem with one of the above commands.
> 4. Restore the backed up data to the newly optimized filesystem

Some examples follow:

> **mkfs -f EAFS /dev/man 40000 1   550**
>
> > Builds a 20000KB (approx. 20MB) EAFS filesystem, allocating the default ratio of inodes to blocks (5120 inodes), a 1:1 logical interleave, while assuming 550 physical blocks per logical cylinder.
>
> **mkfs /dev/u   360000:65488 1 256 -E**
>
> > Builds a near 180MB EAFS filesystem, allocating the maximum number of inodes (65488), a 1:1 logical interleave, while assuming 256 physical blocks per logical disk cylinder.

Chapter 5   Configuring Your System

    mkfs /dev/tmp   20000

        Builds a 10MB AFS filesystem with a 7:1 logical interleave, allocating the default ratio of inodes to blocks (2560 inodes), while assuming 400 physical blocks per logical disk cylinder.

Configuring Filesystem Backup

The most important periodic task you'll perform is backing up your filesystems.

Table 5-27:   **Three Reasons to Perform Periodic Filesystem Backups**

1. Disk data can be corrupted or destroyed by:
   - unexpected or undetected hardware failure
   - application or system software failure
   - administrator/operator error
   - natural disaster
2. Users frequently want to restore previous versions of files or files they've deleted
3. Archival data (e.g. quarterly reports) may need to be saved for long periods.

The following types of backup will be addressed:
- periodic scheduled filesystem backup
- unscheduled filesystem backup
- unattended filesystem backup

☞   The first two backup methods require operator intervention.

[Full and partial filesystem restore are addressed in Chapter 6].

Whatever the type of backup, try to heed these helpful rules.

The Rules of Filesystem Backup

   A. Retensioning a tape increases its reliability.
   B. Bad tape blocks can appear suddenly, without warning.
   C. The restore tape you most desperately require is the one that can't be read.
   D. An unlabelled backup tape is not worth the plastic it's written on.
   E. Backing up without verifying is a thrilling form of "russian roulette".

Essential SCO System Administration

> Many users swear by third-party backup products, some of which provide bit-level verification (e.g. CTAR). You may well consider one of these, since no equivalent function is provided by SCO UNIX. Bit-level verification carefully
> I ` h h j j h ! h ` $
> ts counterpart on the disk.

Scheduled Filesystem Backup

The key tasks here are creating the backup schedule and initiating daily execution of the backup facility. *[Consult the* SCO UNIX Operating System System Administrator's Guide *for details on creating the schedule].*

Before creating the backup schedule, you'll need to know:
- the names of your filesystems (raw device names)
- the name of the tape backup device
- the capacity of the tape (in KB)

> The filesystem raw device is the name of the filesystem preceded by 'r'.

To modify the backup schedule: <u>edit</u>   **/usr/lib/sysadmin/schedule**

    From **sysadmsh**, go to: *Backups ▷ Schedule*

Guidelines on How Frequently to Back Up Filesystems
- user home filesystems should be backed up daily,
  with full backups run at least once per week.
- production database filesystems should be fully backed up
  at least once a day.
- the root filesystem should be backed at least once per week,
  with full backups run at least once a month

To run the scheduled backup facility: **cd /usr/lib/sysadmin**
    ./fsphoto

    From **sysadmsh**, go to: *Backups ▷ Create ▷ Scheduled*

Chapter 5   Configuring Your System

The scheduled backup facility is designed to be run daily, except weekends. Every instance that the facility is run constitutes one "day" in the schedule. When multiple filesystems are scheduled for a given day, that day will not complete until every filesystem has been backed up.

Table 5-28:	Relevant Files in the Scheduled Backup Facility
./schedule	the filesystem backup schedule
./last/past	indicates that a postponed backup is pending
./last/r*filesystem*	contains the numerical "day" of the last backup for *filesystem*
./cstamps/dev/*filesystem*/N	contains the calendar date that a level *N* back up was completed for *filesystem*

(all files are relative to **/usr/lib/sysadmin**)

Tape Backup Labels

Since a backup is only as good as the label that identifies it, here are some suggested ways to sensibly label your tapes.

For multi-volume backups of large filesystems, consider the format below:

```
Filesystem1     Level              Creation Date
                Mount Point        Expiration Date
                Block Size
                Archive Format                      Volume ?? of ??
```
Archive Format: CPIO, TAR, CTAR, etc.

For multiple filesystem backups on a single large volume, consider this:

```
Filesystem1     Level            Mount Point    Creation Date
                Archive Format   Block Size     Expiration Date
Filesystem2     Level            Mount Point
                Archive Format   Block Size
```

Multiple Volume Backups

To store two or more filesystems on a single tape volume, you must explicitly insert filemarks between the archives. Use the no-rewind device to perform the backup, and tape wfm to write the filemark. The following example shows how /dev/root and /dev/u can be archived to the same tape.

```
tape  rewind  /dev/xStp0
cd / ; find . -mount -print | cpio -oBv -O/dev/nrStp0
tape  wfm    /dev/xStp0
cd / ; find . -mount -print | cpio -oBv -O/dev/rStp0
```

5-85

Essential SCO System Administration

Unscheduled Filesystem Backups

Unscheduled filesystem backups can be used to perform the following:
- resizing or reconfiguring a filesystem
- duplicating a tested configuration
- extracting data to restore on a remote system
- updating the operating system version

Before performing an unscheduled filesystem backup, you'll need to know:
- the name of the filesystem
- the filesystem's mount point
- the type of tape backup device to be used
- the preferred tape block size in bytes
- the capacity of the tape (in KB)

To perform an unscheduled filesystem backup, use **sysadmsh**.
Proceed to: *Backups* ➪ *Create* ➪ *Unscheduled*

> **Procedure for Unscheduled Filesystem Backup**
>
> Hardcore users may want to try the commands below instead:
>
>   **cd** *mount point*
>   **find . -mount -print | **
>   **cpio -ocmv -C** *blocksize* **-K** *capacity* **-O** *raw tape device*
>
> For example, the commands:
>
>   **cd /u**
>   **find . -mount -print | **
>   **cpio -ocmv -C 10240 -K 150000 -O/dev/rStp0**
>
> backup the **/dev/u** filesystem on the default SCSI device using a block size of 10KB and a tape capacity of 150,000KB (~ 150MB).
>
> *You are strongly advised to use pathnames relative to the mount point, as in these examples. You can incur serious problems restoring absolute pathnames.*

5-86

Chapter 5   Configuring Your System

Unattended Filesystem Backups

Unattended filesystem backup lets you backup filesystems without having to manually intervene. One possible drawback is that the filesystems to be backed up must fit on one tape.

To configure unattended filesystem backup, you'll need to know:
- the capacity (in KB) of your backup tape
- the name of the no-rewind tape device
- the filesystem's device file name
- the level of the backup being performed
- how to schedule tasks with **crontab** *[see "Configuring Processes"]*

Effectively, you configure the unattended backup command to run at a specific time. This involves creating an entry in the system crontab file.

The unattended backup component will look like:

/usr/lib/sysadmin/cbackup   *level   tape capacity   tape device   filesystem device*

For example, consider the command:

/usr/lib/sysadmin/cbackup 0 535000 /dev/nrStp1 /dev/u

This backs up the **/dev/u** filesystem onto a 535MB tape loaded in the second SCSI tape device, using no-rewind operation. The no-rewind device lets another filesystem be archived on the same tape.

The **crontab** entry will look like:

*minutes   hour   * * *   days of week   unattended backup command*

For example, consider the entry:

30 2 * * * 1-5 *unattended backup command*

This would run *unattended backup command* at 02:30 every weekday (Mon-Fri).

If multiple filesystems are to be backed up, you should consider scheduling an appropriate shell script for **crontab** execution. For instance, the shell script, sback0, below accomplishes the following:

> A.   Backs up **/dev/util** onto a 1GB tape loaded in the third SCSI tape device, using no-rewind mode.
> B.   Backs up **/dev/dbms** onto the remainder of the 1GB tape, still using no-rewind mode.
> C.   Rewinds the tape after the second filesystem.

Essential SCO System Administration

```
# sback0:   unattended backup script (to be run by cron)
#
PATH=/usr/lib/sysadmin:$PATH
export   PATH
TAPE=/dev/nrStp2                         # tape device
XTAPE=/dev/xStp2                         # tape control device
TYPE=-s                                  # device type flag
CAPACITY=1000000                         # tape capacity in KB
LEVEL=0                                  # backup level (0-9)
#
tape    $TYPE    reten    $XTAPE
tape    $TYPE    rewind   $XTAPE
cbackup $LEVEL   $CAPACITY  $TAPE   /dev/util
tape    $TYPE    wfm      $XTAPE             # write tape file mark
cbackup $LEVEL   $CAPACITY  $TAPE   /dev/dbms
tape    $TYPE    wfm      $XTAPE
tape    $TYPE    rewind   $XTAPE
tape    $TYPE    unload   $XTAPE
```

  cbackup is a shell script which uses a fixed block size of 10240.

A sample crontab entry follows: 0 4 * * * 6 /usr/local/bin/sback0

In this case, the script would run at 4:00am every Saturday.

Verifying Filesystem Backups

No less important than creating a backup is verifying that accurate data resides on it. As SCO lacks a true tape verification capability, you are obliged to rely upon third-party products for complete assurance.

Table 5-29:	Some Third-Party Tape Backup Products
Product	**Vendor/Phone/City**
CTAR	Microlite Corp. / (412) 771-4901, (800) 992-2827 / Pittsburg, PA
BRU	Enhanced Software Technologies Inc. / (602) 820-0042, (800) 998-8649 / Tempe, AZ
DBR	DMS Systems Inc./ (801) 484-3333 / Salt Lake City, UT
Lone Tar	Lone Star Software inc. / (301) 829-1622 / Mt. Airy, MD

Yet, there are some strategies that you can pursue using the standard SCO UNIX tools. These are summarized below.

Chapter 5 Configuring Your System

Backup Verification Strategies

1. Use an ECC (error correction) tape device.

    For about 10% overhead, you get good error protection. Combine with some of the other strategies. *[see "Configuring Tape Devices" for details]*

2. Attempt to read the file headers (inode data) from the backup.

    This provides a basic level of verification. The assumption is that if a file's header is readable, so, probably, is the file.

    > From **sysadmsh**, go to: Backups ⇨ Integrity
    >
    > From the command line, use:
    >   (multi-volume backups)   **cpio -itv -C blocksize -I device**
    >   (single volume backups)   **cpio -itkv -C blocksize -I device**
    >
    > **Notes**:
    >   1. The **-k** option does not work well with multi-volume backups
    >   2. Supplying the correct block size expedites data recovery

3. Compare random files from the backup with their disk counterparts.

    This provides a random sample of backup integrity. The assumption is that as more samples are taken, the level of confidence increases.

Quick Recipe SR5.6   Budget Backup Verify

Verifying random files from the backup may increase your level of confidence. Note the mount point of the filesystem you will be "verifying".

1. Run: **cd /usr/tmp**
2. From **sysadmsh**, go to: Backups ⇨ View

    Randomly select files as you scroll through the list. Record the names.

3. Next, go to: Backups ⇨ Restore ⇨ Partial

    This lets you extract a file or directory from the backup

4. Fill in the form as follows:

    File to restore   enter file names exactly as listed in step 2 separated by spaces

    Directory to restore to   **/usr/tmp**

    Process the form.

5. Repeat steps 3 and 4 until you've extracted every file selected in step 2.
6. Exit from sysadmsh.

5-89

Essential SCO System Administration

7. For each file, run:

        cmp -s *./file mount_point/file* **|| echo "bad tape data"**

Replace *file* with the pathname of your extracted file, and *mount_point* with the full pathname of the mount point.

For example: **cmp -s ./jdr/report /u2/jdr/report || echo** ....

Successful file compares do not print a message.

Quick Recipe SR5.7   Positioning a Multi-Filesystem Backup

Many users are backing up several filesystems on a single tape. This recipe provides some hints on how to position the tape to the right filesystem.

```
┌──────────────────────────────────┐
│          Filesystem 1            │
├──────────────────────────────────┤
│          Filesystem 2            │
├──────────────────────────────────┤
│          Filesystem 3            │
└──────────────────────────────────┘
```

The above diagram shows three filesystems separated by filemarks. The dark ends are the tape boundaries, beginning and end.

We will use **tape rfm** and the no-rewind device, **nrStp0** to position the tape.

1. Rewind the tape: **tape rewind /dev/xStp0**
2. To read filesystem 2, run: **tape rfm /dev/xStp0**
                                                  cpio -itv -I/dev/nrStp0
3. To next read filesystem 3, run: **tape rfm /dev/xStp0**
                                                  cpio -itv -I/dev/nrStp0
4. Rewind the tape again: **tape rewind /dev/xStp0**
5. To read filesystem 3, run: **tape -a 2 rfm /dev/xStp0**
                                                cpio -itv -I/dev/nrStp0

> ✈ Multiple filemarks can be read on SCSI devices using: **tape -a** *N* **rfm**.

6. To next read filesystem 2, run: **tape -a -2 rfm /dev/xStp0**
                                                tape rfm /dev/xStp0
                                                cpio -itv -I/dev/nrStp0

> Reverse file movements (i.e. **tape -a 2 rfm**) read past the filemark to abut the end of the previous archive. To position to the start of the next archive, you must read the filemark again in the forward direction.

Configuring The Print Spooler Service

The print spooler service has more features than can be comfortably discused here. This section summarizes the most important information and the key configuration commands.

Quick Backgrounder SB5.5   **How the Print Service Works**

The print spooler service queues user print requests for destinations that may be printers or classes or **any**.

Destination	Queued Result
printer	request queued for *printer*
class	request queued for first available printer in *class*
any	request queued for first available printer on the system

Destination Status	Spooler Response
accepting	queues request for destination
rejecting	rejects (and discards) request
enabled *	invokes printer interface to print request
disabled *	preserves requests already queued for printer; makes printer queue unavailable to classes (and **any**)
	* - applies to printers only

Users submit print requests to the spool service with **lp***(C)*. The system default destination is assumed unless the user specifies a destination with the **-d** option.

Users supply printer options using the **-o** flag to **lp**.

For example, the following command submits the file **tucson.rpt** to the spooler, along with the options **landscape**, **nobanner**, and **cpi=12**. The destination is a printer (or class) named "laser5".

                lp -o "landscape,nobanner,cpi=12" -d laser5 tucson.rpt

Other options that users can request are: forms, character sets, and print-wheels.

Essential SCO System Administration

Even when not queueing print reqeusts, the print spooler is rarely idle. It listens for printer status messages (e.g. job completion, print problems) to determine printer availability. It mails print status messages to users who request them. It alerts the administrator to a variety of conditions including printer faults, print wheel requests, and queued jobs awaiting a specific form.

What's What: Print Spooler Configuration

Spooler *filters* convert print request content from one type to another. Several print filters may be linked together to convert a print request to a type acceptable by the target printer. Filters must be explicitly added to the spooler's pool of filters. Effectively, a filter is a brief definition that references the actual filter executable. The type of filter may be *slow* or *fast*. Fast filters run quickly, with low conversion overhead. Because they access printers directly, only fast filters can detect and respond to printer faults. Slow filters run in the background due to their higher overhead.

Spooler *forms* define the printing and size characteristics of pre-printed hardcopy forms. An important element of a form is the alignment pattern. The alignment pattern helps you align pre-printed forms in the printer. Once you have loaded and aligned the pre-printed paper in the printer, you logically *mount* the form on the printer, so that requests specifying the form can print.

Print request *content types* are user-defined names that are recognized by defined print filters and printers. You can configure printers to accept certain content types. You can configure filters to accept certain content types as input, and generate others as output. The default content type is **simple**.

Filter Definition Entries

Input types:	content type list
Output types:	content type list
Printers:	list of printers
Filter type:	*fast* or *slow*
Command:	full pathname of executable
Options:	user-defined options

Form Definition Entries

Page length:	scaled decimal integer
Page width:	scaled decimal integer
Number of pages:	integer
Line pitch:	scaled decimal integer
Character pitch:	scaled decimal integer
Character set choice:	character set
Alignment pattern:	
one or more lines of the alignment pattern	

A *scaled decimal integer* is a number followed optionally by **i** (for inches or cpi), c (for centimeters). Depending upon the context, unscaled integers are interpreted as lines, columns, or cpi.

Chapter 5 Configuring Your System

Print Spooler Configuration Tips

The specific commands for print spooler configuration are listed in the tables that follow. These general tips are intended to help you take advantage of the most useful print spooler features.

- define classes to group your printers
- define a dummy printer (with device **/dev/null**) for general spool maintenance (e.g. cancelling all jobs on a printer)
- define a special printer type for PostScript printers; use the above type as the content type for PostScript documents
- configure the printer fault alert facility to mail messages to you
- use the environment variable, **LPDEST**, to set up different default destinations for the various user clusters at your site.

Table 5-30: General Spooler Configuration

Command *	Function
lpsched	starts the print spooler service
lpshut	terminates the print spooler service
accept *destination*	accept requests in the queue for *destination*
reject *destination*	reject requests for *destination*
reject -r "*message*" *destination*	reject requests for *destination*; mail message to users
enable *printer*	enables *printer* for printing requests
disable *printer*	stops requests from printing on *printer*; places request currently printing on hold
disable -r "*message*" *printer*	stops printing requests on *printer*; *message* displayed by **lpstat**
disable -c *printer*	cancels requests before disabling *printer*
disable -W *printer1* ...	wait for requests to complete printing before disabling listed printers
lpadmin -d *destination*	makes *destination* the default spool destination
lpadmin -d	ensures that no default destination is defined
lpadmin -x *destination*	removes *destination* from the spooler service
lpadmin -x all	removes all spooler service destinations
lpfilter -f *filter* **-C** *pathname*	installs definition for filter from pathname
lpfilter -f *filter* **-x**	uninstalls spooler filter
lpforms -f *form* **-F** *pathname*	installs definition for form from pathname
lpforms -f *form* **-x**	uninstalls a spooler form

* most spooler commands reside in **/usr/lib**

Essential SCO System Administration

> From **sysadmsh**, use: *Printers ➪ Configure*
> *Printers ➪ Schedule*
> *Printers ➪ Auxiliary ➪ Filter*
> *Printers ➪ Auxiliary ➪ PPForms*

Table 5-31: Print Request Configuration

Command	Function
lpadmin -p *printer* **-c** *class*	assigns *printer* to *class*; *class* is created if new
lpadmin -p *printer* **-r** *class*	removes *printer* from *class*
lpadmin -p *printer* **-T** *type*	assigns printer type to *printer*
lpadmin -p *printer* **-I** *type list*	assigns a list of acceptable content types
lpadmin -p *printer* **-M -f** *form*	logically mounts *form* on *printer* [pre-printed form must be manually loaded]
lpadmin -p *printer* **-M -f none**	logically unmounts *form* from *printer* [pre-printed form must be manually unloaded]
lpadmin -p *printer* **-M -f** *form* **-a**	logically mounts *form* on *printer*, and prints the alignment pattern defined in *form*
lpadmin -p *printer* **-u allow:***list*	assigns a list of users allowed to use *printer*
lpadmin -p *printer* **-f allow:***list*	assigns a list of compatible forms to *printer*

> From **sysadmsh**, use: *Printers ➪ Configure ➪ Parameters*
> *Printers ➪ Configure ➪ Content*
> *Printers ➪ Configure ➪ Users*
> *Printers ➪ Auxiliary ➪ PPForms ➪ Configure*

Lists requested by the various spooler administration commands are simply names separated by commas. Optionally, the list can enclosed by quotes.

Table 5-32: Printer Alert Configuration

Command	Function
lpadmin -p *printer* **-A** *mail*	mails fault alerts for *printer* to invoking user
lpadmin -p *printer* **-A** *write*	writes *printer* alerts on invoking user's terminal
lpadmin -p *printer* **-A** *quiet*	terminates alerts for the current problem
lpadmin -p *printer* **-A** *none*	disables all alerts for *printer*
lpadmin -p *printer* **-A** *command*	invokes *command* w/ alert message as input
lpadmin -p *printer* **-A** *opt* **-W** *num*	periodically sends relevant alert (*opt*) every *num* minutes
lpforms -f *form* **-A** *mail*	mails form mount alerts to invoking user
lpforms -f *form* **-A** *write*	writes form alerts on invoking user's terminal
lpforms -f *form* **-A** *opt* **-W** *num*	periodically sends relevant alert (*opt*) every *num* minutes

Chapter 5   Configuring Your System

> From **sysadmsh**, use: *Printers* ➪ *Auxiliary* ➪ *PPForms* ➪ *Alerts*

Table 5-33:	User Options Supported by lp(C)
Option	**Result**
-d *dest*	request is queued for destination
-o *list*	option list is passed to the printer interface
-n *number*	the number of copies is passed to interface
-f *form* **-d any**	queues job for first available printer that has the form mounted, or that can mount the form
-S *character set*	tells printer to use *character set*; character set must be an alias or one defined in the printer's **terminfo** entry; the interface can access it as CHARSET (shell variable)
-T *content type*	request is queued for first printer that supports the type

User-requested Forms and Content Types

When a print request specifies a form, the system searches for any printers that can mount the form. If the form is already mounted on a printer, the request is queued for that printer. If the form is not mounted, and a printer supports the form, an alert is sent to the print administrator to load the pre-printed forms into the paper tray, and to mount the requested spooler form for the printer. If no printer supports the form, the request is rejected.

When a request specifies a content type, the system searches for printers that support the content type. If no printers, support the type, then the installed filters are searched for one that can convert the content type to one that is supported. Several filters may need to be piped together to successfully convert the type. If, after this, the spooler is unable to process the content type, the request is cancelled.

Essential SCO System Administration

Configuring Outbound Modem Dialing

The first part of modem configuration was registering your modem as a dial-out device. You specified the serial port and a dialer to manage the modem connection. The next part is defining the remote sites you wish to dial. The OS package that we use to configure modem communications is **uucp**.

The relevant **uucp** files are listed below:

File *	Function
Devices	database of outbound serial lines and connection methods; modem ports and dialers are specified here
Systems	database of defined outbound sites
Permissions	database of site access controls; primarily applied to inbound **uucp** connections

                      * - These files are located in **/usr/lib/uucp**.

The system supports the following types of outbound modem connections:

- manual connections using **cu**
- scheduled (or manual) connections using **uucp**
- connections to dial-up printers using the **lp** print service

Dial-up printer connections are addressed in "Configuring Printers". The immediate focus is on manual connections using **cu**(C) (call UNIX). *[Consult the SCO System Administrator's Guide to configure uucp connections].*

Defining a Remote Site

When you specify the name of a remote site in a **cu** (or **uucico**) command, the system looks up the site name in the **Systems** file. It then uses the desired indicated speed to cross-reference the Devices file. The goal is to locate a unengaged modem that can handle the requested speed.

You need to create a **Systems** file entry for each of your remote sites. **Systems** entries look like this:

    sitename   schedule   device   speed   phone   login-script

> ☞ The *schedule* regulates when outbound calls are allowed. The device is typically '**ACU**'. The *login-script* is used primarily with **uucp** connections.

Chapter 5 Configuring Your System

Let's create entries for three sites in Tucson, New York, and London.

Site	Phone Number	Connection Speed	When to Call
Tucson	1-602-773-9987	9600-14400	any time
New York	1-212-638-2234	14400-28800	5pm-8am,Sat,Sun
London	011-44-081-943-7654	2400-9600	3pm-8am Tue-Fri

Converting those into **Systems** entries (and adjusting for supported speeds), yields:

```
tucson     Any                    ACU   9600-19200  16027739987
new_york   Wk1700-0800,Sa,Sun     ACU   9600-38400  12126382234
london     TuWeThFr1500-0800      ACU   2400-9600   011440819437654
```

The SCO dialers only recognize the following speeds as valid:

    300   1200   2400   4800   9600   19200   38400

The above entries are quite acceptable to the SCO dialers, but there is a problem because of the way we have configured the modem. To solve the problem, we need to set the artificial speed values. To determine what the artificial speed should be, we must consult the **Devices** file.

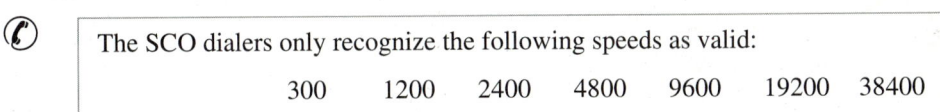

SCO Dialer Serial Port Speed Problems

When specifying a sitename to the **cu** command, the SCO dialer takes the following actions:

1. Extracts speed range (speed1) and phone number from **Systems** entry.
2. Searches **Devices** for first entry intersecting the extracted speed range.
3. Computes a new speed range (speed2) from the intersection of speed1 and the speed range in the **Devices** entry.
4. Resets the serial port rate to the highest speed in the intersection, speed2. This is the serial speed that the modem initially senses when fixing its transmission speed to the port.
5. Resets serial port rate again if perceived modem connect rate is different.

Actions (4) and (5) seriously decrease the efficiency of the modem link, particularly if the link uses data compression. Optimally, you want your serial port rate fixed as high as possible. The remedy is to trick the SCO dialer into seeing only one very high baud rate. The highest supported rate is 38400.

5-97

Assume that the following **Devices** entries are defined:
  ACU tty10A - 2400-9600 dialHA96V
  ACU tty22A - 38400   atdialUSR

Aha! The high speed modem entry, tty22A, is using the **atdialUSR** dialer with the special configuration *[described in "Modem Configuration"]*. As long as the modem connect speed is between 9600 and 38400 baud, the 38400 baud is always reported to the SCO dialer. Lower speeds report the correct baud rate. We need to set the speed at 38400 for any entries that could use this **Devices** entry.

Here are the revised **Systems** entries:

```
tucson     Any                    ACU   38400   16027739987
new_york   Wk1700-0800,Sa,Sun     ACU   38400   12126382234
london     TuWeThFr1500-0800      ACU   38400   011440819437654
```

Supporting Lower Speed Modem Connections

With the above artificial speed setting, modem connections at 4800 baud or lower will fail. This is good if you don't want to pay for slow connections. Problems may arise, though, when it isn't possible to guarantee a high-speed connection. For example, the london site's real connect range is 2400-9600. With a poor phone connection it may only be possible to support 2400 baud. In that case the connection would fail.

If you could tolerate a lower connection rate to london, you would need to:

1. Select or configure a new **Devices** entry with a different speed. You could even use the same modem (by using the same modem port)!
2. Modify the artificial speed for the london entry in **Systems** to match the speed in your new **Devices** entry.

Whenever possible, use fixed speeds in **Systems** file entries. You will avoid many frustrating connection problems later on.

Remote sites can be explicitly set up to use specific modems. A specific entry for the site can be placed in the **Devices** file as follows:

  sitename   modem port   -   speed   modem dialer   \D

Sample **Devices** entry: chicago tty11A 19200 dialTBIT \D
Companion **Systems** entry: chicago Any chicago 19200 13129996735

Instead of **ACU**, this **Systems** entry specifies the *sitename* for device type.

> **What's What: Trusted Security**
>
> Underlying SCO trusted security is the concept of *accountability*. Accountability ensures that every action can be traced to an individual person.
>
> *Discretionary Access Control* (DAC) is the ability of the owner of information to provide controlled access to others. SCO file permissions are a prime example of DAC.
>
> An *authorization* is a permission to do or access something. Authorizations complement file permissions in that they apply to actions and access to resources.
>
> *Identification* provides a way to uniquely specify users of a system. On SCO this is provided by the user ID.
>
> *Authentication* attempts to verify the identity of the user attempting to access the system. SCO login passwords offer a simple level of authentication.
>
> Primary access to system resources is restricted to the system administrator. *Protected subsystems* give users controlled access to system resources and functions. For example, users are not allowed to edit directories. Only via specific tools allowing a controlled range of actions (eg mkdir) can users do so. On SCO protected subsystem access is implemented with *subsystem authorizations* combined with the SUID and SGID file permissions.
>
> *Auditing* provides a way to record every access between a user and a system resource. Effectively, it generates a trail of records for each user and system action. A skilled administrator can then replay this audit trail to determine the who, what, and how behind any system problem or anomaly.

Trusted Security States

SCO provides four predefined trusted states. In order of level of trust they are:

        high <- *improved* <- *traditional* <- *low*

The *high* and *improved* states implement C2 trusted specifications. The *traditional* state corresponds to the level of security offered by typical UNIX systems. The *low* state provides very little security and is not recommended for multiuser environments.

Comparative features of the four states are summarized in table 5-36.

Essential SCO System Administration

Table 5-36:	Comparison of Trusted Security Levels			
Security Parameter	**Low**	**Traditional**	**Improved**	**High**
Login password required	no	no	yes	yes
Password expiration (days)	infinite	infinite	42	42
Minimum password length	1	3	5	8
Obvious password checks	no	no	yes	yes
Maximum unsuccesful logins	infinite	99	5	3
Delay between attempts (secs)	0	1	2	2
Primary password database	UNIX	UNIX	TCB	TCB
Action when database corrupted	recover	recover	lockout	lockout
User IDs can be reused	yes	yes	no	no
Default permissions umask	022	022	027	077
SUID/SGID clear on write	no	yes	yes	yes
STOPIO on devices	no	yes	yes	yes
LUID enforcement	no	no	no	yes
Use of **su**(C) logged	no	yes	yes	yes
Password for **asroot**(ADM)	no	no	no	yes
Dialup printers allowed	yes	yes	no	no

> **What's What: Trusted Security Technical Features**
>
> SCO trusted security implements many features new to UNIX users. The heart of the system is a security policy implemented by a integrated package of files and utilities called the *trusted computing base* (TCB).
>
> The TCB implements a *protected password database* to process user authorizations and authentication. This database can only be read by the system administrator. The system is intricately designed to detect any tampering of its files or data. In the event of password database corruption, the system locks out all login attempts, except on the special override device. The protected password database is located under **/tcb/files/auth**. It is organized by the first letter of the login.
>
> Another special feature of the TCB is the *LUID* (login user ID). The LUID does not change even when the user runs **su** to switch (user) identity. This helps to improve accountability on the system.
>
> The *STOPIO* feature prevents multiple processes from writing to a device (e.g. a printer) at the same time. Once a process has invoked STOPIO on a device, any other process that tries to write to it will be killed.
>
> The *SUID* (set user ID) and *SGID* (set group ID) permissions can be quite dangerous if misused. Clearing these bits when a file is written prevents privileged files from being subverted to new uses.

Chapter 5 Configuring Your System

> Under C2 security user IDs cannot be reused. The reasoning is that accountability is undermined when there is no assurance that a given user ID will always refer to the same individuals. Instead of being removed, user IDs can be retired.

Security Tips and Recommendations

Although you have a choice of four trusted security states, my recommendation is to select either *improved* or *traditional*, then customize. My preference is *improved*, since the C2 functionality is already integrated. The *high* state is far too restrictive for most users.

You should consider implementing the recommended guidelines below.

```
Table 5-37:            Guidelines for a Trusted System
```
- require login passwords
- assign a standard password for all new users;
  forced a password change at first login
- check all passwords for obviousness
- age all passwords periodically
- enforce an effective limit on terminal access attempts
- restrict root logins to the console;
  place the console in a locked room
- log off all idle users (except at the console)
- restrict the assignment of the **su** (ability to run **su**(*C*)) authorization
- log all attempt to run **su**(*C*)
- designate special administrative users for:
    filesystem backup
    printer administration
- set the sticky bit on shared directories
- configure the kernel for STOPIO

> Do not let users run the password generator. The passwords are obscure and difficult to remember. Some may not even be suitable for civilized company.

Essential SCO System Administration

> **Selecting Effective Passwords**
>
> The most effective passwords mix lowercase and uppercase letters with digits and punctuation. The combination must not form a simple word, but it should resemble something intelligible; so that your users can remember it. Some examples follow:
>
> Fun2B40   aLi54Cn!   Stop;relaX   1Der@Noon

Some of these guidelines can be implemented from **sysadmsh**. Proceed to the following menus:

    Accounts ⇨ Defaults ⇨ Password
    Accounts ⇨ Defaults ⇨ Login
    Accounts ⇨ Defaults ⇨ System

Security Monitoring Configuration

Outside of auditing, there are some nominal security monitoring functions that you can configure.

To log use of su(C)	*[see recipe SR5.8]*
To monitor TCB status	*Accounts ⇨ Check*
	[also see table 4-25]
To report suspicious SUID/SGID files	*[see recipe SR5.9]*

> **Proper Use of su(C)**
>
> The su(C) command lets users temporarily "switch" to another user ID. This can be dangerous if you have restricted root logins to the console, but still allow unauthorized users to **su** to root from unsecured terminals. On the other hand, su(C) is very useful for administrative users who perform selected system tasks, and need to access system files as the system owner.
>
> Consider, for example, printer administration. All printer subsystem files are owned by system ID **lp**. Most of the files and directories can only be opened by **lp**. To access those files, the administrative user must be able to switch identity to **lp** (or **root**).

Chapter 5   Configuring Your System

Quick Recipe SR5.8   Logging Attempts to Use su(C)

Potential security breaches can be identified by monitoring the use of su(C).

1. Edit the file: **/etc/default/su**
2. Search for the line: `SULOG=/usr/adm/su`
   If found, exit. Attempts are already being logged.
3. Insert the above line in the file.
   Close and exit.

Quick Recipe SR5.9   Preparing to Identify Suspicious SUID/SGID Files

Strange executables with the SGID or SUID bits set can be potential security holes. this recipe will help to easier identify them. <u>This procedure should be performed as soon as you have installed your system and applications.</u>

1. Run: **find / \(-perm -2000 -o -perm -4000 \) -print > /usr/adm/sugid**
   This creates a master log of SUID and SGID files.
2. To identify new SUID/SGID files from now on, run the same command as above, except redirect the output to **/tmp/sugid**;
   then run: **diff /usr/adm/sugid /tmp/sugid**

System Access Security

Securing access to your system involves a lot more than just passwords. There are unscrupulous individuals who would try anything to gain access to your system. You need to protect it on the following fronts:

- require login passwords: *Accounts ➪ Defaults ➪ Password*
- configure account and terminal locking: *Accounts ➪ Defaults ➪ Login*
- deny unauthorized uucp access: *[see SCO System Admin Guide]*
- deny unauthorized tcp/ip access: remove untrusted systems from
                                        /etc/hosts.equiv and **/.rhosts**
- put port passwords on dial-in lines: *[see **passwd**(C)]*

5-107

Essential SCO System Administration

Protected Subsystem Security

Protected subsystem security is based upon authorizations. The table below summarizes the authorizations required to administer various subsystems:

Table 5-38: Required Authorizations For Subsystem Administration

	Authorizations	
Subsystem	**Subsystem**	**Kernel**
print spooling	lp	chown
filesystem backups	backup	execsuid
system accounts	auth	chown, execsuid
account passwords	passwd	execsuid
terminal devices	terminal	chown, execsuid
task scheduling (cron and at)	cron	execsuid, chown, chmodsugid
system process information	mem	execsuid
auditing	audit	configaudit, writeaudit, execsuid

Kernel Authorizations

Kernel authorizations grant user processes the ability to perform restricted tasks. These are summarized below:

execsuid	ability to run SUID programs
chmodsugid	ability to set the SUID or SGID bit on files
chown	ability to change ownership of files
...audit	*[various audit-related authorizations]*

Most users require only **execsuid**.

Discretionary Access Control (DAC)

Discretionary access control is just another name for UNIX file permissions.

There are 12 UNIX file permission bits. They are assigned as follows:

4	2	1	4 2 1	4 2 1	4 2 1
SUID	SGID	sticky	*owner* r | w | x	*group* r | w | x	*others* r | w | x

Chapter 5 Configuring Your System

☞ **Setting File Permission Bits**

Use chmod(C) to set permission bits for files and directories. Bits to be set may be specified as octal digits. Examples follow:

chmod 700	...	sets the read, write, and execute bits for the file owner
chmod 444	...	sets the read bits for owner, group, and others
chmod 511	...	sets execute bits for owner, group, and other; and sets read for owner
chmod 4511	...	sets SUID bit, in addition to those set above

Permissions for existing files and directories can be set with **chmod**(C). Permissions for new files and directories are determined by the active *umask*.

 The Sticky Bit

Historically, the sticky bit was important for executables, especially since paging used to used raw I/O (instead of the disk buffer cache). When set, once a process died, it's text (code) region was moved over to swap for faster loading the next time the process was executed. Now, the sticky bit mainly affects directories. On executables, the effect of the bit has changed. When set, once a process dies, its text region persists in memory until the paged memory software (i.e. **vhand**) reclaims it. If the process is executed again before the memory is reclaimed, it should theoretically run faster. Of course, with modern disk caching techniques, the efficiency advantage of the sticky bit is minimal.

Regarding directories, the sticky bit prevents anyone but the user of a file from deleting it. This is critical in shared directories, where many users may be saving valuable data and temporary files.

☞ **How umask(C) Works**

The umask masks out selected permission bits; so that they are not set for new files and directories. Without the umask, new directories are created with permission 777. New files are created with permission 666. Some examples follow, demonstrating the effect of the umask.

	Resulting Permission	
Umask	**File**	**Directory**
0000	0666	0777
0007	0660	0770
0022	0644	0755
0266	0400	0511

Essential SCO System Administration

Table 5-39:	Recommendations For File and Directory Permissions
user files and directories	**umask 077**
shared system directories	**chmod 1777** *directory*
shared group directories	**chmod 1770** *directory*

> ### System File Permissions
>
> System file permissions and ownership are defined and maintained by the **fixperm** database, **/etc/perms**. When using trusted security, the TCB redefines the permissions and ownership of selected system files.
>
> *[See recipe SR5.10 for instructions on how to restore system file permissions].*

Configuring Groups

Groups have traditionally been an underappreciated security feature of UNIX. SCO has changed that. As before, groups can be sued to restrict access to specific files and directories to members of the group. And as before, users can belong to any number of groups, but under SCO UNIX they can have up to 128 of those group memberships active at one time. Here's how this works:

Quick Demo SD5.1   **Supplemental Groups**

SCO's implementation of supplemental groups injects new power into the UNIX group concept.

Consider the user tina, with group membership in general, gremlins, finance, and strategic. These are her current supplemental groups. This is shown in the following output from **id -s**:

```
uid=6243(tina) gid=210(general), groups=210(general), 227(gremlins),
                         350(finance), 402(strategic)
```

Now consider the following files that tina has encountered today.

```
-rwxr-x---   1  finadm    finance     1756943 Nov 17  1994 report4.94
-rw-rw-r--   1  markj     gremlins      35002 Dec 21 10:43 plan_sheet
drwx--x---   2  lexis     strategic       800 Dec 02  1994 Factors
```

By virtue of her supplemental group list, Tina has some form of access to each of the files above. She can run **report.94**, update **plan_sheet**, and change directory to **Factors**. She can do all this without running a single **newgrp***(C)* command.

5-110

Chapter 5   Configuring Your System

> **Some recommendations for configuring groups:**
> - create specific groups for each functional area on your system (or network)
> - record the name and function of each of your groups in a specially created file.
> - designate a special administrative user to own the files for a group
> - when adding a new user, let the manager suggest the appropriate groups
> - do not create a default supplemental group list; instead allow supplemental groups to be added as users require them

The system group file, **/etc/group**, has the following format:

        group name **::** *group ID* **:** *list of users*

Examples include: `bin::2:bin,daemon`
                         `mem::20:`
                         `group::50:lexis,juliek,markt`

Default/maximum limit of supplemental groups:	**8/128** *
Setting the number of supplemental groups:	**/etc/conf/bin/idtune** NGROUPS *value*
Defining groups:	edit **/etc/group**
Setting the default group:	<u>edit</u> **/etc/default/authsh**
Setting the default supplemental group list:	<u>edit</u> **/etc/default/authsh**

                                        * maximum is 16 w/o special QFS *[see Appendix C]*

> **Links and Security**
>
> Links can be a security feature as well. Security applications include:
> - Maintaining the integrity of non-searchable directories, while providing access to key files.
> - Providing local access to far-flung system and group files without compromising the security of system directories.

<u>**Quick Recipe SR5.10**</u>   **Setting System File Permissions**

The TCB alters the permissions of many system files. This modified procedure restores the file permissions to a safe TCB state.

1. Run: **cd / ; /etc/fixperm -cs /etc/perms/rts /etc/perms/ext** *others*
   This restores the installed run-time and extended system file permissions.

2. Run: **fixmog**
   This resets the correct TCB file permissions.

5-111

Essential SCO System Administration

Configuring SUID and SGID Files

If your site develops applications, you can build your own protected subsystems by skillful application of the SUID and SGID permission bits.

> **Table 5-40:** **Protected Subsystem Design Criteria**
> - a common database of files are owned by a single administrative user; the files are also "owned" by a single "subsystem" group.
> - only the owner and the group have write permission on any of the database files;
> - others may be allowed read permission on some files, but no higher access.
> - a set of applications (binaries and shell scripts) have been created to selectively and securely modify data in the database.
> - the applications are owned by both the administrative user and the group.
> - the SUID bit may be set on some application binaries to allow users controlled read and write access to the database.
> - the SGID bit may be set on some application binaries which allow data to be read, but not modified.

> **The Group "Owner" of a File**
>
> To say that a group owns a file is inaccurate. In effect, what the group "owns" are specific access rights to the file. The group is designated access-holding group (or "group of record") with respect to the three group permission bits.

> **SUID, SGID, and the Effective UID (EUID)**
>
> While running an SUID application, the user temporarily acquires the UID of the application owner. His effective user ID (EUID) is that of the application owner. He is effectively the owner for the duration of the program, enjoying all of the owner's file access privileges. It is still possible for the application to determine that he is not the real owner, since his real user ID (UID) does not change, but most applications are designed to respond to the EUID.
>
> While running an SGID application, the user temporarily becomes a member of the access-holding group. His effective group ID (EGID) and supplemental groups are those of the access-holder. For the duration of the program, he enjoys all of the file access privileges of that group. As with the UID, the user still retains his real group ID (GID).

The following exercise demonstrates the concept:

Chapter 5   Configuring Your System

Quick Demo SD5.2   **Using SUID and SGID**

SUID and SGID can be used to implement protected subsystems.

Consider the following listing for imaginary directory, **/v/lib/lexis/data**:

```
drwxr-x---   4   lexis   legal      2048 Oct 16  1994 .
dr-x--x--x  15   lexis   legal      1296 Oct 16  1994 ..
-rw-------   1   lexis   legal   5580996 Dec 21 04:00 case_data1
-rw-r-----   1   lexis   legal    831251 Dec 21 03:57 casesummary
-rw-------   1   lexis   legal   1298532 Dec 21 04:03 clients
```

Now consider the applications directory, **/v/lib/lexis/bin**:

```
drwxr-x--x   2   lexis   legal       512 Oct 16  1994 .
dr-x--x--x  15   lexis   legal      1296 Oct 16  1994 ..
-rwx--x---   1   lexis   legal    379846 May 05  1994 lxadmin
-rwx--s--x   1   lexis   legal    379846 May 05  1994 lxexcerpt
-rws--x---   1   lexis   legal    379846 May 05  1994 lxreview
-rws--x--x   1   lexis   legal   1298532 Dec 21 04:00 updclients
```

Finally consider the **id -s** output for users ray and laura:

```
uid=1086(ray) gid=401(legal), groups=401(legal)
uid=1014(laura) gid=200(general), groups=200(general),228(minks)
```

Now here are the situations, and the results.

a) Ray desperately needs to access critical case data in **case_data1**.
b) He is unable to use standard tools to inspect that file.
c) He can however run the application, **lxreview**, which then lets him inspect **case_data1** in a controlled fashion. His EUID becomes **lexis**.
d) Ray is also able to run **lxadmin** to perform some administrative functions on the case database, but he will be denied any administrative access to **case_data1**. His EUID remains **ray**.
e) Laura needs to enter some new client infomation into the file **clients**.
f) Laura is not even able to access the directory, let alone the file.
g) She can, however, run the application, **updclients**, which then lets her add new client records to **clients**. Her EUID becomes **lexis**.
h) Laura is unable to run **lxadmin** to check her work, but she can run **lxexcerpt** to selectively peruse **casesummary** while she drinks her coffee. Her EGID becomes **legal**.

Essential SCO System Administration

Configuring Privileged System Access

Configuring privileged access to the system is probably the most crucial aspect of system security. In most cases, privileged access addresses how users acquire root privileges. Generally, privileged access concerns any change of user ID on the system.

Note, how in table 5-41, the user, maria, is seen differently by the system depending on how she acquires root access.

Table 5-41:	User IDs and Privileged Applications			
Action taken by sample user Maria	**UID**	**EUID**	**LUID**	**LUID***
Maria logs in as herself	maria	maria	maria	maria
Maria runs an SUID program owned by root	maria	root	root	maria
Maria runs **su**(C) as root	root	root	root	maria
Maria runs an **asroot**(ADM) command	root	root	root	maria
Maria logs in as root	root	root	root	root

* - high and improved security only

The LUID

The LUID (login user ID) is a C2 concept. No matter how the UID or EUID changes, the ID at login (LUID) enables full accountability. In **improved** security, the LUID is tracked, but not enforced. It is enforced only under **high** security.

Table 5-42:	Comparison of Methods Used to Grant Root Access	
Method	**Advantage**	**Containment**
logging in as root	full root capability	none (poor)
running **su**(C) root	full root capability *	none (poor)
running SUID root binary	high root capability within controlled scope	good
running **asroot**(ADM) shell script	full root capability * within controlled scope	fair +

* - programs that enforce LUID may fail
+ - programs with shell escapes can grant full capability

The preferred methods of giving **root** access to users are: SUID and **asroot**(ADM).

Chapter 5 Configuring Your System

Quick Recipe SR5.11   Making Commands Executable by asroot(ADM)

The **asroot***(ADM)* command lets you implement SUID shell scripts

1. Log in as root.
2. Determine the desired command; and copy it to **/tcb/files/rootcmds**.
   Rename it as appropriate. This is your new command.
3. Run: **fixmog -v**

   This gives the new command permissions consistent with the TCB.
4. Edit: **/etc/auth/system/authorize**
   Find the line that starts: "root:shutdown". Add the name of your new command, preceded by a comma. You have just created a new authorization.
5. From **sysadmsh**, use: *Accounts* ⇨ *User* ⇨ *Examine* (⇨ *Privileges*)
   to assign this authorization to the designated user (or users).
   The user runs the command as follows: **/tcb/bin/asroot** *command*

> To avoid the mandatory user password requested by **asroot***(ADM)*, place the following entry in **/etc/default/su**:   ASROOTPW=NO

Quick Recipe SR5.12   Restricting root logins to the console

Many potential security threats can be avoided by physically protecting the console and only allowing root access on the console.

1. Edit: **/etc/default/login**

   Add the following line: CONSOLE=/dev/tty01

> This device is the only logical choice, since it is also the OVERRIDE device. The OVERRIDE device is critical, because it is the sole enabled system port when the protected password database is corrupted. The OVERRIDE device is defined in **/etc/default/login**.

Root logins are now restricted to **/dev/tty01**.

Essential SCO System Administration

Creating Administrative Users

Administrative users exist primarily to manage subsystems. Admin users like **lp** are dedicated to a specific subsystem. Designating administrative users is an effective way to delegate some of the tasks normally doen by **root**.

There are two main methods to create administrative users under SCO.

- assign the required authorizations to a normal user
- create a real administrative user (type: pseudo-user) with the required authorizations, and designate a normal user as able to **su** to that account.

> The second method is more consistent with C2 guidelines, but under the current implementation is difficult to properly configure.

Quick Recipe SR5.13 **Designating a Backup Administrative User**

You can create administrative specialists to offload some of the burden of system administration. A designated backup administrator is a very useful specialist.

1. From **sysadmsh**, go to: Accounts ⇨ User ⇨ Examine (⇨ Privileges)
   Assign the backup authorization to the selected user.
2. Change the group ownership of each filesystem to backup.
   The user is now ready to perform filesystem backups.

> **/etc/checklist** contains a full list of filesystems.

Table 5-43:	Configuring Key TCB Components
Database	**Configuration Command**
Audit	System ⇨ Audit ⇨ Collection
Device Assignment	Accounts ⇨ Terminal ⇨ Assign
Protected Password	Accounts ⇨ Defaults ⇨ Password
	Accounts ⇨ Defaults ⇨ Logins
	Accounts ⇨ Defaults ⇨ System
	Accounts ⇨ Defaults ⇨ Authorizations
	System ⇨ Configure ⇨ Defaults ⇨ Home
Terminal Control	Accounts ⇨ Terminal ⇨ Examine
Subsystem	[configured as users are created]
File Control	[not configurable]

Chapter 5   Configuring Your System

Configuring Processes

Configuring processes involves determining what to run and when you would like to run it. Although most processes running on the system are unconfigured as such, there are tools you can use to schedule specific ones of your own.

The tools are **crontab**(C) and **at**(C). Since **crontab** is the more flexible of the two, we address it here. For those new to the process concept, here's a quick intro.

Quick Backgrounder SB5.6   **Introduction to Processes**

A process is task that communicates with the system. Interactive processes, like your shell, communicate with you as well. Since nearly all system operations are defined in terms of processes, a quick introduction would be helpful.

Consider the following table of processes, excerpted from the command, **ps -ef**:

```
   UID    PID   PPID   C   STIME      TTY    TIME   COMMAND
   root   234      1   0   Aug 27      ?     0:31   cron
 lesley  8210      1   0   08:34:00   008    0:20   -ksh
 lesley  9637   8210  22   09:15:25   008    1:58   Tframe
```

Notice that the command **Tframe** has a PID of 9637. That is its process ID. We can use this process ID to control or terminate the process. Note that **Tframe** also has a PPID of 8210. That is the parent process ID. **Tframe** was originated by the process whose process ID is 8210. The parent process must be **-ksh**. Both processes have the same UID as well. That is the UID of the process owner, in this case lesley.

The other information we can deduce is that Lesley's processes are running on tty008. It also appears that Lesley has been very busy with the **Tframe** application, since her C value (CPU utilization) is relatively high.

If Lesley were to encounter a problem with **Tframe**, for example, garbling her display, you as administrator could *kill* her process. The command below would allow you to do that:

>   **kill 9637**

This version of the command gives the process a warning that we'd like it to clean up after itself, then die. It is relatively polite, compared to the alternative. But if Lesley's process still persists, it may be hung. You'll need a stronger form of **kill**(C).

>   **kill -9 9637**

The **-9** is the *death* signal. The **kill** command sends a signal (in this case, the death signal) to a process. This signal is final, and is usually sufficient to terminate most processes.

Essential SCO System Administration

Quick Backgrounder SB5.7   How Processes are Initiated

Processes are initiated on the system as follows:

After **boot**(M) completes, the kernel builds the process table, and loads the scheduler and 3 initial processes. One of these is **init**(M), process 1. The init process then initializes the system from the process initialization table, **/etc/inittab**. This file tells **init** what to run when. Among others the files that initially get run are:

/etc/bcheckrc	cleans and mounts /dev/root
/etc/smmrc	runs initial TCB check
/etc/sulogin	prompts for single-user prompt *[not in /etc/inittab]*
/etc/asktimerc	initializes system time and date
/etc/rc2	spawns system and application daemons; mounts filesystems *[see **rc2**(ADM)]*

The file **/etc/rc2** executes the files in **/etc/rc2.d**. These files initiate the various system and application daemons.

Finally, **init** spawns a **getty** processes on each enabled terminal. getty(M) displays the login prompt, and waits for input. Upon receiving a name **getty** then execs **/bin/login**. The login program tries to authenticate the name; and if successful, *execs* the login shell.

> When a process *execs* another, it effectively overlays itself with the code from the file being *exec'd*. A *fork* is a duplicate of a process. The forked process is known as the *child*. By convention the *parent* process sleeps until the child *dies* (completes).

Each time you enter a command, the shell forks a child shell which execs the command. The parent shell then wakes and waits for the next command. When you terminate the shell, **init** reclaims the line and spawns another **getty**.

> In practice, you'll only edit **/etc/inittab** to add or modify serial port entries.

Chapter 5 Configuring Your System

Configuring the Scheduled Job Daemon, Cron

The **cron**(C) daemon is one of the processes started by **init** from /etc/rc2.d. It is a quite special. It's job is to wake up every minute and look for work. It looks in one of two places for things to do.

> /usr/lib/cron/crontabs cron tables submitted by **crontab**(C)
> /usr/lib/cron/atjobs   at jobs submitted by **at**(C) or **batch**(C)

Job entries created by **at** are one-shots. Only the crontabs are configurable.

Quick Demo SD5.3 **Crontab Entries**

Cron tables (crontabs) contain one or more entries with the following format:

❶   ❷   ❸   ❹   ❺   *command*

❶ minute (0-60)
❷ hour (0-23)
❸ day of the month (1-31)
❹ month of the year (1-12)
❺ day of the week (0 - Sunday, 1 - Monday, ... 6 - Saturday)

Each of the five numeric fields can be:
- a single number (e.g. 15)
- a range (eg 2-6)
- a list of numbers or ranges separated by commas
- an asterisk * (for all values)

Fields are separated by spaces or TABs.
Some examples:

10,30,50 6-21 * 11-12 1-6 seasonal.help

> The command **seasonal.help** runs at 10, 30, and 50 minutes past the hour, between 0600 and 2100 every weekday and Saturday during November and December

15 9 13 * 5 mass.mailing

> At 0915 on Friday, the 13th (every 13th day of the month that is also a Friday), **mass.mailing** will run.

Crontabs are submitted with **crontab**(C). The system maintains a separate crontab for each user who submits one. Normal users, though, must have explicitly permission to use crontab. The following recipe demonstrates how to use crontab to specify and schedule tasks.

5-119

Essential SCO System Administration

Quick Recipe SR5.14   **Submitting Jobs with Crontab**

You will update an existing crontab with a new crontab entry. You want to submit the following entry:

    30 8-17 * * 1-6 collect.stat diskuse >> /usr/local/dsklog

1. Run: **crontab -l > .mycrontab**
   This will copy your current crontab to an ordinary file.
2. Edit this file to add the above crontab entry. Be careful not to remove any existing entries in the file.
3. Resubmit the modified crontab: **crontab .mycrontab**
   Verify the changes with: **crontab -l**

Although, you may not have any jobs to configure now, you will be using this facility frequently. There are many existing cron entries already submitted. You can use the above technique to customize those entries.

Configuring the Default User Account Environment

> General user account creation and configuration is covered in the section "Configuring User Accounts" in Chapter 3. This section addresses the configuration of the default user account environment.

To lay the best foundation for managing user accounts, you'll want to configure appropriate account creation defaults. Some of the considerations you'll want to address include:

- determining the default login shell   *[see Chapter 3]*
- specifying the UID range for this system *[see Chapter 3]*
- configuring access groups   *[see "Configuring Security"]*
- selecting the default group (and GID)
- determining the location of user home directories   *[see also Chapter 3]*
- configuring mail delivery to user home directories

Chapter 5 Configuring Your System

Where to Locate User Home Directories?

Determine the location of user home directories by specifying the *parent home directory* in **/etc/default/authsh**. For example, **/u** is the parent of the user home directory **/u/sandra**. Ideally, **/u** should be mounted on its own filesystem (i.e. **/dev/u**). *[Exercise SR3.9 offers detailed instructions]*.

Where to Locate User Mailboxes?

As discussed elsewhere, there are drawbacks to keeping user mailboxes in the default location – **/usr/spool/mail** (on the root filesystem!), especially since user mailboxes can grow quite large.

The alternative is to maintain mailboxes in user home directories. This should keep them off the root filesystem. It will also improve privacy. To implement this, **mmdf***(ADM)* (the default mail delivery software) must be reconfigured *[see recipe SR5.15]*.

Quick Recipe SR5.15   **Configuring User Mailbox in the Home Directory**

You need to reconfigure mmdf to deliver mail to each user's home directory.

1. Login as **mmdf**.
2. Edit the following file: **/usr/mmdf/mmdftailor**
   Add the following entries: MDLVRDIR ""
                                 MMBXNAME ".mailbox"
                                 MMBXPROT "600"
3. Run: **cd /usr/mmdf/table**
                                                     ./dbmbuild

   This configures the changes into the mmdf database.

Table 5-44:   **Recommended User Account Defaults**
- Designate **/bin/ksh** as the standard login shell.
- Locate home directories away from **/dev/root** (the root filesystem).
- Set user authorizations as listed in Table 3-4.
- Set password and login controls as listed in Table 3-4.
- Specify a unique ID range between 200 and 60000
- Predefine groups for the systen.

Essential SCO System Administration

Table 5-45:	Configuring User Account Defaults
Account Attribute	**Command/Procedure**
UID range, GID	System ⇨ Configure ⇨ Default ⇨ Home
home directories	System ⇨ Configure ⇨ Default ⇨ Home
authorizations	Accounts ⇨ Defaults ⇨ Authorizations
password controls	Accounts ⇨ Defaults ⇨ Password
login controls	Accounts ⇨ Defaults ⇨ Logins

Once you have assigned the default shells, add environment definitions and login session startup commands to the appropriate file.

Table 5-46:	New Account Profiles
Shell	**Master Profile File**
/bin/sh	/usr/lib/mkuser/sh/profile
/bin/ksh	/usr/lib/mkuser/ksh/profile
/bin/csh	/usr/lib/mkuser/csh/login
	/usr/lib/mkuser/csh/cshrc

Recommended environment definitions include:

- standard user-friendly prompt   (PS1 for **sh** and **ksh**)
- standard command search path   (PATH for all shells)
- reasonable **ulimit**   (not supported in **csh**)

Customize the following environment variables in the created home directories:

TERM	user's terminal type
HUSHLOGIN	whether or not to display message of the day and last login messages
LPDEST	user's default print destinationaside trailer

To enable *hushlogin*, the following entry must be set in **/etc/default/login**:
ALLOWHUSH=YES

Chapter 5   Configuring Your System

Configuring SCO Shell as Login Shell

The SCO shell, **scosh**(C), is a suitable environment for some users. It is menu-based and has a friendly text editor. A key disadvantage is that there is no simple way to customize the startup environment.

To configure **scosh** in administrative mode, run: **scosh   desktop   -a**
[See SR3.8 for specific instructions].

For **scosh** to be treated like the other shells, you'll need to replace the initial colon '**:**' in **/usr/bin/scosh** with the line below.

                #!/bin/sh   *[see the box below]*

Useful tip: You can prevent shell escapes out of the menus by adding an empty file named **/usr/lib/scosh/allowshell** as follows:

       cd /usr/lib/scosh ; touch allowshell ; chmod 444 allowshell

Executable Shell Scripts

SCO supports a capability called *hashpling*, which effectively enables executable shell scripts. By inserting a special string as the first line of a shell script, we transform it. Programs that normally would not execute a shell script (e.g. **exec**(S)) now will.

The hashpling line has three forms: **#!/bin/sh**   **#!/bin/ksh**   **#!/bin/csh**
[See SR5.16 to enable hashpling].

Quick Recipe SR5.16   **Enabling Hashpling**

Hashpling effectively bestows "binary" file status upon shell scripts. This exercize describes how to configure it.

1. Change directory to: **/etc/conf/pack.d/kernel**
2. Edit **space.c**, as follows:
   - locate the line: **int hashplingenable=0;**
   - change this to: **int hashplingenable=1;**
3. To relink the kernel, run: **cd /etc/conf/cf.d**
                                          ./link_unix
4. Reboot to realize the changes.

Essential SCO System Administration

Review of User Account Creation

The recommended account creation procedure is:
- create the account, accepting the creation defaults
- assign a standard "new user" password to the account
- force a password change at first login
- customize the user account as desired

To create a user, proceed to: Accounts ⇨ User ⇨ Create
To customize a newly created user, proceed to: Accounts ⇨ User ⇨ Examine

> The creation of administrative users is discussed in "Creating Administrative Users" in the section "Configuring System Security".

Configuring the Kernel

> Specific applications of kernel tuning are addressed in Chapter 6.

After using your system for a while, you may discover some aspects that you'd like to fine-tune. For typical systems, these include:

- adjusting resources used by processes   *[see Chapter 6]*
- adjusting file and filesystem resources   *[see Chapter 6]*
- adjusting system performance   *[see Chapter 6]*
- adjusting hardware resources
  (e.g. disk and tape buffers)

The key tools for monitoring tunable system resources are listed in Table 4-7.
The key tools for modifying tunable system resources are listed in Table 5-47.

Table 5-47:   **Kernel Tuning Tools**

Tool	Function
configure*(ADM)*	inspecting and modifying kernel parameters by group
sysdef(*ADM*)	listing run-time values of kernel parameters
idtune*(ADM)*	modifying individual kernel parameters
tunesh*(ADM)*	automatically tailoring kernel parameters to reflect system configuration and usage
sar*(ADM)*	reporting system activity
crash*(ADM)*	inspecting system tables (especially streams: ⇨ *strstat*)

Chapter 5 Configuring Your System

Table 5-48 summarizes the most useful tunable kernel parameters.

Table 5-48: Summary of SCO Tunable Kernel Parameters

Parameter	Default	Min/Max	Determines
NDISK	4	1/50	number of disk drives
NBUF	*	0/65536	number of 1K disk buffers
CTBUFSIZE	128	0/256	size of the tape buffer in K
MAXBUF	600	0/65536	maximum number of allocated disk buffers
NAUTOUP	10	0/60	buffer age in seconds for automatic update
BDFLUSHR	30	1/300	frequency that bdflush daemon runs in seconds
NCLIST	120	120/16640	number of 64byte character buffers to allocate
TTHOG	256	256/8192	size of the raw queue for the tty driver
NINODE	300	100/16000	number of inode table entries to allocate
NHINODE	128	64/8192	size of the inode hash table (power of 2)
NFILE	300	100/16000	number of open file entrie to allocate
NMOUNT	8	4/50	number of mount table entries
ETRUNC	0	0/1	if 1, silently truncate too long filenames
NOFILES	60	60/11000	number of open files per process
NMPBUF	0	0/100	number of 16K AFS cluster buffers
S5CACHEENTS	256	1/4096	size of directory -> inode name cache
S5HASHQS	61	1/8191	size of hash table used with S5CACHEENTS
S5OFBIAS	8	1/256	search optimization control for S5CACHEENTS
NGROUPS	8	0/128	maximum number of supplemental groups
NPROC	100	50/3000	number of process table entries
MAXUP	25	15/200	maximum processes per non-root user
NREGION	300	100/10000	number of region table entries to allocate
MAXSLICE	100	25/100	maxium time slice for user processes (ticks)
TBLNK	0	0/32767	number of seconds before screen blanks
NSPTTYS	16	1/256	number of pseudo-ttys
NBLK4	40	0/2048	number of 4-byte streams message blocks
NBLK16	40	0/2048	"" "" 16-byte "" "" ""
NBLK64	40	0/2048	"" "" 64-byte "" "" ""
NBLK128	8	0/2048	"" "" 128-byte"" "" ""
NBLK256	8	0/2048	"" "" 128-byte"" "" ""
NBLK512	8	0/2048	"" "" 512-byte"" "" ""
NBLK1024	20	0/2048	"" "" 1024-byte "" "" ""
NBLK2048	20	0/2048	"" "" 2048-byte "" "" ""
NBLK4096	0	0/2048	"" "" 4096-byte "" "" ""
EVQUEUES	16	1/256	number of event queues
EVDEVS	16	1/256	number of event devices
SECLUID	*	0/1	enforces LUID
SECSTOPIO	*	0/1	implements stopio
SECCLEARID	*	0/1	clearing of SUID/SGID bit on write

Chapter 6

The Art of System Administration

	Page
Introduction	6-4
Road Map	6-5
The Art of Maintenance	6-6
Maintaining Filesystems	6-7
Maintaining the Process Environment	6-13
Maintaining the Print Spooler System	6-15
Maintaining Trusted Security	6-16
Maintaining User Accounts	6-18
Supporting System Users	6-19
Customizing User Environments	6-19
User Monitoring and Communication	6-20
Ad Hoc Archival and Restore	6-21
Emergency System Recovery	6-25
Emergency System Access	6-28
Selected Hardware Troubleshooting	6-30
Selected Problems with Hard Disks	6-30
fdisk Limits SCO Partitions to 2GB	6-30
Disk Buffers Flush Every Minute	6-30
Selected Problems with Printers	6-30
Slow or Erratic Parallel Printing	6-31
Slow PostScript Printing	6-32
Selected Problems with Mice	6-33
Errors Configuring Multiple Mice of the Same Type	6-33

Essential SCO System Administration

	Page
Performance Notes	6-34
Optimizing Disk Paging and Data Access	6-36
Caching	6-36
The SCO Disk Buffer Cache	6-37
Optimizing Directory Searches	6-38
The File Name Lookup Cache	6-38

Survival Recipes

		Page
SR6.1:	Freeing Filesystem Space	6-8
SR6.2:	Freeing Filesystem Inodes	6-9
SR6.3:	Looking for Large Files	6-9
SR6.4:	Reinitializing A Filesystem	6-11
SR6.5:	Restoring a Full Filesystem from a Backup	6-12
SR6.6:	Restoring a Partial Filesystem from a Backup	6-12
SR6.7:	Restoring the System Bootstrap	6-25
SR6.8:	Restoring a Corrupted /boot	6-26
SR6.9:	Restoring masterboot	6-26
SR6.10:	Restoring the Root Filesystem	6-26
SR6.11:	Recreating the Root Filesystem	6-27
SR6.12:	Emergency System Access	6-29
SR6.13:	Setting Up Printer Polling	6-31
SR6.14:	Fixing the PostScript Filter	6-32
SR6.15:	Patching the Mouse Configuration Code	6-33

Procedures and Strategies

	Page
Creating an Ad Hoc Archive	6-22

Titled Digressions

		Page
☞	A Report Log Directory	6-6
☞	Logging Suggestion	6-7
ⓒ	SCO Filesystems and dcopy(ADM)	6-10
✈	AFS and EAFS Filesystem Structure	6-10
☞	Reinitializing a Filesystem	6-11
✈	The sar(ADM) Utility	6-13
✈	Suspending and Resuming Processes	6-15
✈	Changing Print Request Priorities	6-16
✈	Automatic Monitoring of Critical TCB Processes	6-17

Chapter 6   The Art of System Administration

Page

Digressions   [continued]

✈	Retire or Remove?	6-18
✈	/etc/motd and /etc/issue	6-20
☞	Archival to Hard Disk	6-21
☞	Recommended Blocking Factors	6-22
✈	Formatting Floppies for Use with copy(C)	6-23
☞	Restoring Parts of an Archive	6-24
✈	Typical Causes of TCB Database Corruption	6-28
✈	Fixing Trusted Security Problems	6-29
✈	RAID and Fast Hard Disks	6-35
✈	Tight Looping	6-37

Tables

6-1:	Filesystem Maintenance Commands	6-7
6-2:	Other Relevant Filesystem Commands	6-9
6-3:	Ten Things You Can Do to SCO Filesystems	6-10
6-4:	Process Status Commands	6-13
6-5:	Kernel Parameters Affecting Processes	6-14
6-6:	Summary of Print Spooler Administration Commands	6-16
6-7:	Commands for Maintaining Trusted Security	6-16
6-8:	Trusted Security Recovery Commands	6-18
6-9:	Account Maintenance Commands	6-18
6-10:	Selected User Support Commands	6-19
6-11:	Global Login Startup Commands	6-19
6-12:	User Communication Tools	6-20
6-13:	User Monitoring Tools	6-20
6-14:	Floppy Disk Media Comparison	6-22
6-15:	Comparison of SCO Archive Utilities	6-23
6-16:	Sample Commands to Archive Current Directory to	6-24
6-17:	Sample Commands to Inspect Archive on	6-24
6-18:	Sample Commands to Restore *Archive from*	6-24
6-19:	Managing Resource-intensive Activities	6-35
6-20:	Comparison of Memory Speeds	6-36
6-21:	Tunable Parameters Affecting the Disk Buffer Cache	6-37
6-22:	Tunable Parameters Affecting the File Name Lookup Cache	6-38

Essential SCO System Administration

Introduction

"I'd rather drink from the Hudson!", Sarah Shaw complained as she fled the office coffee machine. The redhead was having a wretched day; and the bleak Brooklyn evening couldn't get much worse. As new system administrator on the firm's UNIX server, this was her shift. Now, she, Sarah, had inherited the host of evils spawned by her predecessor, Paul.

As she approached her console, it emitted several loud beeps. Sarah snapped to attention. The console was now crying continuously. Heads shot up nearby. Almost immediately, the room rocked with language not heard since lunchtime in the cafeteria. "~@^#%! my resume! 3 hours lost!" "@^%#*! where's my report?" "Data unavailable! I'll kill the @#*!% responsible!"

"Ooo, that's not good", Sarah worried; then she saw the display.

```
Out of space on EAFS dev hd (1/40)
Out of space on EAFS dev hd (1/80)
Out of space on EAFS dev Sdsk (56,104)
    . . . .
```

"Oh no!", she sighed, "the filesystems are full." Yes, this was clearly much worse than a bad cup of coffee. ... Meanwhile ....

No system problem will frustrate your users more than losing data or being unable to access it. This is certainly not an normal occurrence on SCO systems, but these things can happen.

As an SCO UNIX system administrator you will be motivated to ensure that users not lose productivity or data due to resource problems or system downtime. In fact, you should usually expect to foresee and remedy potential problems long before they manifest. But when things do occur you'll want to recover in a hurry. Such is the art of system administration.

By the way, Sarah freed up disk space quickly enough to hear sighs of relief in the office. Only the resume guy lost any data; but he was leaving anyway.

Chapter 6   The Art of System Administration

Road Map

 This chapter is suitable for all system administrators.

This chapter offers tools and strategies to administer and troubleshoot your base SCO system. Although some of the sections included may not be relevant to you now, you will certainly find them useful later.

 System monitoring tools are presented in Chapter 4.

Essential Sections for All New Administrators

The Art of Maintenance

Essential Recipes: SR6.1: Freeing Filesystem Space
                             SR6.6: Restoring a Partial Filesystem

Highly Recommended: Emergency System Recovery

Recommended Topics for Experienced Administrators

Emergency System Access
Performance Notes

SR6.10:   Restoring the Root Filesystem
SR6.12:   Emergency System Access
℗   SCO Filesystems and dcopy(ADM)
✈   Suspending and Resuming Processes
✈   Retire or Remove
Table 6-3: Ten Things You Can Do to SCO Filesystems
Table 6-15: Comparison of SCO Archive Utilities

 For comprehensive performance tuning strategies, the PTR Prentice-Hall book *SCO Performance Tuning Handbook* by Gina Miscovich and David Simons is strongly recommended.

Essential SCO System Administration

The Art of Maintenance

"So this is how it all works!" That sentiment has been shared countless times by scores of system administrators who've finally learned the ropes, and now have smoothly running, trouble-free SCO systems.

Actually, though, system maintenance never stops. It's much like owning a vintage automobile. Once you've secured the right components and installed and adjusted them properly, you still need to check under the hood on a regular basis for any warning signs.

A Report Log Directory

Although most subsystems maintain their own log files *[see table 4-26]*, it is quite useful to maintain some of your own. The specific logs to be created can vary with the source of the data. Initially, though, you'll want to consider where to keep these logs.

One suggestion is to create a dedicated log directory (**e.g. /usr/spool/local**). Ideally, the directory should reside on a filesystem other than **/dev/root**.

To assist you in mastering the art of maintenance, the following topics are addressed in this section.

- maintaining filesystems
- maintaining the process environment
- maintaining the print spooler system
- maintaining trusted security
- maintaining user accounts
- supporting system users

Chapter 6   The Art of System Administration

Maintaining Filesystems

Maintaining filesystems is simple. The key things to check are listed in Table 6-1.

Table 6-1:	Filesystem Maintenance Commands	
Condition to Check	**Command/Procedure**	**When to Run**
filesystem integrity	**fsck -Dy** *filesystem*	once/week *
	fsck -Db **/dev/root**	
filesystem free space	**df -v**	frequently
filesystem free inodes	**df -i**	daily
	* - must be in single-user mode	

fsck(ADM) performs the integrity check in six stages. The following options apply:
-**y** (accept all fsck decisions)
-**b** (reboot if changes were made)
-**D** (check and repair bad directories)

Logging Suggestion

Add the following **crontab**(C) entry, which logs **df** output every 30 minutes to the file **df.rpt**:

3,33 6-20 * * * 1-5 (date; df -v) >> /usr/spool/local/df.rpt

Healthy Results

- all filesystems repaired by **fsck**
- no more than 85% used disk space in any filesystem.
- no more than 90% used inodes in any filesystem.

If less than 15% of a filesystem is free, system performance can become slow and erratic. Furthermore, filesystem fragmentation worsens. If the filesystem is out of space, users may lose data, and the system may crash.

Indications

- ✉ NOTICE: `clalloc - No space on` fstyp dev name (maj,min)
- ✉ NOTICE: `s5alloc - No space on` fstyp dev name (maj,min)
- ✉ NOTICE: `s5ialloc - Out of inodes on` fstyp dev name (maj,min)

`EAFS dev hd (1,40)` indicates the root filesystem, **/dev/root**.

Essential SCO System Administration

Recovery

- no recovery is necessary for **fsck**, since it repairs most inconsistencies it finds
- if less than 15% of a filesystem is available, consult SR6.1 to free up space
- if less than 10% of a filesystem's inodes are free, consult SR6.2 to free up inodes

---

Quick Recipe SR6.1   **Freeing Filesystem Space**

This recipe lists a variety of strategies to free up filesystem disk space

1. Delete unnecessary files:

   - **core** files: **find / -name core -print | xargs rm**
   - strange /dev files   **find / -type f -print | xargs rm**
   - **tmp** files   **find /tmp /usr/tmp -print | xargs rm -f**
   - audit trails   **find /tcb/audittmp -print | xargs rm -f**
   - orphaned files   **rm -f /lost+found/* */lost+found/***

2. Check and truncate system log files: **cat /dev/null >** *file*
   [See Table 4-x for list]

3. Resize large directories: **find / -depth -type d -size +5 -print |** *resizedir*
   *[See the box below for the code to **resizdir**]*

   ☞
To resize directories manually:	**cd** *dir*; **cd ..** **copy -roml** *dir dir*.**new** **rm -r** *dir* ; **mv** *dir*.**new** *dir*

4. If user filesystems are affected, ask users to remove any unneeded files. Advise them that any files older than 30 days can be restored from level 0 backups.

```
: resizdir -            Resize Directory
#
while read DIR
do  NDIR=${DIR}+
echo  Resizing  $DIR  1>&2
cd  $DIR/..
#  This procedure will not resize the root directory
#
copy  -roml  $DIR  $NDIR  ||  { echo  "Cannot resize root dir!";
                                exit  2; }
rm  -rf  $DIR
mv  $NDIR  $DIR
```

Chapter 6   The Art of System Administration

Quick Recipe SR6.2   **Freeing Filesystem Inodes**

Although enough inodes are allocated for normal use, shortages can occur, especially if many small or empty files have been created. Here are some recovery strategies.

1. Delete unnecessary files as in SR6.1.
2. Remove empty files in *user* accounts:

   find *dirs* **-type -f -size 0 -print | xargs rm -f**

&   Try not to remove empty system files (especially on **/dev/root**). The presence of most of these files is mandatory for system function.

Quick Recipe SR6.3   **Looking for Large Files**

Another possible way to free up system space is to look for abnormally large files. Often these files are created through inadvertent user error (esp. typos).

1. Run: **find / -size +1000 -print > bigflog**
   This command finds all files larger then 500KB.
2. Next, you must determine which of these files are legitimate system files.
   For each suspicious file run: **fgrep -l** *full pathname* **/etc/perms/***
   Any files found are probably system files; and should not be deleted.
3. Remove any files not identified as system files.

Table 6-2:	Other Relevant Filesystem Commands
Command	**Function**
dcopy*(ADM)*	builds a reorganized UNIX filesystem from a copy
dtype*(C)*	determines filesystem type or disk format
ff*(ADM)*	lists filesystem filenames and statistics
fsdb*(ADM)*	filesystem debugger
fsstat*(ADM)*	determines filesystem status
fstyp*(ADM)*	determines filesystem type
fuser*(ADM)*	identifies processes (and users) using listed files
ncheck*(ADM)*	reports filesystem inode numbers and names
pipe*(ADM)*	assigns filesystem on which pipes will reside

Essential SCO System Administration

> **SCO Filesystems and dcopy(ADM)**
>
> Beware of using **dcopy**(ADM) on EAFS (and AFS) filesystems. Although it claims to generate an optimal filesystem organization, some users have reported filesystem corruption after using on AFS filesystems.

> **AFS and EAFS Filesystem Structure**
>
> Unlike XENIX or S51K filesystems, which maintain an actual free block list, EAFS and AFS filesystems maintain a bitmap instead. In fact, there are multiple bitmaps regularly spaced throughout the filesystem block area at 8192 block intervals. Each bit corresponds to a data block. A block is free if the corresponding bit is 1. The bitmap allows the use of fast machine bit instructions to locate suitable clusters of free blocks for allocation to new or growing files. The default cluster size for EAFS filesystems is 32.

Restoring and Modifying Filesystems

Any significant modification to a filesystem requires you to backup and restore. After backing up the filesystem to tape (or disk), you make the desired modifications, then restore.

Table 6-3:	Ten Things You Can Do To SCO Filesystems
Operation	**Tool/Procedure**
rename	**divvy**(ADM)
restore structural integrity	**fsck**(ADM)
repair/rewire	**fsdb**(ADM)
change mount point	edit **/etc/default/filesys**
resize	backup -> **divvy**(ADM) -> restore
defragment	backup -> restore
physically relocate	backup -> **divvy**(ADM) -> restore
adjust logical interleave	backup -> **mkfs**(ADM) -> restore
change inode/block ratio	backup -> **mkfs**(ADM) -> restore
restore corrupted files	restore

[See "Configuring Filesystem Backup" in Chapter 5 for filesystem backup details].

Chapter 6   The Art of System Administration

> **Reinitializing a Filesystem**
>
> To expedite a full filesystem restore, you should consider reinitializing it to a virgin state. This effectively wipes the filesystem clean. That way, any unwanted (and possibly corrupted) directories and files are removed. To reinitialize a filesystem see SR6.4.

Quick Recipe SR6.4   Reinitializing a Filesystem

Reinitializing a filesystem speeds the restore process and removes corruption. Beware that it also removes any files and directories not on the backup.

> See SR6.10 to initialize and restore a full root filesystem.

1. Unmount the filesystem.
2. Run: **divvy**   filesystem device
3. At the prompt, select: **c[reate]**
   Enter the division of the filesystem to be reinitialized.
   Verify that the <u>New FS</u> field indicates "yes" for your filesystem.
4. At the same prompt, enter q (to quit).
5. At the next prompt, select: **i[nstall]**
   This will reinitialize your filesystem and exit to the shell.
6. Run: **mkdev fs**
   This is necessary to rebuild the lost+found directory.
   At the first prompt, select: **1** (to add a filesystem)
7. In response to device name, enter the filesystem device.
   Respond "yes" to continue despite the warning about conflicts.
8. In response to directory name, enter: **/mnt** (or any free mount point)
   Verify that it reports "reserving slots in lost+found"
9. At the next prompt, press the DEL key to abort. We're done.
10. Remount the filesystem if desired.

Essential SCO System Administration

Quick Recipe SR6.5 — Restoring a Full Filesystem from a Backup

There is probably no more critical system administration skill than this. Just pray that you have verified the backup you are about to restore.

1. Ensure that the filesystem to be restored is mounted at its proper mount point.
2. For the filesystem you are about to restore, note the following:
   - the device filename
   - the archive format   *[should be* **cpio** *or "sysadmsh"]*
   - the level   *[should be 0 for the initial restore]*
   - the block size   *[this is important]*
3. Load the backup media. If applicable, position it to the correct filesystem *[see SR5.7 for details]*.
4. From sysadmsh, go to: Backups ⇨ Restore ⇨ Full

   Enter the relevant information.

   ☞ Make sure that your tape device (e.g. **/dev/enrStp0**) is linked to one of the devices in the list that F3 displays. Yes, this list is non-configurable.

5. Your successful restore displays the names of the files being installed.

Quick Recipe SR6.6 — Restoring a Partial Filesystem from a Backup

A partial restore of a filesystem backup extracts one or more files or directories. Just remember that the files on the backup are relative to the mount point.

1. Ensure that the filesystem is mounted at its proper mount point.
2. For the filesystem you are about to partially restore, note the following:
   - the device filename
   - the archive format   *[should be* **cpio** *or "scheduled backup"]*
   - the level   *[should be 0 for the initial restore]*
   - the block size   *[this is important]*
   - the mount point
3. Load the backup media. If applicable, position it to the correct filesystem *[see SR5.7 for details]*.
4. From **sysadmsh**, go to: Backups ⇨ Restore ⇨ Partial

   Enter the requested information as follows:

   File to restore: one or more relative pathnames, separated by commas
   Directory to restore to: the filesystem mount point

Chapter 6 The Art of System Administration

☞
> File pathnames are relative to the filesystem's **root** (its mount point). For example, with: mount point: **/u2**
> and normal file name: **/u2/norma/diary**
>
> the relative pathname is: **norma/diary**
>
> To extract a directory, append "/*" to the relative pathname, as below:
>
> relative directory name: **norma/***

☞
> Make sure that your tape device (e.g. **/dev/enrStp0**) is linked to one of the devices in the list that F3 displays.

5. A successful partial restore displays the names of the files being extracted.

Maintaining the Process Environment

You can measure the efficiency of your system by how well processes run. Maintaining processes involves collecting the information to measure this. *[See Table 6-4 for a list of key commands]*.

Table 6-4:	Process Status Commands	
Statistic to Check	**Command**	**Frequency**
process table utilization	sar -v | cut -c1-16	daily
process load average	sar -q	daily
	w	hourly
process resource use	sar -v	daily
free memory	sar -r	daily
individual process status	ps -ef | pg	hourly

> **The sar*(ADM)* Utility**
>
> **sar***(ADM)* creates reports from data regularly collected by the kernel. It can be used to monitor system activity currently or historically (up to 30 days back). By default, sar monitors the current day's history. Day history files are located in **/usr/adm/sa**. They are generated by **sa1***(ADM)*, running in the crontab of user **sys**. The names of the files correspond to days of the month. For example, **sa17** is generated on the 17th of the month.
>
> To look at a given day's report, simply run **sar** as follows:
>
>   **sar** *flags* **-f /usr/adm/sa/sa**XX

Essential SCO System Administration

Healthy Results

- average load factor less than 2.0 per CPU
- average process table occupancy less than 80%
- average inode and file table occupancy less than 80%
- at least 10% of memory free (1 processor page = 4KB)
- no process exhibits both high CPU utilization and system time
  [in other words, there are no runaway processes]

Indications

- No more processes
- File table overflow
- CONFIG: falloc - File table overflow
- CONFIG: allocreg - Region table overflow
- CONFIG: newproc - Process table overflow
- CONFIG: ifreeget - Inode table overflow
- CONFIG: s5iread - EAFS inode table overflow
- Too many open files

Recovery

- The first 7 error messages indicate resource problems. *[See the table below for tips on increasing the relevant resources]*
- The last error message refers to a limit on open files per process
  If this occurs frequently, you may need to increase the value of the NOFILES kernel parameter
- In the case of a runaway process, you can simply **kill** it. If you have doubts about the origin of the process, or if it can be run at a time when the system is less busy, you can suspend it, and resume it later. *[See the relevant box]*

Table 6-5:   Kernel Parameters Affecting Processes

Process Resource	Parameter	Default	Min/Max
inode table size	NINODE	300	100/16000
file table size	NFILE	300	100/1600
process table size	NPROC	100	50/3000
region table size	NREGION	300	100/10000
open files/process	NOFILES	60	60/11000
max user processes/UID	MAXUP	25	15/200

Chapter 6   The Art of System Administration

> To reset a kernel parameter, run: **/etc/conf/bin/idtune** *parameter value*
> From **sysadmsh**, go to: *System ⇨ Configure ⇨ Kernel (⇨ Parameters)*

Suspending and Resuming Processes

Busy or CPU-intensive processes can be suspended for later execution with the **kill**(C) command. Normally **kill**(C) is used to terminate processes, but two special signals support suspend and resume. These are demonstrated below.

To suspend a process: **kill -23** *process id*
To resume a process: **kill -25** *process id*
Use **ps -l** to identify suspended processes. Look for a 'T' in the status field.

Maintaining the Print Spooler System

Printers can keep you very busy. These are some of the tasks required to maintain efficient print spooling:

- checking print queues and printer status for possible problems
- rerouting jobs from busy print queues to other printers
- holding large print requests for execution at less busy times
- giving high-priority to urgent print requests
- taking printers off-line for repair or maintenance
- terminating selected print jobs
- loading pre-printed forms on printers

Knowing the rules of the road can make life much easier for you and your users.

The Honorable Rules of Print Spooling

A. Print requests are queued in the order submitted
B. Print requests are queued only for printers that can support their options (e.g. content type, form name, character set)
C. In the event of printer failure, printing jobs are interrupted, but not discarded.
D. Interrupted print requests, by default, restart from the beginning when resumed
E. Print requests specifying forms remain queued until an administrator mounts the form on the printer.
F. Few ever fully master SCO print spooler administration.

Essential SCO System Administration

Table 6-6:	Summary of Printer Spooler Administration Commands
Operation	**Command**
checking print queues	**lpstat -o**
checking printer status	**lpstat -p -l**
Making a request high-priority	**lp** *requestID* **-H immediate**
Resuming a print request	**lp** *requestID* **-H resume**
interrupting a printing request	**lp** *requestID* **-H hold**
holding a queued print request	**lp** *requestID* **-H hold**
checking the alert log	**mail -u lp**
moving a print job	**lpmove** *requestID printer*
moving requests between queues	**lpmove** *printer printer*
terminating the current request	**cancel** *printer*
terminating a specific request	**cancel** *requestID*
stopping printers	**reject -r** "*reason*" *printer*
	disable *printer*
restarting printers	**accept** *printer*
	enable *printer*

Changing Print Request Priorities

Print jobs normally have equal priority, and typically print in the order submitted. This can be altered with **lp -H**. Print requests prioritized as *immediate* print next. Any currently printing job must be explicitly interrupted (or complete) before an *immediate* job gets printed.

Maintaining Trusted Security

Monitoring security need not be a full-time occupation. Simply keep track of the conditions listed in Table 6-7.

Table 6-7:	Commands for Maintaining Trusted Security
Condition to Monitor	**Command/Procedure**
TCB password database integrity	**authck -avn**
	Accounts ⇨ *Check*
TCB file control database integrity	**integrity -e**
terminal lock status	*Accounts* ⇨ *Report* ⇨ *Terminal*
account lock status	*Accounts* ⇨ *Report* ⇨ *Login* ⇨ *User*
su activity	view **/usr/adm/sulog**

Chapter 6 The Art of System Administration

While **su** logging is enabled, the file **/usr/adm/sulog** logs all **su**(ADM) attempts, all **asroot**(ADM) attempts, and all attempts to login as **root**. Logging is enabled by inserting the following entry into **/etc/default/su**:
SULOG=/usr/adm/su

Automatic Monitoring of Critical TCB Files

TCB files critical to access security are checked automatically by **tcbck**(ADM), before allowing multi-user logins. If any checks fail, the system goes into single-user mode. The command will indicate which files need to be restored for safe operation.

Healthy Results

- TCB password database consistent
- TCB file control database consistent
- no reported login problems

Indications

- ⊠ `Terminal is disabled -- see Account Administrator`
- ⊠ `Account is disabled -- see Account Administrator`
- ⊠ `Cannot obtain database information on this terminal`
- ⊠ `useshell: File Control database inconsistency`
- unusual or unexpected **su** activity

Unexpected **su** activity is any recorded access that does not normally appear in the sulog. This should include all accesses outside of normal operating hours.

For access-related security error messages, see "Emergency System Access".

Recovery

- consult Table 6-8 to remedy terminal or account locking problems
- to remedy terminal database problems, run: **tcbck**
- the useshell problem surfaces when creating users; to fix run: **fixmog -i**
- to remedy unusual **su** activity, you may need to change the root password, and remove **su** capability from those who do not need it

Essential SCO System Administration

Table 6-8:	Trusted Security Recovery Commands
Function	**Command**
to repair TCB password database	**fixmog -i**
to repair TCB file control database	**authck -ay**
to repair TCB tty database	**tcbck**
to unlock terminals	Accounts ⇨ Terminal ⇨ Unlock
to unlock accounts	Accounts ⇨ User ⇨ Examine (⇨ Logins)

Maintaining User Accounts

Once created, user accounts require little maintenance. As for the users, themselves, that's another story. *[See "Supporting System Users" for details]*.

These are some of the tasks you'll perform in the service of user account maintenance:

- retiring or removing the accounts of departing users
- relocating user home directories
- locking the accounts of users on leave

Retire or Remove?

Traditionally, once a user leaves the system, the account is simply removed. Removal clears the user's password entries and group memberships. Only the files owned by the user remain. The problem is that, technically, C2 systems disallow user removal. Fortunately, for traditionalists, SCO does allow it.

Proper C2 procedure is to retire the account. All traces of the user remain, except for his or her ability to log in. This prevents the all-important UID being assigned to another user. It is consistent with the accountability requirements of trusted systems. Yet, once a user is retired, supposedly they can never come back. Fortunately, SCO provides **unretire**(ADM).

Table 6-9:	Account Maintenance Commands
Function	**Command**
to remove a user account	**/tcb/bin/rmuser** *user*
to retire a user account	**/tcb/bin/unretire -t retired** *user*
	Accounts ⇨ User ⇨ Retire
to unretire a user account	**/tcb/bin/unretire** *user*
to disable/lock an account	Accounts ⇨ User ⇨ Examine (⇨ Logins)
to move a user home directory	Accounts ⇨ User ⇨ Examine (⇨ Identity)

6-18

Chapter 6 The Art of System Administration

Supporting System Users

Users have a way of really making you feel needed. At the very least, they keep you busy. Who else, but users would:

- occasionally forget their passwords
- occasionally get locked out of their accounts
- sometimes warrant increased system privileges
- frequently need to have deleted files restored
- sometimes encounter terminal or display problems
- always need more disk space
- often encounter application limitations
- usually require training to fully utilize application software
- eventually require expanded access to application software
- sometimes desire to have additional hardware configured
- eventually require expanded access to networks

And that's just a small sample of the support that system users require. *[See table 6-10 for selected support commands]*.

Table 6-10:	Selected User Support Commands
Function	**sysadmsh Menu**
resetting user account passwords	*Accounts ⇨ User ⇨ Examine (⇨ Password)*
adjusting user authorizations	*Accounts ⇨ User ⇨ Examine (⇨ Privileges)*
adjusting user group membership	*Accounts ⇨ User ⇨ Examine (⇨ Identity)*

Customizing User Environments

User environments are replete with shell variables controlling various aspects of shell, system, and application function. Certain commands also help to initialize the user environment. Typically, these variables and commands are customized by account. You can perform some customization globally, though.

You can put global customization values in one of two login startup files.

Table 6-11:	Global Login Startup Files
File	**Shells Affected**
/etc/profile	sh, rsh, ksh, rksh
/etc/cshrc	csh

Essential SCO System Administration

User Monitoring and Communication

As users make demands upon your time, so can you demand theirs. Occasionally, you'll need to communicate important information to individual users or the entire user community.

Some of the things you may want to inform them to do include:
- closing all files due to an impending filesystem backup
- freeing disk space by removing unused or unwanted files
- logging off due to impending system shutdown
- consulting news for details of system changes

Table 6-12:	User Communication Tools
Tool	**Purpose**
mail(C)	composes, sends, and displays electronic mail
news(C)	maintains a simple local bulletin board
wall(ADM)	sends message to all user terminals
write(C)	sends message to individual user terminals
/etc/motd	holds message-of-the-day (displayed after login)
/etc/issue(F)	holds prelogin message (displayed before login)

> **/etc/motd and /etc/issue**
>
> **/etc/motd** is the system "message of the day" file. It is displayed after just prior to reading the user's home directory startup file (but after /etc/profile or /etc/cshrc). Although, it is not read if *hushlogin* is active for the user.
>
> **/etc/issue**(F) contains the message (or screen) displayed right before the login prompt. Every user sees this file before logging in.

Table 6-13 lists some of the commands that track what users are doing.

Table 6-13:	User Monitoring Tools
Tool	**Purpose**
finger(C)	lists detailed user info and idle time
w(C)	summarizes system and user activity
who(C)	lists statistics for logged-in users
whodo(C)	reports user login and process information

Chapter 6   The Art of System Administration

Ad Hoc Archival and Restore

Sometimes you simply want to extract a few files or a directory, without having to backup a whole filesystem. Yes, you can do this.

For most ad hoc archiving you'll use floppies. That's the focus here, but similar considerations apply to tape, as well.

Archive hardware can be any device with removable media. These can include:
- floppy disks (1.2MB, 1.44MB, 2.88MB)
- optical floppies *[proprietary driver needed]*
- tape (cartridge, 8mm, DAT)

> **Archival to Hard Disk**
>
> You can also create archives as hard disk files. This is ideal for transmitting archives over a network. Simply specify the pathname of a disk file, instead of an archive device. Make sure of the following:
> - that there is sufficient disk space for your archive
> - that the archive does not reside in the directory being archived.

A few rules of the desert will help to keep you on track.

The Fundamental Rules of Ad Hoc Archival
A.   Keep plenty of formatted floppies handy.
B.   Portable (character) archives are more reliably understood between systems.
C.   Determine an appropriate blocking factor.
D.   Use default blocking factors at your peril.
E.   Try to configure device defaults (in advance) to simplify commands.
F.   Whenever possible, change to the directory being archived or restored.
G.   Always inspect an archive after creating it.
H.   Archives are best restored using the initial blocking factor.
I.   Always make backup copies (just in case ...).

Now all that remains are some tips to help you successfully archive your files.

Essential SCO System Administration

Creating an Ad Hoc Archive

1. Determine the total size of the files to be archived.
   The fastest way to do this is to run: **du -s** *directory or file*
   Do this for each file or directory, then total the amounts.

2. Format a sufficient number of floppy disks.
   To format a floppy, run: **format /dev/rinstall**

> To designate a default format device, edit **/etc/default/format**.

3. Determine an appropriate blocking factor.

> **Recommended Blocking Factors**
>
> Consult Table 6-14 for recommended floppy blocking factors. For tape use the value specified by the vendor. If none is specified, optimally use any value that divides the kernel parameter, CTBUF.
>
> Note that blocking factors tend to be even numbers. This is consistent with the size of a block (512 bytes). Two blocks are 1KB (filesystem block size).

4. Change to the directory being archived.
5. Insert the first floppy to written.
6. Create the archive *[consult table 6-16 for appropriate commands]*.

> Always use relative instead of absolute pathnames (e.g. **./file**, **./u/file**, **./u/***).

7. Inspect the archive to verify readability *[see Table 6-17]*.
8. Label the archive with archive type, blocking factor, title, and date.

Table 6-14: Floppy Disk Media Comparison

				Recommended Blocking Factor	
Capacity	**Form**	**Sectors/Track**	**Tracks**	**With tar**	**With cpio/pax**
360KB	5.25"	9	40	18	18
720KB	3.5"	9	80	18	18
1.2MB	5.25"	15	80	10	30
1.44MB	3.5"	18	80	18	36
2.88MB	3.5"	36	80	18	72

6-22

Chapter 6 The Art of System Administration

Table 6-15:	Comparison of SCO Archive Utilities					
Attribute	**tar**	**cpio**	**pax**	**ptar**	**pcpio**	**copy**
simple to use	yes	no	yes	yes	no	yes
accepts source pathname	yes	no	yes	yes	no	yes
default archive supported	yes	no	no	yes	no	no
sensibly handles links	yes	no	yes	yes	yes	yes
copies each separate link	no	yes	no	no	no	no
retains symbolic links	no	yes	yes	yes	yes	no
backs up empty directories	no	yes	yes	yes	yes	yes
backs up special files	no	yes	yes	yes	yes	yes
space efficiency	fair	fair	good	fair	good	fair
can append or update	yes	no	yes	yes	no	yes
accepts shell wildcards	no	yes	yes	no	yes	yes
error recovery on read	no	yes	yes	no	yes	yes
detects blocking factor	yes	no	yes	yes	yes	--
detects end of medium	no	no	yes	no	no	yes
multiple volumes supported	yes	yes	yes	no	no	no
tape supported	yes	yes	yes	yes	yes	no
recognized by **dtype**(C)	yes	yes	no	no	yes	yes
special notes	①		②	③		④

① default file is **/etc/default/tar**
② can archive in ptar or pcpio format
③ default is TAPE= or **/dev/fd096**
④ target must be a mounted filesystem

Formatting Floppies for Use with copy(C)

The **copy**(C) command be used to archive files on mounted, filesystem-formatted floppies. To put a blank filesystem on a floppy, first format the floppy, then impose a blank filesystem onto it. Use the command below.

   mkdev fd

Select the media type, then select **1** (Filesystem).

Notes on the Following Command Tables

Whenever two command lines are listed (in Tables 6-16, 6-17, and 6-18), the first uses the applicable defaults. The second explicitly specifies the essential options. When only one command line is listed, it specifies the most essential command options. Special notes include:

① uses the default device (archive=...) in **/etc/default/tar**.
② uses the device defined as TAPE=... in the environment
   /dev/fd0135ds18 refers to the high-density 3.5" floppy on drive 0

Essential SCO System Administration

Table 6-16: Sample Commands to Archive Current Directory to /dev/fd0135ds18

Format	Archive Commands	
tar(C)	tar cv .	①
	tar cnbkfv 18 1440 /dev/rfd0135ds18	
cpio(C)	find . -print | cpio -oBcv -K 1440 -O/dev/fd0/fd0ds18	
	... | cpio -ocv -C 9216 -K 1440 -O/dev/fd0135ds18	
pax(C)	pax -w -v -f /dev/fd0135ds18 .	
	pax -w -v -b 9k -f /dev/fd0135ds18 .	
pcpio(C)	find . -print | pcpio -ocv > /dev/fd0135ds18	
ptar(C)	ptar -cv .	②
	ptar -cbfv 18 /dev/fd0135ds18 .	
copy(C)	mount /dev/fd0135ds18 /mnt ; copy -romv . /mnt ; umount /mnt	

Table 6-17: Sample Commands to Inspect Archive on /dev/fd0135ds18

Format	Archive Commands	
tar(C)	tar tv	①
	tar tfv /dev/rfd0135ds18	
cpio(C)	cpio -itv -I/dev/fd0/fd0ds18	
	cpio -itv -C 9216 -I/dev/fd0135ds18	
pax(C)	pax -v -f /dev/fd0135ds18	
pcpio(C)	pcpio -itv < /dev/fd0135ds18	
ptar(C)	ptar -tv	②
	ptar -tfv /dev/fd0135ds18	
copy(C)	mount /dev/fd0135ds18 /mnt ; l -R /mnt ; umount /mnt	

Table 6-18: Sample Commands to Restore Archive on /dev/fd0135ds18 to the Current Directory

Format	Archive Commands	
tar(C)	tar xv	①
	tar xfv /dev/rfd0135ds18	
cpio(C)	cpio -iBcdmukv -O/dev/fd0/fd0ds18	
	cpio -icdmuv -C 9216 -O/dev/fd0135ds18	
pax(C)	pax -r -v -f /dev/fd0135ds18	
pcpio(C)	pcpio -icdmuv < /dev/fd0135ds18	
ptar(C)	ptar -xv	②
	ptar -xfv /dev/fd0135ds18	
copy(C)	mount /dev/fd0135ds18 /mnt ; copy -romv /mnt . ; umount /mnt	

Restoring Part of an Archive

Except for **tar**(C), parts of an archive can be restored using shell wildcard patterns. Separate patterns with spaces. *Remember to quote all patterns!*

Chapter 6   The Art of System Administration

Emergency System Recovery

The day that you've dreaded has finally arrived. Your system is corrupted and you can't log in. What are you going to do? I hope you heeded the warnings to make root/boot floppies and a system backup! *[See SR2.9 to make them].*

 For security problems see "Emergency System Access".

Indications

- ✉ `No OS`
- ✉ `/boot not found`
  `Stage 1 boot failure: error loading /boot`
- ✉ `EEEEEEEEE....`
- `system hangs unexpectedly`

Recovery

- "No OS" indicates that the bootstrap files are corrupted or missing. *[Consult SR6.7 to restore the bootstrap files].*
- If /boot is corrupted, you'll need to replace it. *[Consult SR6.8 for details].*
- A series of **E**s indicates a corrupted or missing **masterboot**. *[Consult SR6.9 to replace **masterboot**].*
- System hangs suggest that either there is a hardware problem or that one or more system files are corrupt. The solution may be to restore the root filesystem. *[See SR6.10 for instructions].*

<u>Quick Recipe SR6.7</u>   **Restoring the System Bootstrap**

The bootstrap files are low-level binaries that load the SCO boot program, /boot.

1. Reboot the system from the root/boot floppy set.
2. At the boot prompt press ENTER.
   The shell "#" prompt follows the initial startup messages.
3. Run: **cp /etc/hdboot0 /dev/hd0a**
              dd if=/etc/hdboot1 of=/dev/hd0a seek=2
              haltsys
4. Eject the floppy, then reboot the system.

Essential SCO System Administration

Quick Recipe SR6.8   Restoring a Corrupted /boot

The SCO boot program, /boot, initializes the system and loads the kernel.

1. Reboot the system from the root/boot floppy set.
2. At the boot prompt, type: **hd(40)unix**
   This loads the SCO kernel from the hard disk.
3. Supply the root password to enter single-user mode.
4. Run:
            mount /dev/install /mnt
            cp /mnt/boot /
            umount /mnt

   This mounts the boot floppy, copies /boot to the hard disk, then unmounts the boot floppy.
5. Eject the floppy, then run: **haltsys**
6. Reboot the system from the hard disk.

Quick Recipe SR6.9   Restoring masterboot

The **masterboot** program manages the partition table, and executes the bootstrap on the active partition.

1. Reboot the system from the root/boot floppy set.
2. At the boot prompt press ENTER. Wait for the "#" prompt.
3. Run:
            cp /etc/masterboot /dev/hd00
            haltsys
4. Eject the floppy, then reboot the system.

Quick Recipe SR6.10   Restoring the Root Filesystem

The bootstrap files are low-level binaries that load the SCO boot program, **/boot**.

1. Reboot the system from the root/boot floppy set.
2. At the boot prompt press ENTER. A "#" prompt follows the startup messages.
3. Initialize the hard disk root filesystem.
   Run:
            fsck -s -y /dev/hd0root
            mount /dev/hd0root /mnt
            cd /mnt
            rm -rf .

Chapter 6 The Art of System Administration

☞
> If any of the above commands fails, you may need to rebuild the root filesystem *[see SR6.11]*.

4. Place your root filesystem backup in the tape drive.
5. If applicable, initialize the tape:
   tape load
   tape rewind
   tape reset
6. Restore the root filesystem backup to disk.
   Run: **cpio -icBudv -I/dev/rct0**

☞
> If restoring from a mini-cartridge, use **/dev/rctmini**, instead.

   When the restore completes, the shell prompt returns.
7. To wrap up, run:
   cd /
   umount /mnt
   haltsys
8. Eject the floppy, then reboot the system.

Quick Recipe SR6.11   Recreating the Root Filesystem

If the root filesystem becomes unrecognizable, it will need to be recreated.

You'll need your N1 and N2 installation floppies and distribution media.

1. Reboot the system from the N1 installation floppy.
2. At the boot prompt, type: **restart**
3. Proceed through the hard disk initialization, as follows:
   - select the preserve installation option (or respond "yes" when asked to preserve existing filesystems)
   - reallocate root filesystem and swap space using values from your log
   - when the system starts reading from the tape or CD-ROM (or asks for the M1 floppy), press DEL to abort.

   Wait for the "Safe to Power Off" message.
4. Insert the boot floppy from your root/boot floppy set.
5. At the boot prompt, press ENTER. Wait for the "#" prompt.
6. With the exception noted below, continue from step (3) of SR6.10.

☞
> Replace: **rm -rf .**
> with: **rm -rf inst***

6-27

Essential SCO System Administration

Emergency System Access

It can be a cold day, indeed, when you are denied system access due to corruption in the TCB trusted security database. Even so, there are strategies you can pursue to restore access.

> **Typical Causes of TCB Database Corruption**
>
> - a privileged user has tampered with a file in TCB file control database
> - a privileged user has edited **/etc/passwd**, **/etc/group**, or the protected password database
> - a TCB file is missing or has been deleted
> - the system crashed (or halted) with TCB files in an inconsistent state
> - a bad binary has trashed disk buffers and corrupted the TCB

Indications

- ✉ The security databases are corrupt. However, login at terminal tty*XX* is allowed.
- ✉ Account is disabled, but console login is allowed
- ✉ Terminal is disabled, but root login is allowed
- ✉ Can't rewrite terminal control entry for tty
- ✉ Cannot obtain database information on this terminal
- ✉ Authorization name file could not be allocated due to: cannot open
- can log in as root, but lack root authorization
- all login accesses (even root) repeatedly denied

Recovery

- once logged in on the OVERRIDE terminal (usually **tty01**), you can fix most security database corruption by running the commands in Table 6-8
- to resolve root login problems, log in on the OVERRIDE terminal, then apply the appropriate command from Table 6-8
- remedy a bad terminal control entry by restoring **/etc/auth/systems/ttys** from your root filesystem backup; *[consult SR6.6 for instructions]*
- unavailable terminal database information is fixed by running: **tcbck**
- restore a bad authorization name file, **/etc/auth/system/authorize**, from a root filesystem backup
- to remedy a loss of root authorization, run: **su root** then run the commands in Table 6-8
- if unable to enter single-user mode to remedy total user lockout, see SR6.12

Chapter 6   The Art of System Administration

Quick Recipe SR6.12   **Emergency System Access**

Use this procedure if all other attempts fail to resolve your system access problems.

This procedure requires a root/boot floppy set.

1. Reboot your system from the root/boot floppy set.
2. At the boot prompt, press ENTER. Wait for the "#" prompt.
3. Run:
   fsck -s /dev/hd0root
   mount /dev/hd0root /mnt
   /mnt/bin/chroot /mnt/ /bin/su root -c sh

   This creates a subshell that makes you **root** on your hard disk, just as if you had logged in.
4. Run any required commands to remedy the problem at hand.
5. To wrap up, run:
   exit
   umount /mnt
   haltsys
6. Eject the floppy and reboot from the hard disk.

Fixing Trusted Security Problems

Single-user mode if the preferred place to remedy TCB trusted security problems. It is ideal because few trusted security mechanisms are enabled before entering multiuser mode.

There are two files, in particular, that you may want to remove after making changes to the password file, the group file, or any other file in the file control database (**/etc/auth/system/files**). These are:

　　　　　　pw_id_map　　　　　　　　　**gr_id_map**

They both reside in **/etc/auth/system**. Both are rebuilt automatically when entering multiuser mode. In multiuser mode, these are the key files that the system uses to detect account or password tampering.

Essential SCO System Administration

Selected Hardware Troubleshooting

> This section may not be appropriate for novice system administrators. the presentation is terse, because the solutions presented tend to be technically obscure. Unfortunately, such is the nature of hardware troubleshooting.

Although most hardware problems can be avoided through proper installation and configuration, inevitably some difficulties may occur. This section deals with the most troublesome hardware problems in the current version.

Selected Problems with Disks

Here are two troublesome problems that affect hard disks.

fdisk Limits SCO Partitions to 2GB

Even though SCO now supports disks up to 56GB, this problem limits maximum accessible capacity to 8GB. There is a revised fdisk(ADM) available from SCO Support to remedy this problem.

Disk Buffers Flush Every Minute

This becomes a problem when the BDFLUSHR kernel parameter is set to more than 60 seconds. It is caused by /etc/inittab being read every minute. The fix is to increase the value of the SLEEPTIME parameter in /etc/default/boot from 60 to a high value like 10000. Apparently SLEEPTIME controls flushing behavior independently of BDFLUSHR.

Selected Problems with Printers

Parallel printers have been a major headache for SCO since day one. For all of the revised parallel device drivers over the years, none has successfully solved all the problems. The main problem symptoms are listed below.

- printer is slow or erratic
- printer is deselecting itself after printing a full line of data
- jobs are hanging in the spooler and refuse to print
- printout is missing characters

Chapter 6   The Art of System Administration

Slow or Erratic Parallel Printing

Slow or erratic printing is usually associated with cheap parallel adapters that do not properly generate interrupts. These may work well under DOS, which uses polling. One solution is to set up printer polling in SCO. This will force the system to periodically poll the printer to determine if more characters can be sent. As you might expect, overall system response can suffer when polling is enabled. [See SR6.13 to set up printer polling].

Quick Recipe SR6.13   **Setting Up Printer Polling**

Some parallel print adapters do not properly generate interrupts. Polling may improve printer performance.

1. Shutdown to single-user mode: **shutdown su**
2. Determine the device file of the slow printer.
3. Edit **/etc/conf/node.d/pa** to include one of the following lines.

   (for lp0)   pa lp0p c 64 bin bin 600
   (for lp1)   pa lp1p c 65 bin bin 600
   (for lp2)   pa lp2p c 66 bin bin 600

4. Reset the configuration. Run: **cd /etc/conf/cf.d**
   touch /etc/.new_unix
   ../bin/idmkenv

   When asked to rebuild the kernel environment, respond **Y**.

5. Enter: **haltsys**

   and reboot the system.

6. Reconfigure the printer to use the new polling device: **mkdev lp**

If the printer seems to be selecting and deselecting itself, you can change the value of the MODE_SELECT kernel parameter. This will eliminate the delays incurred by checking the printer mode. Enter the command below, then relink and reboot the kernel.

   cd /etc/conf/cf.d ; ../bin/idtune MODE_SELECT 0

If neither of these problems seems to work, there could be timing issues. This is especially common with the faster 486 and Pentium processors. In that case, you may need to procure the latest parallel printer QFS from SCO *[see Appendix C]*.

Essential SCO System Administration

Slow PostScript Printing

Although slow PostScript printing may be associated with parallel port problems, it is more likely that a simple fix to the default PostScript filter will remedy the problem.

Quick Recipe SR6.14   **Fixing the PostScript Filter**

By default, the Postscript filter tries to use the ISO 8859 international character set. This has to be downloaded to the printer. But because, downloaded fonts tend to create large output files, it is much faster to use an internal printer font like Courier.

1. Change directory to: **/usr/spool/lp/bin**
2. Edit **text2post** as follows:
   a) insert a comment character '#' before the following line:

                         cat /usr/spool/lp/bin/iso8859.ps

   b) replace all occurrences of **ISO8859** with **Courier**
3. Save the file and exit.

Chapter 6   The Art of System Administration

Selected Problems with Mice

The mouse problem addressed here concerns configuring multiple mice of the same type.

Errors Configuring Multiple Mice of the Same Type

This problem is caused by a bug in the mouse configuration procedure. The patch to remedy the problem is presented in SR6.15.

Quick Recipe SR6.15   **Patching the Mouse Configuration Code**

1. Excepting the first instance, deconfigure any extra mice of the same type.
   Run: mkdev mouse
2. Edit /usr/lib/mkdev/mouse as follows:
   - find the line starting with: **LASTKEY=**
   - on that line only, replace   **$THISKEY**   with   **"^$THISKEY[]"**
     (all characters are significant)
   - on the same line, between [and],
     insert these three characters: SPACE TAB UNDERSCORE
     (the third character is '_')

   The resulting line should look like:

   | LASTKEY=`grep "$THISKEY[_]" $DEVFILE | awk .... |

3. Save and exit the file.
4. Reconfigure the extra mice.

Chapter 6   The Art of System Administration

Performance Notes

Lynn: *Just look at that CPU utilization curve! And what incredible network throughput! As for the disks, I've never seen such low seek latency! Tony, its enough to make you proud. We've done a really good job here.*

Tony: *[cautiously] Lynn, I really wouldn't get too excited about those results. At least not yet. It's probably going to take a good four weeks before we'll have an accurate reading on these performance hacks.*

Lynn: *Hacks? Hacks, Tony!? I'll have you know that this has been the result of long, hard hours of painstaking analysis and tuning. This is science at its best... Uh ohh! What's happening to my beautiful numbers? Why is the disk making that crazy noise? Tony, who's killing my system?!*

Tony: *Umm Lynn? I hate to break the bad news, but it was the second user logging in. ... There, there. Here, take my hanky. It's not so bad. Just one of those days. Actually, I was thinking we should take a break and order out for some beer and pizza. It looks like we might be here a while.*

 | For an excellent, comprehensive presentation of SCO system performance tuning strategies, you are strongly advised to consult the PTR Prentice-Hall book, *SCO Performance Tuning Handbook*, by Gina Miscovich and David Simons.

It's important, it's essential, and, also a black art, this ... performance tuning.

Exactly which factors are critical to tune? Which tuning strategies give the biggest bang for the buck? Perhaps it might be better to ask which system activities are most expensive to support in terms of compute resources, then work backwards. Let's see...

Chapter 6   The Art of System Administration

Here's a list of some of the activities placing the greatest load on SCO systems.

- video processing   *very resource costly*
- serial interrupt processing   *very resource costly*
- disk paging   *moderately resource costly*
- swapping   *depends on RAM size*
- device polling   *very resource costly when used*
- tight looping   *extremely resource costly when active*
- inbound network processing   *very resource costly*
- directory searches   *quite resource costly*
- data accesses   *extremely resource costly*

Table 6-19:   Managing Resource-intensive Activities

Costly System Activity	Management Solution
Video processing	high speed local data buses
Serial interrupt processing (terminals, modems, streams)	intelligent serial adapters
disk paging	caching processors and motherboards fast disks, **data organization**
swapping	ample RAM
device polling	dedicated co-processors
tight looping	**vigilant detection and elimination**
inbound network processing	dedicated co-processors and fast DMA
directory searches	**intelligent configuration**
data accesses	SRAM caching of RAM data, **RAM caching of disk data**, fast disks, **data organization**

RAID and Fast Hard Disks

Hard disks are possibly one of the prime bottlenecks on Intel-based systems. Speed is paramount as far as disks are concerned. But given the technical limits to physical disk speed, other techniques must be used to speed up disk data access. One answer is RAID (redundant arrays of inexpensive disks). RAID uses parallelism to yield very high disk data access rates.

For example, by spreading data across 10 multiple disks, you can now access 10 times the amount of data during (the time of) a single disk access.

There are many levels of RAID, each offering different uses for the extra hard disks in the array.

As you may be able to tell from Table 6-19, there are reasonable hardware solutions to most of the costly activities on the system. The ones that remain we address here.

> harddisk paging
> tight looping
> directory searches
> data accesses

Optimizing Disk Paging and Data Access

Disk paging and data access both depend on fast disks and optimal data organization. Optimizing your filesystems *[see Chapter 5]*, while not glamorous, can yield significant performance benefits. The result is shorter *seek latency* (the time it takes to find the next disk data block).

Caching

The other aspect that must be addressed is *caching*. The whole intent of caching is to minimize the access time to data. As Table 6-20 demonstrates, there is a significant speed increase as you move up the memory ladder. Unfortunately, the cost of faster memory greatly outpaces the speed advantage.

Table 6-20:	Comparison of Memory Speeds		
Memory type	**Access Speed**	**Clock Cycles**	**Relative Speed**
processor register memory	5-10ns	1	24-120
SRAM cache	20-25ns	2	6-12
DRAM (main memory)	50-80ns	6	1
hard disk (virtual memory)	9000-15000ns (9-15ms)		.002

The greatest speed gain is realized from moving data from disk to DRAM (or RAM). Hardware solutions such as caching disk controllers can be mighty tempting, but since they use DRAM as their cache medium, you might be just as well off using SCO's disk buffer caching facility.

Chapter 6   The Art of System Administration

The SCO Disk Buffer Cache

SCO allocates a fixed amount of RAM as a disk buffer cache to hold data blocks read in from the hard disk. The kernel uses a read-ahead algorithm to preload disk blocks into the cache. Data is also written to blocks in the disk cache. The kernel block flushing process, **bdflush**, makes sure that these blocks eventually get physically written to the hard disk. You'll need to monitor the utilization of these buffers regularly to maintain good performance.

Run the following command to monitor disk buffer statistics: **sar -b**

The relevant kernel parameters affecting disk caching are listed in Table 6-21.

Table 6-21:			Tunable Parameters Affecting the Disk Buffer Cache
Parameter	**Default**	**Min/Max**	**Function**
NBUF	0 +	0/65536	number of 1K disk buffers
MAXBUF	600	0/65536	upper limit on NBUF
NHBUF	256	32/131072	number of hash buckets for buffer cache
NMPBUF	0	0/100	number of 16K AFS cluster buffers
NAUTOUP	10	0/60	buffer age (in seconds) eligible for flushing
BDFLUSHR	30	1/300	frequency (in seconds) that bdflush runs
SLEEPTIME *	60	0/65536	frequency of filesystem syncs
	+	by default, takes the value of MAXBUF	
	*	SLEEPTIME is a parameter in **/etc/default/boot**	

> NMPBUF is most useful when there is heavy disk access from lots of users. Optimally, the kernel reads an entire filesystem cluster per disk access.
>
> BDFLUSHR is the key flush control parameter affecting performance. The more often **bdflushr** runs, the more time is consumed searching for eligible buffers to write to disk.

> **Tight Looping**
>
> This is something to eliminate, rather than tolerate. At the code level, most kernel and processors can detect and recover from tight looping.
>
> At the process level, this manifests as a runaway process. Once detected, you'll want to eliminate this as soon as possible.

6-37

Essential SCO System Administration

Optimizing Directory Searches

High-speed hardware aside, directory search optimization could be where the greatest performance improvement is realized.

> A typical UNIX system spends 15-25% of its processing resources searching directories and resolving pathnames. Each component of the pathname may require a disk access to get the inode and another to get the directory file. Each directory file is searched sequentially for the next component of the pathname.

Simply by making directory searches more efficient, you can significantly boost system performance. So what does an efficient directory structure look like?

- directories have minimal size
- frequently accessed subdirectories appear first in the directory table
- frequently accessed files immediately follow the directories

> You can use **cpio -pld** and **link**(ADM) to reconstruct directories. The general procedure is to create a new directory and link in the desired entries from the target directory. Finally you remove the target directory, then rename the new directory with the original directory's name.

The Filename Lookup Cache

Another way to shorten directory searches is to cache the directory inodes of frequently accessed pathnames. This is what the file name lookup (**namei**) cache does. The **namei** cache hashes the inode numbers so that pathname searches can take place almost entirely in RAM rather then using the much slower disk.

Table 6-22:	Tunable Parameters Affecting the File Name Lookup Cache		
Parameter	Default	Min/Max	Function
S5CACHEENTS	256	1/4096	number of **namei** cache entries
S5HASHQS	61	1/8191	size of the hash table used with the cache
S5OFBIAS	8	1/256	controls search time for free cache entries

> Recommended starting point for S5CACHEENTS is 3 * NINODE.

Appendix A

List of Supplemental Resources for SCO Systems

Periodicals

SCO World Magazine   monthly independent magazine of SCO products, reviews, tips, and commentary

   SCO World
   PO Box 59662
   Boulder, CO 80322-9662
   (303) 447-9330
   (800) 879-3358 [toll-free North America]
 (415) 941-1504 [fax]

DISCOVER SCO   quarterly newsletter of SCO-related news and activities

   contact: Lesley MacDonald
   email: discoversco@sco.com

[for mailing address and phone numbers see SCO U.S. listing below]

Shareware

SCO Skunkware 2.0   CD-ROM of entertainment, tools, images, and new technology

   contact: Dion L. Johnson
   email: dionj@sco.com

[for mailing address and phone numbers see SCO U.S. listing below]

Online Resources

Intenet Newsgroups

biz.sco.announce	SCO and SCO Developer product announcements
biz.sco.general	questions, answers, and comments on SCO products
biz.sco.opendesktop	technical questions and answers relevant to Open Desktop
biz.sco.wserver	questions, answers, etc. on the SCO widget server
biz.sco.magazine	online interaction with SCO World magazine readers, writers, publishers, and editors
biz.sco.binaries	binaries compiled from SCO-compatible source code
biz.sco.sources	UNIX source code for useful programs modified to compile and run on SCO systems

Compuserve Discussion Group

SCO Forum   questions, answers, and comments on SCO products

contact: Compuserve
(604) 457-0802
(800) 848-8199 [toll-free North America]

Mailing Lists

scoann-request@xenitec.on.ca	mailing list for biz.sco.announce
scogen-request@xenitec.on.ca	mailing list for biz.sco.general
scoodt-request@xenitec.on.ca	mailing list for biz.sco.opendesktop
scowsr-request@xenitec.on.ca	mailing list for biz.sco.wserver
scomag-request@xenitec.on.ca	mailing list for biz.sco.magazine

☞ To subscribe, mail the following line to the relevant address above:
Add: *your login name @ your site domain*

Appendix A: List of Supplemental Resources for SCO Systems

Bulletin Boards and Software Archives

SCO BBS ftp: ftp ftp.sco.com
   => **get info**

   uucp: uucp:sosco!/usr/spool/uucppublic/info   your file
   [see appendix B for dialup details]

SCO World Wide Web   web address: http://www.sco.com

Anomaly Archives ftp: ftp ftp.anomaly.sbs.com (155.212.2.2)
   => **get SOFTLIST**

   uucp: uucp anomaly!/usr/spool/uucppublic/ls-lR *file*
   (401) 455 0347   2400-19200   Telebit Trailblazer Plus
   (401) 331-3706   300-9600   Hayes-compatible
   site name: **anomaly**
   login: **xxcp**
   password: **xenix**

Xenitec Archives ftp: ftp xenitec.xenitec.on.ca (192.75.213.1)
   => **get /archive/pub/index**

   uucp: uucp xenitec!/archie/pub/index   your file
   (519) 743-5247   2400-19200   Telebit Trailblazer Plus
   (519) 743-4697   2400   Hayes-compatible
   site name: **xenitec**
   login: **nncp**
   password: **fall89**

Celestial Archive ftp: ftp ftp.celestial.com   (192.136.111.2)

biz.sco.* Archive ftp: ftp vanbc.wimsey.ba.ca (192/48.234.1)

A-3

Essential SCO System Administration

> **Connecting to Anonymous ftp Sites**
>
> Use the listed **ftp**(TC) command to establish the connection. *[ftp is SCO TCP/IP, a component of Open Server and Open Desktop].*
>
>   use for login name: ftp
>   use for password: *your name @ your site*
>
> Sample **ftp** commands:
>
> | | | |
> |---|---|---|
> | **help** | - | lists available commands |
> | **help** *command* | - | lists format and function of command |
> | **dir** | - | lists table of files and directories |
> | **cd** <u>directory</u> | - | changes directories on the remote system |
> | **lcd** directory | - | changes directories on the local system |
> | **bin** | - | puts ftp into binary transfer mode |
> | **get** *file* | - | downloads file to your system |
> | **mget** *files* | - | downloads files to your system |
> | **quit** | - | terminates the ftp phone commnection. |

> **Connecting to Anonymous uucp Sites**
>
> To connect to an anonymous **uucp** site, you must add appropriate entries to the uucp **Systems** and **Permissions** files. You'll need the telephone number, baud rate, login, and login password to create these entries.
>
> To create the **Systems** entry consult *Configuring Outbound Modem Dialing* in Chapter 5. You'll need to add a *login script*. It may be easiest to uncomment and modify the entry for *samplesite* in **Systems**. If so, substitute the remote system's login name for "uucp", and the remote password for "frogin".
>
> To quickly create a **Permissions** entry, follow the steps below.
>
> 1. Copy the 5-line entry that begins:
>
>   `MACHINE=samplesite     LOGNAME=uucp`
>
> 2. Change "samplesite" to the name of the remote system;
>   change "uucp" to the login name listed for the remote system
>
> 3. Save the file and exit.
>
> You will now be able to receive files in **/usr/tmp** or **/usr/spool/uucppublic**.

A-4

Appendix A: List of Supplemental Resources for SCO Systems

SCO Resource Products

- SCO Directory [Windows version]   directory of 3000+ products and vendors
- SCO Hardware Compatibility Guide   catalog of compatible hardware
- SCO Price and Availability Guide   ordering and background information on SCO products
- SCO Support Online Service (SOS)   online access to the BBS and the information tools (IT) database
- SCO Support Library (SSL)   SOS information on CD-ROM
- *other SCO support products*

SCO Addresses

The Santa Cruz Operation, Inc.
400 Encinal St.
Santa Cruz, CA 95061-1900
    (408) 425-7222
    (800) 726-8649 [toll-free North America]
    (408) 458-4227 [fax]
    email: info@sco.com   uunet!sco!info

The Santa Cruz Operation, Ltd.
Croxley Centre, Hatters Lane
Watford WD1 8YN   United Kingdom
    +44 923 816344
    +44 923 813808 [fax]
    TELEX: 917372 SCOLON G
    email: info@sco.com   uknet!sco!info

The Santa Cruz Operation (Asia), Ltd.
04-01A Inchcape House
450-452 Alexandra Road
Singapore 0511
    +65 471 2221
    +65 471 2223 [fax]

Appendix B
SCO Online Support BBS Access

Access via ftp: **ftp ftp.sco.com**

☞
> For login, use: **ftp**
> For password, use: *your email address*

To get information on down-loadable files, enter the commands below:

```
get info info.sos
get SLS/info info.sls
get EFS/info info.efs
get TLS/info info.tls
quit
```

Access via uucp:
     uucp *SCO!*/usr/spool/uucppublic/info info.sos
     uucp *SCO!*/usr/spool/uucppublic/SLS/info /tmp/info.sls
     uucp *SCO!*/usr/spool/uucppublic/EFS/info /tmp/info.efs
     uucp *SCO!*/usr/spool/uucppublic/TLS/info /tmp/info.tls

where *SCO* is **sosco** or **scolon**

☞
> **Setting up uucp for SCO Access**
>
> The uucp entries for *sosco* (North America, Latin America, Asia, Pacific Rim) and *scolon* (Europe, Middle East, Africa) already exist in the **Systems** file. These entries are for 2400 baud connections. Consult Table B-1 for phone numbers to support higher speed connections.
>
> An entry for sosco exists in **Permissions**. To add scolon to **Permissions**:
>
> 1. edit **/usr/lib/uucp/Permissions**
> 2. find the entry starting with: **MACHINE=sosco**
> 3. change **MACHINE=sosco** to **MACHINE=sosco:scolon**
> 4. save and close the file

Table B-1: SCO Phone Numbers for uucp Connections

System	Baud	Phone Number	Answering Modem
sosco	9600	(408) 427-4470	Hayes V Series 9600
	9600	(408) 425-3502	Telebit 1500 V.32
	9600-19200	(408) 429-1786	Telebit Trailblazer Plus
scolon	9600	+44 923 210911	Dowty Trailblazer
	9600	+44 923 222681	Miracom V.32

B-1

Appendix C:
Relevant SCO Software Supplements

The tables below list the key SCO software supplements that apply to SCO UNIX Version 4.2 and Open Desktop/Open Server Release 3.0.

The main supplement categories are listed below:

- Support Level Supplements (SLS) — *fixits, updates*
- Extended Feature Supplements (EFS) — *improved product components*
- Quick Fix Supplements (QFS) — *unsupported quick fixes*
- Technical Library Supplements (TLS) — *unsupported technical and miscellaneous code*

 The supplements listed below can either be ordered from SCO or they can be down-loaded onto your system. See Appendix B for details on connecting to the host SCO BBSs.

Table C-1:	Relevant Support Level Supplements (SLS)
uod368a: Security Supplement	new **passwd** code; fixes problems with account locks and users with **auth** capability
uod369b: Console Keyboard Supplement	new console keyboard drivers; fixes stuck CTRL and ALT keys, hung keyboards
uod374a: CD-ROM Executable SLS	allows execution of CD-ROM binaries; removes trailing dot from CD-ROM filenames
uod376a: Enhanced SCSI Tape Drivers	supports variable tape block length support; and skipping multiple file marks
uod381a: AIO Driver Enhancements	fixes problems with aio driver under heavy load
uod383a: IBM Hardware Supplement	supports IBM SCSI-2 Fast Wide Adapter/A host adapter, new IBM SCSI tape drivers
oda377a: Security Enhancement SLS	fixes problems where non-root users can become root via certain utilities

Table C-2:	Relevant Extended Feature Supplements (EFS)
EFS140:	Advanced Hardware Supplement 3.3 (3.5" disk image)
EFS141:	Advanced Hardware Supplement 3.3 (5.25" disk image)
EFS???:	Advanced Hardware Supplement 3.4 (3.5" disk image)

Essential SCO System Administration

Table C-3: Selected Quick Fix Supplements (QFS)

QFS21:	New **ksh** binary	new XPG-compliant ksh
QFS30:	New parallel driver	fixes some printing problems on fast machines
QFS35:	New parallel driver	fixes some slow printing on IBM port hardware
QFS39:	New shared mem driver	allows multiple large shared memory segments
QFS44:	New **mscreen** binary	fixes a flow control problem
QFS46:	New **mapkey** binary	works correctly with certain X clients
QFS112:	New time binaries	prevents time from going backwards
QFS136:	New **login** binary	fixes problem with OVERRIDE device
QFS137:	New DOS driver	fixes problem with DOS partitions with more than 32767 files
QFS143:	NGROUPS enhancement	enables up to 128 supplemental groups
QFS148:	keyboard mouse	new driver fixes selected mouse problems
QFS150:	New floppy driver	supports FIFO on devices with Intel 82077/8477 chip
QFS157:	New **uucp** binary	fixes cu and uucp to support all baud rates between B50 and B38400
QFS159:	New parallel driver	fixes certain types of slow printing problems
QFS160:	New **init** binary	allows init to fork more than 400 processes
QFS163:	New SCSI tape driver	enhancements and fixes to (SLS) UOD376B

Table C-4: Selected Technical Library Supplements (TLS)

TLS018	system trace and monitor utilities
TLS029	SCO Directory - 1994 edition
TLS035	Widget Server and Tool Command Language
TLS044	improved PostScript printer driver
TLS045	Lynx character-mode browser for the Internet (like Mosaic)
TLS047	BSD-style dump/restore
TLS059	**nwho** command - extended **who**

Index

CD-ROM
  configuration and mounting 5-67
CMOS
  configuration 5-27 5-29
  recommended settings 5-28
DCE *See* Data communications
DMA
  defaults 5-15
  defined 5-11
DCE *See* Data communications
DTE *See* Data communications
EUID and EGID 5-112
HCR *See* Hardware configuration report
IRQ
  conflicts 5-13
  defaults 5-13
  defined 5-11
LUID 5-104
LUID 5-114
MS-DOS
  SCO command mapping 1-26
  creating a partition 2-16
  differences from SCO 1-20 1-26
  port mappings 1-25
Permissions *See* **uucp, Permissions** file
RAM
  caching 6-36
  controller, defined 5-11
  maximum supported 4-17
  shadow, defined 5-28
  speed 6-36
ROM
  shadow, defined 5-28
ROM BIOS
  extensions 5-28

Essential SCO System Administration

SCO
    cancel key   1-23
    command line features   1-19
    differences from MS-DOS   1-20, 1-26
    disk allocation guidelines   2-11
    filenames   1-22, 1-23
    required system resources   2-11
    software, packages   3-8, 3-9
    software, removal   3-7
    software, supplemental   3-14
    supported hardware   2-10, 2-14
SCO shell   *See* **scosh**
SCSI   2-9
    CD-ROM, device names   4-9
    LUN   5-16
    adapter   *See* SCSI adapter
    cabling and termination   5-17
    configuration file   4-9, 5-21
    hard disk, as boot disk   5-27
    hard disk, automatic write/read remapping   5-34
    hard disk, badtracking   5-34
    overview   5-16, 5-18
    peripheral, configuration   5-20
    tape, device names   4-9
    tape, drive numbers   4-9
    target ID   5-16
SCSI adapter
    configuration   5-19
    maximum supported   5-19
    supported   5-20
SUID and SGID   5-112, 5-113
UID   *See* Account, UID
Account   1-11
    UID, determination   3-22
    UID, ranges   3-21, 4-18
    backup user creation   5-116
    creation   3-22
    creation, defaults   4-18
    creation, recommendations   5-124
    environment configuration   5-120, 5-123
    home directory   4-18
    list   4-18

Index

Account [continued]
  logins, idle   4-26
  mailbox, location   4-23, 5-121
  mailboxes   3-21
  maintenance   6-18
  monitoring   4-18
  profile, display   4-18
  recommended defaults   5-121
  retiring or removing   6-18
  shell selection   3-18
  status, monitoring   4-18 4-19
  user monitoring and communication   6-20
  user support   6-19
Addressing
  high memory area   5-15
  segment   5-15
Archival and restore   6-21 6-24
  archive utility comparison   6-22
  floppy disk media comparison   6-22
  hard disk archival   6-21
  partial restores   6-24
  recommended blocking factors   6-22
  sample commands   6-24
  use of **copy**(C)   6-23
Backup user creation   5-116
Backup   *See*   Filesystem backup
Base address
  defaults   5-14
  defined   5-11
  supported   5-14
Baud rate   5-44
Boot prompt   2-28
Booting   2-8
  boot strings   2-14
  defaults   4-23
  information   4-23
  masterboot   2-8
  override terminal   4-21, 4-22, 6-28
  startup files   4-23
  tutorial   2-28 2-32

Cabling
   SCSI   5-17 5-18
   modem   5-53
   serial   5-50
   serial, terminology   5-51
   terminal   5-50
Cache   *See* RAM, cache
        See Hard disk, buffer cache
Command   1-12
Console
   configuration   5-101
   device names   4-8
   function key mapping   4-15
   restricted root logins   5-115
cron
   configuration   5-119 5-120
   determining if running   4-15
   list of periodic jobs   4-19
   status   4-19
   submitting jobs   5-120
Cursor size   5-101
Data communications
   DCE   5-51
   DTE   5-51
   EIA-232-D   5-51
   RS-232-C   5-51
   hardware handshaking   5-51
Default
   TCB user profile   4-24
   account recommendations   5-121
   autoboot timeout   4-23
   backup device   4-21
   boot device   4-23
   buffer flush frequency   6-37
   configured hardware   5-23
   filesystem parameters   5-81
   group   4-18
   kernel parameters   3-16
   login environment   4-21
   login prompt   4-21
   login shell   4-18
   parent home directory   4-18

Default [continued]
  printer   4-19
  printer, assigning   5-93
  run level   4-23
  scancode map   4-22
  startup script   4-23
  system sync frequency   6-37
  tar device   4-21
Device driver   1-13
  boot-time loadable   2-15
  configuration, information   4-30
  removal   4-30
Device drivers
  default   4-31
  listing   4-30
Device file
  block and character   5-77
  names   4-8 4-9
  nodes   5-25
Device nodes   5-25
Device
  major numbers   5-26
  minor numbers   5-26
Directory   1-9
  defined   5-74
  moving   5-78
  permissions   5-108 5-110
  resizing   6-8
  search optimization   6-38
  symbolic links to   5-79
Discretionary access control   *See*   Trusted security, DAC
Disk quotas   3-20
Dump device   5-26
Emergency system recovery   6-25 6-27
Emergency root/boot floppies   2-26
  creation   2-39
Emergency system access   6-28 6-29
  bad bootstrap   6-25
  bad or missing masterboot   6-26
  corrupted **/boot**   6-26
  corrupted root filesystem   6-26 6-27
File name lookup cache   6-38

Essential SCO System Administration

File   1-9
   archiving   *See*   Archival and restore
   defined   5-74
   group owner   5-112
   link   *See*   Link
   link   5-75
   log   *See*   Log files
   message-of-the-day   6-20
   pathname   5-70
   permissions   5-108 5-110
   permissions, integrity   4-25
   permissions, sticky bit   5-109
   permissions, umask   5-109
   restoring from archive   *See*   Archival and restore
   restoring from backup   *See*   Filesystem, maintenance
   size   4-20
   size, maximum   5-78
   types   5-77
   recently changed   4-24
Filesystem backup
   administrative user creation   5-116
   configuration   5-83 5-90
   default device, configuration   2-37
   labels   5-85
   multiple volume   5-85
   positioning   5-90
   schedule   4-21
   scheduled   5-84 5-86
   tutorial   3-24
   unattended   5-87 5-88
   unscheduled   5-86
Filesystem   2-7
   backup   *See*   Filesystem, backup
   checking with **fsck**(*ADM*)   6-7
   cluster   5-81
   commands   6-9
   creation   5-34 5-35, 5-82
   default parameters   5-81
   finding large files   6-9
   freeing inodes   6-9
   freeing space   6-8
   initialization   3-11

Index

Filesystem [continued]
    limits   5-81
    list of processes using   4-20
    maintenance   6-7 6-13
    modification   5-82, 6-10 6-13
    mount, attributes   5-72 5-73
    mount, terminology   5-70
    mount point   5-70
    mount point, configuration   5-71
    optimization   5-80 5-82
    optimization, directory searches   6-38
    optimization, terminology   5-80
    reinitialization   6-11
    restore, full   6-12
    restore, partial   6-12
    restoring   6-10 6-13
    status, monitoring   4-20
    structure, EAFS and AFS   6-10
    structure, diagram   5-75
    terminology   5-74
    troubleshooting   6-7 6-9
    types   4-21
    verification   5-88 5-90
    warning about **dcopy**(ADM)   6-10
Floppy disk
    archival   *See*   Archival and restore
    IRQ   5-13
    device names   4-8
Flow control   5-54
    stty parameters   5-59
gettydefs file   5-47
group file   3-17
    adding   3-18
Groups   3-17
    configuration   5-110 5-111
    supplemental   5-110

Hard disk
  IRQ   5-13
  RAID   6-35
  active partition   2-6
  alias tracks   5-32
  available space   4-17
  badtracking   5-34
  base address   5-14
  buffer cache   6-37
  buffers, monitoring   6-37
  capacity   4-17
  configuration   5-30 5-35
  configuration, commands   5-31
  configuration units   5-33
  controller, configuration   5-19
  device names   4-8, 5-31
  divisions   2-7
  fragmentation   5-81
  geometry   5-31
  interleave   5-80
  management with filesystems   5-35
  maximum supported size   5-31
  parameters, displaying   5-31
  partition structure   5-32
  partitions   2-5
  partitions, creation   5-33
  partitions, guidelines   5-33
  partitions, using for data backup   5-33
  seek latency   6-36
  testing   4-11
  tracks   2-6
  troubleshooting   6-30
Hardware adapter
  ROM, conflicts   5-12
  base address   *See* Base address
  base address, defined   5-11
  configuration   5-10 5-24
  configuration, definitions   5-11
  configuration, parameters   5-10
  configuration, procedure   5-11 5-13
  controller RAM, determination   5-12

Index

Hardware configuration report   2-29, 4-6
   configuration   4-6
   diagnostics   4-29   4-30
   omissions   4-7
   problems   4-7
Hardware handshaking   5-39, 5-51
   cabling   5-50
Hardware services
   list   4-13
   testing   4-12
   testing   4-15
Hardware
   adapter   *See*   Hardware adapter
   configuration, commands   3-10
   configured for installation   5-24
   default   5-23
   inspection strategy   4-6
   status, determination   4-6   4-26
Hashpling feature   5-123
Hushlogin   5-122
init process   5-118
inittab file
   respawn state   4-16
Inode
   defined   5-74
   structure, diagram   5-76
Inodes
   list of multiply linked   4-20
Installation   2-10   2-27
   checklist   2-23
   configured hardware   5-24
   customization   3-16
   hardware preconfiguration   2-13   2-15
   preventative tips   2-27
Job scheduler   *See*   Cron

Kernel   1-11
    configuration   5-124, 5-125
    creation, post-installation   3-16
    environment   4-31
    linking   5-25
    parameters, buffer cache   6-37
    parameters, processes   6-14
    parameters, table of   5-125
    process table size   4-20
    region table size   4-17
    relinking   3-17, 4-31
Limits
    filesystem   5-81
    maximum RAM   4-17
    maximum hard disk size   5-31
    maximum usable disk   5-31
Line discipline   5-22
Link
    hard   5-75
    symbolic   5-75
    symbolic, configuration   5-79
Log file
    management   4-28
    monitoring   4-27, 4-28
    trimming   4-28
Logical block   5-74
Login
    information   4-21
    scosh configuration   5-123
    idle, configuration   4-26
    idle, detection   4-26
Mail
    control file for **mail**(C)   4-23
    mailbox location   5-121
Major number   5-26
Mapping
    character I/O   4-22
    scancode   4-22
    screen   4-22
Memory cache   5-29
Memory   *See* RAM
Memory speed comparison   6-36

Index

Messages *See* Troubleshooting
 "10 bits of I/O addressing"   4-29, 5-14
Minor number   5-26
Modem
 NVRAM   5-56
 atdial configuration   5-41
 cabling   5-50, 5-53
 configuration, commands   5-62
 configuration, recommended   5-54
 configuration for outbound dialing   5-96 5-99
 connection testing   5-61
 dialer, configuration   5-57 5-59
 dialer, selection   5-40
 dialer, speed problems   5-97
 dialout registration   5-60
 terminology   5-53, 5-55
 testing   4-12
motd file   6-20
Mount point   5-70
 configuration   5-71
Mounting   *See* Filesystem, mount
Mouse
 configuration   5-68 5-69
 testing   4-12
Multitasking   1-8
 defined   1-7
Override terminal   *See* Booting
Parallel
 IRQ   5-13
 base address   5-14
 device names   4-8
 testing   4-10
passwd file   4-24
Password
 file   4-24
 protected password database   5-104
 setting an effective   5-106
 status   4-19
Pathname   5-70

Essential SCO System Administration

Performance   6-34   6-38
    intensive activity management   6-35
    optimizing data access   6-36
    optimizing directory searches   6-38
    optimizing file name lookup   6-38
    optimizing paging   6-36
Physical block   5-74
Power off message   2-28
Print filter   5-37
Print spooler
    administration, commands   6-16
    configuration   5-91   5-95
    maintenance   6-15   6-16
    status, monitoring   4-19
    terminology   5-92
Printer
    cabling   5-50
    class, defined   5-37
    configuration   5-36   5-43
    configuration, commands   5-43
    configuration, tips   5-38
    configuration, tutorial   3-13
    content type   5-92, 5-95
    default   4-19
    default, assigning   5-93
    default, configuration   3-13
    dialup, configuration   5-40   5-41
    filter specification   5-92
    form specification   5-92
    hardware handshaking   5-39
    hardware handshaking   5-43
    interface, defaults   5-39
    interface, defined   5-37
    interface, key models   5-38
    interface, location   5-37
    local, configuration   5-48
    network, configuration   5-42
    spooler attributes   5-37
    troubleshooting   6-30   6-32
    type   5-37
    user-specified options   5-36

Index

Printing
 changing job priorities   6-16
 user options to lp(C)   5-95
Process   1-10
 bdflushr   6-37
 configuration   5-117, 5-120
 exec and fork   5-118
 initiation   5-118
 introduction   5-117
 killing   5-117
 maintenance   6-13, 6-15
 region, table size   4-17
 runaway   4-20
 scheduled   *See* Cron
 status, monitoring   4-20
 suspending and resuming   6-15
 troubleshooting   6-14
 using sar(ADM)   6-13
Process launch script   4-20
Pseudo-terminals   3-16, 5-100
Region   *See* Process, region
Restoring files   *See* Archival and restore
   See Filesystem, maintenance
Root account
 introduced   1-11
 login   2-31
 password   2-22
 restricted logins   5-115
Root filesystem   2-7
 creation   2-19
 introduced   1-10
Rotational gap   *See* Hard disk, interleave
scosh
 configuration   5-123
 customization   3-19
Security   *See* Trusted security
Segment addressing   5-15
Serial adapter
 configuration   5-21
 dumb   5-21
 dumb, terminal limit   5-22
 intelligent   5-22

Essential SCO System Administration

Serial port
    COM3 and COM4   5-14
    IRQ   5-13
    UART and high-speed   5-52
    base address   5-14
    device names   4-8
    information   4-22
    testing   4-10
Serial terminal   *See*   Terminal
Shell
    SCO   *See*   **scosh**
    command line features   1-19
    executable scripts   5-123
    hashpling feature   5-123
    types   3-18
Single-user prompt   2-29
Software
    installation   3-14
    installed, list   4-14
    monitoring   4-14 4-15
    serial numbers   4-14
    version levels, displaying   4-14
su   *See*   Trusted security, **su**(C)
Swap
    allocation   2-20
    available   4-17
sysadmsh*(ADM)* tutorial   2-34 2-36
System administration
    responsibilities   3-25
    task summary   3-26
System
    access security   5-107
    configuration files   5-25
    emergency access   *See*   Emergency sy
    emergency recovery   *See*   Emergency
    file permissions   5-110
    limits   4-17
    log files   4-27
    messages   *See*   Messages
    monitoring   4-16 4-17
    name   4-16
    power down   1-20

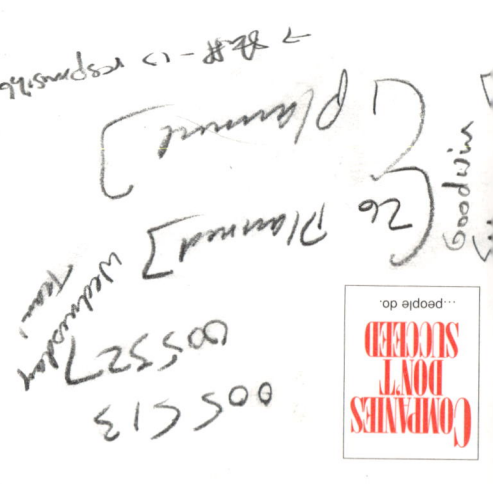

Index

System   [continued]
  power up   1-20
  privileged access configuration   5-114 5-115
  recommended CMOS settings   5-28
  resource, determination   4-17
  shutdown   2-32 2-33
  startup files   4-23
  utilities, monitoring   4-23
  utilities, summary   1-15 1-17
Tape backup   *See* Filesystem backup
tape(C) command options   5-65
Tape
  ECC device   5-65
  QIC, controller configuration   5-22
  QIC, device names   4-8
  SCSI, device names   4-9
  configuration   5-63 5-66
  device files, special   5-64
  device, testing   4-10
  hardware buffer size   4-17
  positioning   5-90
termcap file   5-48
  sample entry   5-49
Terminal
  baud rate   5-44
  cabling   5-50
  configuration   5-43 5-47
  configuration, summary   5-47
  device files   4-8
  gettydefs file   5-45
  inittab file   5-45
  line attributes, scancode   5-45
  line attributes   5-45
  locking   4-26
  logins, enabling   5-47
  multiscreens, configuration   5-100 5-101
  respawn inittab state   5-47
  scancode, configuration   5-44, 5-99
  scancode, problems with **mscreen**(C)   5-101
  scancode, support   4-15
  ttytype file   5-47
  type   5-46

Troubleshooting
   emergency system access   6-28 6-29
   emergency system recovery   6-25 6-27
   filesystems   6-7 6-9
   hard disks   6-30
   hardware   4-29 4-31, 6-30 6-33
   mice   6-33
   printers   6-30 6-32
   processes   6-14
   trusted security   6-17 6-18, 6-28

Trusted security
   DAC   5-108 5-110
   asroot(ADM)   5-115
   causes of database corruption   6-28
   configuration   3-15, 5-102 5-116
   defined   5-102
   kernel authorizations   5-108
   levels   2-23
   levels, comparison   5-104
   levels, determination   4-25
   maintenance   6-16 6-18
   override terminal   4-21, 6-28
   parameters   3-15
   protected subsystem, design   5-112
   protected subsystems   5-108
   recommendations   5-105
   repair   6-29
   restricted root logins   5-115
   status   4-24
   su(C)   5-106
   su logging   5-106, 6-17
   subsystem authorizations   5-108
   terminology   5-103, 5-104
   testing   4-15
   troubleshooting   6-17 6-18, 6-28

User   *See* Account

uucp
   Permissions file   5-42
   Systems file   5-42
   status   4-24

Index

Version level
    operating system   4-14
    software   4-14
Virtual memory   1-25, 2-7